AGE
PROOFING
Jane Ogle

AGE PROOFING

Jane Ogle

Arlington Books
King Street St. James's
London

AGEPROOFING
First published 1985 in the United States of America
This edition first published 1984 in England by
Arlington Books (Publishers) Ltd
15–17 King Street, St. James's
London SW1

© Jane Ogle

Additional typesetting by
Inforum Ltd, Portsmouth
Printed and bound by
Billing & Sons, Worcester

British Library Cataloguing in Publication Data
Ogle, Jane
Ageproofing
1. Health
I. Title
613   RA776

ISBN 85140–676–9

NOTE TO THE READER

The ideas, procedures, and suggestions contained in this book are not
intended as a substitute for consulting with your physician. All matters
regarding your health require medical supervision.

CONTENTS

A Breakthrough for You

Is there anybody who does not worry about aging?

The very word brings to mind a whole spectrum of unwanted changes that are likely to occur at various times of life—from the first signs of wrinkles and flabby muscles to loss of teeth, poor eyesight, stiff joints, failing memory, and chronic disease. These are things that you may assume you have little or no control over, things you feel you just have to be ready to accept as the years go by.

It is becoming increasingly evident, however, that this is not so. The ideas people have about aging tend to be way off target. Most of the deteriorative changes and diseases attributed to aging have little if anything to do with true aging and are not at all inevitable.

The big news coming out of the latest scientific research is that you can prevent almost all of the so-called "aging" changes, or delay them, or mitigate them, or even reverse them. What's more, you can do this without gimmicks, without trade-offs.

Amazingly, a few simple things you do every day can make a lasting difference in your looks, your health, your energy and vitality. They can have a tremendous impact on every aspect of your well-being and are what really count in making you ageproof. They can get you in great shape today and help you stay that way every day of your life.

Ageproofing is, for me, a very exciting discovery. I hope my book will make it as real and exciting for you, too. *Ageproofing* shows you how to do all the simple things that make the big difference in protecting yourself against the changes people mistakenly identify with aging.

You may wonder what gives me my special perspective. Who am I? How do I happen to be writing about ageproofing? Here are a few facts about myself.

I am sixty-two. I am in terrific shape and—knock on wood —plan to stay that way. The same goes for my husband, who is in his sixties. We have two children: a son and a daughter in their twenties. Like many of their friends and contemporaries, they have instinctively hit on what ageproofing is all about: protecting your body. And they realize that this especially means eating right, exercising right, and striking a dynamic balance between work and rest in order to realize your maximum physical and mental potential in the decades ahead.

My family provides me with an excellent vantage point from which to see how people can protect their looks, health, and overall fitness both short-term and long-term. Relatives, schoolmates, neighbors, tradesmen, and the various people I have worked with over the years provide other instances of the ageproofing factors that count most in life.

During the forty years I have been a magazine editor and writer, one of my keenest interests has long been looks, health, and fitness and the way they link together. This link is crucial to ageproofing. The interactions between all three can work for you whether you begin at twenty, thirty, forty, fifty, sixty, or more. I know because I really started only two years ago—on reaching sixty—to put all that I had learned about looks, health, and fitness to the actual test and see for myself how much I could achieve. And I can tell you it is a lot!

One simple principle that is basic to every aspect of ageproofing is Use it or lose it. I call it Your Ageproofing Law. Your body was made to move, to work. You need to use your body the way it is meant to be used, the way it has evolved over millions of years to move and work. Using it is what keeps it in top working order. Every system, organ, and tissue in your body maintains a dynamic balance, constantly adjusting to the needs of the moment with exquisite economy. This means your whole body and every part of it, right down to the individual cells, is in good working order only if you put the kind of demands on it that force it to respond dynamically and continue functioning at optimal levels.

What better example of this response than your diaphragm muscle, to which you doubtless give no thought whatever. From the moment you take your first breath, this muscle contracts and relaxes nonstop, minute after minute, hour after hour, day after day. It never lets up. And it never shows any signs of aging. That muscle is certainly telling you something. It is telling you to do everything you can to keep all the other parts of your body in just as good working order.

As you get in better and better shape, you start to sense a new flow of energy—an exhilarating, all-pervasive vitality. You unlock your body's reserves. You begin to realize your full ageproofing potential. It is a feeling to revel in.

You will need motivation to get started. Motivation is what powers you. It, more than anything else, holds the key to how much you can prevent, delay, mitigate, or reverse deterioration right across the whole spectrum of "aging" changes. There is no hard and fast limit to how much you can do, no set cutoff point to how far you can go in ageproofing your body if you are motivated.

Ageproofing is your chance, your challenge, to discover your enormous untapped potential for maintaining your looks, your health, your total fitness—for life!

PART ONE
Your Ageproofing Basics

CHAPTER 1

Holding the Line Against "Aging"— Your Ageproofing Perspective

You want to hold the line against what is called aging— against the decline in looks, health, and overall fitness that seems to occur as a matter of course over the years and decades. And you want to stop and as far as possible reverse any deteriorative changes that are already under way.

How do you go about it?

The first thing you need is a clear idea of the difference between true aging on the one hand and all the changes that people mistakenly attribute to it on the other.

True aging comprises changes that are bound to occur as you get older. Graying hair is a good example. Just when the graying starts and how far and fast it progresses may seem to vary capriciously from one individual to the next but is in fact taking place exactly as planned by each person's genetic printout and can be neither prevented nor reversed. It is part of true biological aging, a process or group of processes inherent in every form of life and embracing all the normal, progressive, irreversible changes that begin as soon as development and growth cease.

There are many speculative theories about the underlying mechanisms of true aging—as many as a centipede has legs, in the words of one researcher—but these mechanisms remain unknown. At some point, when they have at last been discovered, it may be possible to modify this or that aging process or at least give it a vigorous nudge. For now, however, true aging changes remain unavoidable.

A second group of changes during the adult years may be due in part to true aging but much less so than you may think. A runner in his forties, for instance, cannot sprint as fast as he could when he was in his twenties, even if he keeps himself in peak shape. He can, nevertheless, far outpace a man in his twenties who is out of condition.

Still other changes often blamed on aging have little if anything to do with the true aging process. A good example of this is so-called aging skin, a misnomer if there ever was one. With very few exceptions, "aging skin" changes are not due to real biological aging and are entirely avoidable.

In sorting out age-related changes that invariably occur according to a fixed timetable, scientists have found them to be largely concentrated in the earliest phases of life. A variability factor comes into play more and more as the body grows. Starting from the moment of conception, development of the maturing embryo follows a minutely precise schedule for each specific event. After birth, some leeway begins to appear—in, for instance, the time when the first tooth erupts. The dates at which a baby starts to talk and walk, while still fairly predictable, follow a somewhat less exact schedule. As a child gets older, the changes—such as those associated with puberty—take place within an even more flexible time frame. In adulthood individual variability is quite pronounced, and it increases noticeably from about sixty on. One person will seem to undergo a decline in looks and fitness at a distressing speed. Another will seem to change so subtly and slightly that the differences from year to year are barely perceptible.

What does this tell you? Obviously it says that there is a lot of biological individuality, but it says something else as well—that the changes people think of as due to actual aging processes are in fact much more under your control than you probably realize. Your "age" at any given age depends more on what you do or do not do today than on the passing years or the genetic printout you were born with.

And this brings up another point. Your looks and health are very closely linked. If you want the best indication of your health and how far you have gotten in your lifespan, forget about your birthdays and see what a full-length mirror reveals about your looks. If you look old, you are old. If you look young, you are young.

This is the startling conclusion reached by a major medical study that tracked several thousand individuals for a number of decades. At the periodic physical examinations it was duly noted whether the people looked older or younger than their age in years suggested. When the examinations were finally tabulated, it was found, to the researchers' frank astonishment, that those who looked older than their years tended to die on the early side. Those who looked younger were more likely to enjoy a healthy and fit old age and to live longer.

You can of course argue that men and women who look young for their age and who live longer than most are those fortunate to have picked their parents well. Genetic factors do of course affect how long you live. But staying young is not merely a matter of lucking out genetically. It is much more a matter of what you yourself do throughout your life to help or hinder your chances. How "old" you are at any given point—at twenty, thirty, forty, fifty, sixty, and on— almost always depends on what you do before you get there.

This is why it is so important to start ageproofing yourself now. The sooner you begin, the better edge you have on "aging." Twenty is not a moment too soon to get going; starting early is in fact the best way to help yourself reach an optimal level and maintain that level. You will begin to look and feel and be better in every way right at the outset, and hold that edge in the years that lie ahead.

By the same token, sixty is not too late to get going on ageproofing. As I happen to have started at sixty, I know. The key word is *now*. Start now. Regardless of what decade you are in, you have the means to counter deteriorative changes and the killers and cripplers they can lead to.

The three key ageproofing questions to ask as you get ready to start are:

• What changes are likely to occur in your body over the years and decades?

- Which of these changes are part of true biological aging and therefore inevitable?
- Which of these changes are the avoidable result of abuse, disuse, or chronic disease?

You will get the answers to these three questions in the next two chapters. Chapter Two, How Much Do You Really Age?, shows you what changes are apt to occur in each of the main systems of the body, and how and when among people living the way they ordinarily do today. There are some big surprises; you will see exactly why many of the changes people call aging have nothing whatever to do with true aging and are not inevitable.

In Chapter Three, Preventing the "Diseases of Aging," you see the way deteriorative changes in your body can lead to coronary heart disease, stroke, hypertension, obesity, diabetes, osteoporosis, osteoarthritis, and cancer. These chronic, degenerative diseases are often called the diseases of aging because they usually take two or three decades to develop or to have serious consequences. But, as you will discover, they are not an inevitable accompaniment of advancing years. They are diseases you can largely prevent by making some small but vital changes in things you do as a matter of course each day.

Everything you do to keep your body in good working order helps you protect yourself against all the major chronic diseases; what helps against one helps against others as well. This is a crucial point. It is not as if you had to use different preventive measures for each and every disease and disorder. The same preventive measures hold right across the board. You hear people talk about the simple economy of nature. Well, here you see it at work.

Most of the degenerative changes which people undergo from decade to decade and the diseases they are so closely linked to are brought about by certain lifestyle factors that you can control. As a rule these are common, everyday bad habits that people fall into over the years quite without thinking. It is easier to break yourself of any such habits once you are aware of what you are doing that is bad for you and what you should be getting into the habit of doing instead.

The good habits that count most have to do with your body's most basic needs—food, exercise, sleep, and proper care and protection. Part Two—Your Ageproofing Program for Looks, Health, and Fitness—shows you how to get and keep the best of habits. The program is in fact quite habit-forming. It is meant to be. It gives you everything you need to reach your ageproofing goal and realize to the full your untapped potential.

Ageproofing Your Looks gives you lots of practical advice and quick and easy tips on how to go about making every inch of your body ageproof.

Your Ageproofing Diet Plan shows you how to modify your eating habits in simple enjoyable ways that really work to keep your health and looks and vitality at their peak for life.

Your Ageproofing Exercise Plan gives you a choice of wonderfully energizing ways to keep you fit and healthy without gimmicks or trade-offs. Exercise is, after all, the best anti-aging prescription there is.

Your Ageproofing Sleep Plan shows you how much rest your body needs and why, and how to get it regularly night after night, year after year.

Drinking, smoking, and medical checkups are dealt with in Your Special Ageproofing Guidelines.

The conclusion, Your Ageproofing Potential, shows you how motivation can power you in ageproofing yourself.

Ageproofing gives you a very exciting perspective on all the years that lie ahead. Every piece of information and every bit of advice in my book is meant to work for you.

And if ageproofing can change my whole life, I know it can do as much for you, too.

CHAPTER 2
_____

How Much Do You Really Age?

How much do you really age? There could not be a better time than now to ask this question because scientists are discovering some startlingly unexpected new answers to it. Many changes that have simply been accepted as part of inevitable aging are turning out to be things you can actually prevent, delay, mitigate, or even reverse.

These fresh findings challenge many popular beliefs. And they also mean that many surveys of what happens to people at successive stages of their life have to be reinterpreted. Quite often changes are ascribed to aging just because they appear to be so pervasive among people of a certain age group. This can lead to the quite unwarranted conclusion that various systems and parts of the body decline at fixed, preordained rates over the course of a lifetime.

In this chapter, nine body systems and their component parts are taken up one by one. For each, you will find very helpful information on three key points.

- What changes tend to occur in the average person living in this country today.
- Which of these changes are true biological aging processes and therefore inevitable.
- Which ones are mistakenly attributed to true aging but are in fact the result of avoidable disuse, abuse, or chronic disease.

The main purpose of this entire chapter is to clear away widespread misconceptions about aging and the deteriora-

tive changes mistakenly thought of as genetically programmed aging processes. Here, you have all the facts you
need in order to understand how well you can protect yourself against these changes and the chronic diseases they so
often lead to—the eight big killers and cripplers which, as
you will see in Chapter Three, are such a scourge of life
today. This gives you a good basis for Your Ageproofing
Program for Looks, Health, and Fitness in Part Two, and
enables you to get the most out of all the helpful ageproofing
advice in the program.

Dermal System

Many of the changes that come first to mind when people
think of aging have to do with outward appearance, particularly with the two main parts of the dermal system: skin
and hair. Even though hair is actually an outgrowth of skin,
it is diametrically opposed to skin in its link to true aging. In
hair you have what are probably the most visible manifestations of biological aging seen in any body tissue. In skin
you have what are probably the most visible signs of
chronic, degenerative change that has little if anything to do
with true aging.

Skin

The skin's appearance can be a very misleading gauge of a
person's age in years. The wrinkling, sagging, blotchiness,
"broken" blood vessels, and other signs of so-called aging
that occur in the course of time result almost entirely from
long abuse, not biological aging processes. Chronic sun exposure alone is responsible for an overwhelming proportion
of such ravages, which explains why black skin, with its
greater natural protection against the sun, "ages" so much
less than white skin. Wind, heat, and cold compound the
injurious effects of sun. And various harmful substances,
such as harsh detergents, that your skin is likely to come in

contact with in the course of routine everyday activities, add to the damage decade after decade.

Skin that is adequately cared for and shielded against abuse remains quite unchanged over the years. The few true aging changes that take place—which can be detected at the cellular level early in life—are rarely apparent on the surface of well-protected skin until the very latest years.

It is good to have some idea of just what these true aging changes are so that you understand why you can do so much to ageproof your skin. You can see for yourself how few true aging changes occur and how slight their effects need be if you give your skin the daily care and protection it should have over the years. And in Chapter Four, you will find out how easy it is to do this.

Probably the most significant real aging change is a gradual flattening out of the highly convoluted boundary between the epidermis and the dermis, the skin's two intermeshing layers. This wavy seam gets slowly worn down with time and finally becomes straight as a hem line. But in well-protected skin there is no visible indication of the process until very late in life, and then only a slight looseness is evident.

Another true aging change has to do with losses in collagen, the main connective tissue in the skin's vital supporting structure, the dermis. Collagen fibers get fewer in number with each succeeding decade. The effects of these losses are more apparent in a woman's skin because it is usually thinner to begin with than a man's. You often hear people say that a woman's skin ages faster than a man's, and this is the reason why—the thinner the skin, the more easily it can become wrinkled. Thinness is not the direct cause of the wrinkles, however; it just facilitates their formation, especially in sun-damaged skin.

There is one other genuine aging change that eventually takes place in the skin's dermal layer: loss of elasticity. This results from decreased resiliency in the tiny elastic fibers that thread through the skeins of collagen. In contrast to the collagen fibers, which set a limit to how far your skin can be stretched, elastic fibers are what put a spring in your skin.

They are what make it snap back into place each time it is stretched. A pinch test can show you instantly what aging changes, if any, have taken place in your skin's elasticity. Simply lift a small fold of skin from any part of your body that has not been damaged by chronic sun exposure, hold it a moment, and then let it fall back into place. An older person's skin may take slightly longer to return to its original shape than a younger person's, but in well-protected skin the difference is negligible until very late in life.

Only one significant aging change occurs in the epidermis, the skin's upper layer. This layer is continuously being renewed by the formation of cells at its base, which work their way up to the surface of the skin where they die and are shed, making way for their successors. Over the years the turnover slows somewhat. The cells become larger, thinner, and more irregular in shape. They slough off in disorderly clumps instead of neatly, one by one. As a result the skin may get rough and itchy and develop cracks and fissures. This is the condition that people call dry skin—quite inaccurately, as it happens, because "dry skin" contains just as much moisture as normal skin. Moisture and moisturizers do help relieve the condition, though, by smoothing things over so that the outermost cells lie flat on the surface and lift off in a orderly fashion.

Among the skin's various types of glands, the sebaceous, or oil, glands reach their peak of activity in adolescence and early adulthood, and they continue to go strong for a number of decades. In men the output of sebum—the oily secretion of the sebaceous glands—does not usually fall off much until after about seventy, and at any time is apt to be greater than that of women of the same age. In women the sebum output remains at a fairly constant level until the menopause. Then it drops by about 40 percent, and this is followed by a much slighter decline between the ages of sixty and seventy. The sudden, sharp reduction at the menopause explains why postmenopausal women complain so frequently of "dry skin"; sebum acts as a natural moisturizer.

The sweat glands are another skin structure that undergoes certain aging changes in later years. Among both men and women there is a gradual decrease in the number of active sweat glands as time goes by. Some simply vanish, and almost all the others are reduced in output. The decline in sweat output may be most noticeable between forty and sixty, and it is generally more marked among women than men. As a rule, the older a person is, the longer it takes to reach sweat point. But people who exercise regularly and vigorously from decade to decade keep their sweat glands functioning at a higher level than physically inactive people do. Even those who start exercising later in life can rev up their waning sweat glands if they exert themselves frequently enough.

The apocrine glands, which are located in the armpit and groin and certain other specific regions of the body and are responsible for odor—with its implied sex signals—are somewhat affected by age. They begin to decline in the middle adult years, again more noticeably in women than in men. But individuals vary a great deal in this respect, as in just about every other, and it is not unusual for a person's apocrine glands to function without perceptible letup well into old age.

Hair

The main changes your hair undergoes over the years are programmed in your genes. When these changes start, the extent to which they occur and the rate at which they progress vary tremendously between races, sexes, and individuals. And even though family patterns give you some idea of what to expect, there is still a great deal of individual leeway.

Loss of color. This is a true aging process and one that can start surprisingly early. About 25 percent of British men and women between the ages of twenty-five and thirty-five have gray in their hair. And by age forty nearly 50 percent are partially gray. Whites go gray much earlier than Blacks, and Orientals are somewhere in between.

Regardless of race and sex, scalp hair goes gray in a more or less set pattern. It starts at the temples, spreads across the front of the hairline, and then gradually progresses over the crown and down to the nape. A man's beard usually turns gray before his scalp hair. That is why, if he is clean shaven, his sideburns are almost always the first hair to turn; sideburns are part of a man's beard, appearing at puberty along with facial hair.

Body hair turns gray much later than scalp and beard hair, with one curious male exception. A man's chest hair achieves its fullest coverage during the late fifties, and the newly emerging hairs usually come in gray or white, even though much of his earlier chest hair remains pigmented into old age, as does his underarm and pubic hair. A woman's underarm hair is normally lost shortly after the menopause while it is still pigmented, and the same is true of the hair on her arms and legs. Her pubic hair is lost at a slower rate, however, and it becomes both gray and sparse during the sixties, as a rule, well before either change occurs in a man.

Loss of hair color is due to loss of a pigment called melanin, which is supplied to the hair shaft in shades ranging from black and brown to yellow and red. Melanin production in the hair slows down with time. Although the cells that produce it do not actually atrophy and can be experimentally stimulated to produce color, some functional impairment seems to occur. As the hair turns, you always see a mosaic of color, white, and gray. This is because hairs grow in clusters of four or five, and any one cluster may contain, say, two colored hairs, two white hairs wholly lacking in pigment, and one transitional gray hair that has lost some of its pigment. Other clusters of hair in the area will have much the same kind of mix.

The white color you see in hair devoid of pigment is, incidentally, due partly to the reflection of light from various parts of the hair shaft. Sometimes a person's hair has a central core, or medulla. It then looks very white, since more light is bounced back. This is why the hair of an Arctic fox or a polar bear appears so snowy. White hair that lacks a medulla has a yellowish cast—the intrinsic color of a substance called keratin, of which most of the hair shaft is composed.

Loss of Hair. Like graying, this is a true aging change, except in rare instances when it is caused by a disease. The density of the hairs is what is most visibly affected. Decrease in density is actually an ongoing process during all of adult life, in non-balding as well as in balding scalps. But whereas in a non-balding scalp hair density may drop from, say, about 700 hairs per square centimeter at age twenty to about 500 at age fifty, with only a slight further reduction in density during the years following, the density count goes much lower in a balding scalp, falling to about 350 hairs per square centimeter between ages fifty-five and seventy and down to about 275 between ages seventy and eighty-five.

Baldness affects all white men to some degree and a certain percentage of white women, although to a slighter extent and in a different pattern. Blacks are much less likely to go bald. Orientals are even less prone to balding.

Unlike the pattern of balding seen among men, which progresses from front to back in a fairly direct manner, hair loss among women is not usually marked by a distinct recession. When this does occur in women, there is a slight loss across the hairline in front and a distinct indentation at each temple. The pattern is seen in up to 25 percent of women who lose hair, but some develop it very early in life only to see it reversed during postmenopausal years. A far more characteristic type of hair loss among women is diffuse fallout over the entire front area on the top of the scalp, starting about half an inch behind the hairline. Because as much as 50 percent of a woman's hair can be lost before the results of diffuse shedding are obvious, the changes taking place may not be cause for concern until very late in life.

A combination of distinctive changes occur during hair loss. In any area where such loss is under way, the shaft of the affected hairs gets progressively thinner—because of a decrease in diameter—and the rate of growth slows markedly. The miniaturized wisps that remain resemble downy fuzz. Even in totally bald scalps, however, some dormant full-size hairs still exist among the many miniaturized ones. Because these scattered few can be stimulated to regrowth, people often get false hopes that a cure for baldness is possible with this or that new hair product.

Excess Hair. In contrast to the hair loss seen among men and women as a result of aging, excess hair growth is experienced by a great many women after they pass the menopause. Like hair loss, excess hair growth follows a clear-cut genetic pattern. The key control mechanism in both instances involves androgens, the male sex hormones, which are produced by the testes in men, the ovaries in women, and the adrenal glands in both sexes. Women usually produce more of the weaker male hormones and less of testosterone, the main male hormone. But if women do produce increased levels of testosterone—and possibly other as yet unidentified hormones as well—this can lead to excess hair growth that follows the male pattern. The condition is known as hirsutism. Even though there is a good deal of variation in the amount of body hair characteristic of women in different parts of the world, the appearance of facial hair in Caucasian women after menopause—especially on the upper lip and the chin—is a real concern for those who experience it. On average in Europe over 40% of post-menopausal women are affected. The condition need not be a traumatic occurrence for any woman today, however, because it can be successfully controlled by very simple cosmetic measures as you will see in Chapter Four, just as other hair changes due to aging can be.

Nails

Over the years nails also undergo some quite specific aging changes. The main one seen in this third component of the dermal system is a slowdown in rate of growth. At twenty-five a person's fingernails are likely to grow an inch and a half a year, about twice as fast as toenails. By sixty-five the annual growth rate is a little less than an inch. Oddly enough, the slowdown follows a cyclical pattern, seven years of slowing growth alternating with seven years of stable growth. Men's nails usually grow faster than women's up to about age fifty and women's, faster than men's from about seventy on. The total amount of nail produced always remains the same, however, because slower growth is offset by greater thickness and breadth over the years.

Women's nails often become quite brittle at some point between forty and sixty. The brittleness rarely lasts for more than about four years and may be due to some hormonal change at the menopause. Another frequent development in the course of decades is lengthwise ridging; this is more conspicuous in men than in women. Both these changes can be dealt with easily, as you will see in Chapter Four, and are nothing to worry about.

Musculoskeletal System

Bones, muscles, joints, and teeth together form a unified system because of their intimate mechanical linkage. Other body components are, of course, inextricably involved with each part of this system—just as occurs with all body systems.

Bones

Your looks and health can be dramatically affected if your bones become porous, weak, and fracture-prone in the course of time. Far too many people simply accept this widespread degenerative process as an inevitable part of aging. Very strong evidence now indicates, however, that you can do a lot to prevent it. Your bones are, to a surprising extent, what you choose to make them. There are three basic points you want to understand.

Bone is not the static, lifeless stuff it is usually thought to be. It is an extremely dynamic substance, rich in blood vessels and nerves, which is constantly being torn down and built up again. It gradually increases or decreases in density and even size, depending on the amount of stress you subject it to. It also serves as a working reserve for vital minerals your body needs all the time in order to carry out various essential functions. These stores are drawn upon as required and replenished by supplies from the food you eat.

The daily loss and gain of bone mineral represents but a minute fraction of the total bone mass, but during the adult years there is a chronic tendency for more mineral to be drawn out than is restored. Over the years the cumulative deficit can become quite severe. If the bone loss goes beyond a certain point, it is considered a disease, osteoporosis. Women are affected much more seriously than men, and Whites are affected immeasurably more than Blacks. Spinal crumbling, hunched-over backs, and broken hips are among the end results of osteoporotic degeneration.

Although these disfiguring and crippling afflictions are linked to the later part of life, it is important to understand that bone demineralization usually gets under way when you are very young. The type of bone that is the main component of the spinal vertebrae may, in fact, show signs of demineralization as early as the mid-twenties. The long bones of the body, which have a different structure, do not usually begin to get porous until the early thirties. During the menopause and for several years after, white women lose both kinds of bone at a very high rate.

You can prevent bone loss—or at least slow it down to a rate that is not dangerous—if you eat right and exercise right. As with many other aspects of ageproofing, the sooner in life you start the better, but it is never too late. There is a great deal that can be done even at an advanced age to halt the losses and to some extent reverse them. Women in their eighties have been successful, and there is no reason to believe that there is any specific cutoff point beyond which improvement is ruled out.

Muscles

A look up and down the street or the beach is enough to tell you that most people's muscles eventually undergo a distressing degree of change. What is involved here is of course skeletal muscle, the only visible kind, as distinct from cardiac muscle and from the smooth muscle that lines the walls of the blood vessels, intestines, and other organs. The change you see in skeletal muscle is its diminished mass, but muscle strength and muscle composition are also affected.

Muscle mass usually reaches its optimal level between ages eighteen and twenty-two for men and sixteen and eighteen for women. From this point on, it may remain stable for a couple of decades. Although there may be a slight loss during the thirties, it is too small to be noticeable until some time during the forties. By the mid-sixties, however, a very marked cumulative decrease is likely to be seen.

Changes in muscle strength over the years parallel the increases and decreases in muscle mass. Men usually achieve peak strength between twenty and thirty and women, by about twenty. Little loss of strength occurs before thirty-five or forty. But from then on, strength is apt to gradually decline; a man may lose 10 to 20 percent of his maximum strength by age sixty and a woman, even more. The decrease in both mass and strength takes place because more protein is being broken down and less is being synthesized. This leads to atrophy and loss of muscle fibers. The lost protein, or lean tissue, is largely replaced by fatty tissue.

The change in composition that takes place in skeletal muscle is a shift in the ratio between the two types of fibers it contains. The proportion of slow-twitch fibers, as they are called, increases, and that of fast-twitch fibers decreases. This requires a little explanation. The twitching of fibers is the mechanism that underlies muscle contraction; the duration of the contraction depends on whether slow-twitch or fast-twitch types of fiber are involved. Slow-twitch fibers are best suited for endurance activities. Fast-twitch fibers are for activities involving either power or fine, precise movement. Most skeletal muscle contains a mixture of both types of fiber, but you tend to develop more of the slow-twitch variety if you do mainly endurance kinds of exercise and more fast-twitch if you concentrate on strength and power.

The three kinds of muscle change are often assumed to be part of true aging. In fact, however, there seems to be little if anything about losses in muscle mass and muscle strength that is inevitable. Muscles that are used systematically do not deteriorate. A good example is the diaphragm muscle mentioned earlier, which works without letup throughout life in order to keep you breathing. As for the shift from fast-twitch to slow-twitch fibers, this may in part be linked to genuine aging processes; even athletes who keep themselves in top condition slow down somewhat as they get older. But in most instances the shift certainly comes partly from less frequent use of fast-twitch fibers. The activities that people engage in during their later years do not usually involve this type of fiber so much.

As with just about every other vital function in your body, the message from all this is an emphatic Use it or lose it. In the absence of disease there is no age-linked falloff in the neural control of muscles. And the cardiovascular system can supply ample amounts of oxygen to the working muscles even late in life. A program of usually vigorous exercise is all it takes to prevent the decline of muscle mass and strength and substantially reverse whatever loss may have occurred, regardless of age. There is no indication of any cutoff point as a rule.

Joints

A joint is not a single, distinct object but a complex of two or more bones and various specialized kinds of connective tissue. These include the smooth, shock-absorbing cartilage that covers the ends of the bones, the tough capsule enveloping the joint proper and holding the viscous synovial fluid which lubricates and nourishes it, the fibrous bands called ligaments that lash the bones together, and the cord-like muscle tendons attached to the bones and moving them. There may also be a very small disc made of fibrous cartilage—which amounts to a buffering pad—in the joint cavity.

The relation between joint deterioration and the passing years is one of the most important and least understood aspects of the whole spectrum of changes that the body goes through in the course of a lifetime. Very little is known about how and to what extent a joint actually ages, but much of the deterioration blamed on aging clearly has to do with disuse, abuse, or chronic disease.

How well a joint functions depends a great deal on its related muscles and bones. Disuse can affect a joint indirectly. If the muscles are not used enough, they lose strength, and the joint cannot work as it should. If the bone becomes weak because of physical inactivity, this can lead to deformation of joint surfaces and erosion of the irreplaceable cartilage.

Abuse of a joint can have very harmful consequences. Excessive pounding and unnatural stress—and of course outright injury—are apt to damage the cartilage. This can show up unexpectedly early, while people are in their twenties or even in their teens. But if cartilage is not damaged, it can withstand decades of hard use remarkably well, with no deterioration whatever over the years. The same is true of synovial fluid. It may get increasingly fibrous in later decades as a result of abuse. This leads to inadequate nourishment of the joint and eventually to its attrition. If, however, the joint is not subjected to excessive trauma, the synovial fluid's viscosity, which is so vital to the health and integrity of the joints, can remain unchanged throughout life.

As to chronic disease, the joint changes so frequently attributed to aging are the very ones characteristic of osteoarthritis, which affects practically every man and woman in this country to some degree during their later years. Although the disorder is generally thought to result from long-term mechanical stress, research is now starting to show that the reverse may be true: regular, vigorous use of the joints may, in fact, actually enhance their integrity and functioning and in so doing delay or even prevent osteoarthritis.

Today's sedentary lifestyle probably has a lot to do with the prevalence of joint deterioration. It certainly contributes to loss of flexibility and range of motion during adult years. Disuse and abuse, not use, are the key factors. Exercising the joints regularly and properly is what it takes to keep them from stiffening up and also to help reverse disabilities if stiffness has already begun to set in. With exercise, noticeable improvement in flexibility and range of motion is seen in people of all ages, even those in their eighties and nineties.

Teeth

A great many people assume that some loss of teeth is an inevitable consequence of growing older, but in fact you can keep your teeth for a lifetime if you give them proper care. Here again, the results of avoidable disuse, abuse, and chronic degenerative disease are too often mistakenly attributed to aging.

Surprising as it may seem, insufficient use can pose serious dental health problems. Both your teeth and their bony foundations respond to the stress of chewing. Foods that require biting and crunching strengthen the supporting bone. Vital tissues in the teeth themselves—like the dentin, which makes up the bulk, and the bone-like cementum and the periodontal membrane, which together shield the roots— also benefit from stimulation. Age-linked decreases in the cementum and the periodontal membrane may be largely due to a reduction in the amount of stress placed upon them. When a person loses a tooth and there is no longer any dynamic stress stimulus, a cascade of deteriorative changes is immediately set in motion. The bone around the missing tooth and in the nearby area is weakened, adjacent teeth become loose, and a gradual weakening and loosening spreads throughout the mouth.

Tooth decay, which to some extent or other affects 95 percent of the population in this country, is basically the result of abuse. Good preventive care, as you will see in Chapter Four, can protect against this insidious damage that leads eventually to tooth loss.

Chronic degenerative disease, in the form of periodontal disease, is rampant among British men and women. The loss of bone around teeth, which gives periodontal disease its name, often begins when people are very young. It may undermine the teeth's supporting structure for many years without any outward sign before its effects—loosening and loss of teeth—occur. Another preventable disease process, atherosclerosis, contributes to the degenerative changes in teeth by reducing the blood supply to the dental pulp at the heart of each tooth. This leads to a loss of blood vessels and a shrinking of the pulp volume over the years.

Cardiovascular System

Every cell in your body needs a continuous supply of oxygen in order to live and work, and providing it is the job of the cardiovascular system. The circulating blood does much more, of course, than simply ferry oxygen to the cells from the lungs: it brings nourishment absorbed from the intestines and removes toxic wastes for elimination by either the lungs or the kidneys. But oxygen delivery is by far the main task. Any interruption can have swift and disastrous effects on whatever part of the body is involved.

What happens when oxygen supplies are cut off is seen most dramatically in a heart attack or a stroke. The underlying disorders responsible for them—atherosclerosis and high blood pressure, in particular—are often thought of as largely due to biological aging. Actually, however, such conditions are chronic degenerative diseases that you can do a great deal to guard against. They are not an automatic and inescapable accompaniment of the aging process. All this is spelled out in the next chapter in the sections on cardiovascular disorders.

Quite aside from cardiovascular disease, there is the question of the efficiency of the heart as you get older. Here again, it is widely assumed that heart function invariably declines with the years, but new research shows that this slowdown has been greatly exaggerated. There is no reason why you cannot keep your heart working at optimal levels decade after decade.

What are the age-related changes in cardiac function that do matter? They involve three main factors affecting oxygen delivery. One is the output of the heart. Another is the blood's capacity to transport oxygen to the tissues. And the third is the ability of the tissues to extract the oxygen they need from the circulating blood.

The output of the heart is the product of the heart rate, or number of beats a minute, and the amount of blood propelled out with each beat, otherwise known as the stroke volume. The heart rate during everyday activities changes very little with time. And it does not show age-related change during moderately increased activity. A twenty-year-old and a fifty-year-old with comparable levels of fitness are apt to have comparable heart rates when exercising at a medium level of intensity. But a difference does appear during strenuous, sustained exercise. The older person has a lower maximum rate than the younger one. This difference has been taken to be inevitable. As a matter of fact, the maximum heart rate at any given age is roughly estimated by subtracting a person's age from 220.

The formula may exaggerate the decline in maximum heart rate, but by just how much is not yet clear. In any case, there is a great deal of individual variation. The key thing to keep in mind is that the heart is a muscle. The lower maximum heart rate in an older person may be due to increased stiffness of the heart's muscular wall. The muscular wall may become infiltrated by fatty and connective tissue —the same deterioration as that noted earlier in skeletal muscle. It is especially apt to happen if a person has a sedentary lifestyle. Many people are not aware of this important point. Until quite recently, most experts in exercise physiology believed that the effects of age on heart muscle were inevitable and irreversible. Now direct evidence from human-performance laboratories is starting to show that the tendency of the heart to stiffen and take longer to contract can be countered by regular, vigorous exercise of sufficient duration.

What about stroke volume? It has been known for some time that no significant age change is seen during routine daily activities, but it has been thought that whenever strenuous demands are placed on an older person's heart, the stroke volume is about 10 to 20 percent lower than that of a younger person's. Recent studies show, however, that this is not necessarily true. Healthy older people do have a smaller increase in heart rate during vigorous exercise, but the amount of blood propelled out with each beat is greater, so there is no actual decline in pumping capacity. The heart's ability to pump blood does not drop in fit individuals. The important word here is "fit." Everything hinges on keeping your body in good physical shape.

The oxygen-carrying capacity of the blood may fall off as a person gets older, but it does not have to. Everything depends pretty much on the level of hemoglobin, or red blood cells. The hemoglobin level need not change very much over the years if the daily diet provides sufficient iron. Exercise can help considerably, too—with regular, vigorous exercise there is a sizable increase in blood volume and at the same time a relative increase in red blood cells.

The third aspect of cardiac function that really matters is how much oxygen the body's tissues can draw out of the blood as it comes through the arteries. Oxygen extraction does show a decline with age. At twenty-five a man may absorb up to four-fifths of the oxygen held by a liter of blood. At sixty-five the figure may be down to about three-fifths. One very obvious reason for the decline is the loss of capillaries, the micro-fine branchings of blood vessels that thread through all the tissues and make oxygen delivery possible from blood to cell. Regular, vigorous exercise workouts can, however, increase the density of the capillaries, as part of an overall increase in the number and size of blood vessels that occurs to accommodate the larger blood volume. In this way the increasing distance between the capillaries and the cells that is otherwise seen with age can be reversed, and oxygen extraction, noticeably improved. This benefits cell metabolism throughout every system, organ, and tissue in the body.

Respiratory System

How much oxygen the body gets depends mainly on how efficient the heart is. This is particularly true of young people. But as men and women get older, their lung efficiency may have to be taken into account as well. What kind of changes take place over the years as a rule? To what extent can these adversely affect lung dynamics? Several factors are involved.

Certain anatomical changes that may occur with time do have deteriorative effects on the lungs. The rib cage may become more rigid—its cartilage may show signs of calcifying, and the joints about which the ribs rotate may stiffen. The respiratory muscles may get weaker, particularly if a person has a sedentary lifestyle. Degenerative changes may be seen in the vast network of alveoli, the capillary-laced outpouchings at the furthest ends of the bronchial tree through which gas exchange between lungs and blood takes place. Some capillaries atrophy. And the elastic fibers, so vital in maintaining the resiliency of the lungs' airways, tend to decline in both thickness and number.

Loss of elastic tissue, along with muscular decline and a more rigid rib cage, leads to what is probably the most significant lung change observed as people get older, a decrease in what is called vital capacity. This is the largest amount of air that can be expelled from your lungs after you take the deepest breath you can. As your vital capacity goes down, there is a corresponding increase in residual gas volume, the amount of air still left in your lungs when you have forced out as much air as possible. Total lung capacity— that is, vital capacity plus residual volume—does not change with age.

Is a decline in vital capacity inevitable? Little if any seems to occur among people who keep fit and healthy and do not smoke. The results of two major studies of physical education teachers—who obviously exercised regularly and kept in good condition—over a period of years are quite striking. In one no loss whatever occurred during a span of twenty-one years. In the other only an extremely small decrease was noted over twenty-five years. As these studies clearly show, exercise that is regular and vigorous enough to keep you conditioned has the strongest kind of ageproofing effect on your lungs.

Such exercise can increase vital capacity in healthy young men and women and reverse losses that have occurred in older ones. Tests with the latter have yielded some spectacular results. As much as forty years of cumulative loss was cancelled out by a conditioning program. A six-week stint brought a 5 percent gain, and after a year the gain went up to 20 percent.

These increases reflect strengthened chest muscles and also more elastic rib cartilage. Muscular development—or redevelopment—is still possible at a very advanced age. And although improving chest mobility becomes increasingly difficult late in life, the important thing is that it can be done. Swimming—particularly the crawl and the breast stroke—is unrivaled for preventing loss of vital capacity and reversing any losses that may have already occurred.

All of this takes on tremendous significance in the light of an ongoing study showing consistently inverse relationships between vital capacity and mortality. Four points are emphasized:

- Excess deaths from all major causes occur at low vital capacities.
- Vital capacity is one of the strongest predictors of premature mortality.
- Vital capacity predicts both short-term and long-term mortality.
- Vital capacity seems to be an index of general health and vigor, literally a measure of living capacity.

So keeping up your vital capacity is clearly a very vital fitness priority.

Gastrointestinal System

Changes that can affect people's health often take place in the gastrointestinal, or GI, tract as they get older. But few if any of these changes seem to stem from biological aging processes, and therefore they do not seem to be inevitable. What counts most in order to keep your whole GI tract working well throughout life is to eat properly, exercise regularly, and get enough sleep. A quick glance at the various parts of the system shows you how little change you need expect if the system is not abused.

- *Esophagus*. Usually the only change in healthy older people is less forceful esophageal contraction as food gets pushed downward, apparently because the muscles have weakened. This may be due to eating too-soft foods over too long a period of time. The muscles need something to really work on.
- *Stomach*. Two things usually happen in later decades. The stomach secretes less acid and less of the enzymes that aid digestion. There is a great deal of variation from one individual to the next, however, and most of the time there is no cause for concern.
- *Small intestine*. Age seems to have little or no effect on the absorption of nutrients as long as a person is healthy. If vitamin and mineral absorption is low, this may come from preparing food poorly and eating too little.
- *Colon*. As a person grows older, the main problem in this part of the GI tract is constipation. The condition is linked to reduced food intake, a low-fiber diet, and not enough physical activity—all things that people can easily change as a rule. Everything that is needed to effect such changes can be found in Your Ageproofing Diet Plan and Your Ageproofing Exercise Plan in Part Two. Your Ageproofing Diet Plan can also be very helpful in preventing diverticular disease, the incidence of which increases with age. The disorder, marked by little hernias in the intestinal wall, is prevalent in Western societies and may be linked to diets low in fiber and high in refined sugar and flour. The condition is rarely seen in parts of the world such as South America, Africa, and Asia, where people eat large amounts of high-fiber fruits and vegetables.
- *Liver*. A decrease in size in relation to body weight occurs almost invariably in the liver after people pass fifty or sixty. There may also be certain shifts in enzyme concentrations and their response to stimuli. But despite these changes there does not appear to be any age-linked decline in liver function.

- *Pancreas*. Among healthy individuals there is no significant falloff in efficiency with the years.
- *Gallbladder*. Gallstones are common as people reach the later decades, women being affected twice as much as men. Excessive amounts of saturated fat and cholesterol in the diet are considered the main cause of gallstones. This is but one among a number of reasons why people should reduce dietary fat and cholesterol, as you will see in the next chapter.

Renal System

The kidneys increase in weight from birth to about age thirty, after which a reverse process gets under way. By age eighty a cumulative decline of 20 to 30 percent has usually occurred. The marked drop in weight is due to the loss of close to a third of certain key components in each kidney's one million filtering units, or nephrons. There is a corresponding drop in the filtration rate of substances reaching both kidneys from the bloodstream and also a decrease in renal blood flow.

Just how inevitable is all this? New research indicates that kidney deterioration is due not to aging as such but rather to excessive protein in the diet. A very high-protein meal puts a heavy workload on the kidneys, increasing filtration and renal blood flow by as much as 100 percent. It is one thing when this happens occasionally. But when it occurs daily, the stress can lead to chronic degeneration.

Far too little attention has been paid to the effect that diet has on progressive deterioration of the kidneys. Although doctors take a person's eating habits into account and prescribe changes when the kidneys are diseased or damaged, they may not pay enough attention to the influence of diet on healthy kidneys. Large daily doses of protein are a recent development historically, one that evolution has not prepared people to handle. Bringing the diet more in line with what people are naturally adapted to through evolution can do a great deal to prevent kidney decline.

Besides moderating protein intake, controlling calories can also have a beneficial effect. The idea is to hold them at a level sufficient for proper nutrition but healthily free of any excess, so that the kidneys are not taxed unnecessarily.

Recent findings indicate that too much dietary fat can be as bad for the kidneys as too much protein. So it seems advisable, for this reason as well as for so many others, to cut back on fat too.

The kind of diet that is most helpful for the lifelong health of the kidneys is the very one that protects against so many of today's deteriorative processes and chronic degenerative diseases. You will find the guidelines spelled out for you in Your Ageproofing Diet Plan.

Reproductive System

The menopause can be very distressing for a great many women. And the sense of decreased potency that men often have later in life can also be depressing. Such changes symbolize for most people the end of an optimal period of their life—in many ways quite needlessly.

Women's Changes

The changes that lead up to, accompany, and follow the menopause are of course far more obvious than those which older men may experience. They are genetically programmed and part of true aging processes. They cannot be prevented, delayed, or reversed by any known natural means. And the fact that the menopause occurs at a relatively early age, often well before fifty, compounds its potentially traumatic impact.

Just because the menopause is the end of the childbearing years does not mean it is also the end of sex. So the effect it has on the vagina is a cause for concern as a number of unwelcome changes are apt to occur. The vagina tends to get shorter and narrower and lose elasticity and turgor. And its mucous membranes may get thin and dry because of the drop in circulating estrogen levels. But some intriguing new research shows that women can do far more than they probably realize to prevent and even partially reverse these undesirable side effects, and do so without recourse to estrogen therapy. For the vagina as for other organs, the operating principle is: Use it. The best way to keep the vagina fit and healthy and in good shape for sexual activity is sex. Conditioning, as one authority puts it, is "sport-specific."

Postmenopausal women who keep sexually active—with intercourse at least once or twice a week—have significantly less vaginal atrophy than sexually inactive women. Particularly fascinating is the finding that the activists have much higher levels of androgens, the male sex hormones, and gonadotropins, the sex-priming hormones. It has generally been assumed that vaginal atrophy is due simply to estrogen loss. But it now appears that when estrogen is in low supply, as it is after the menopause, androgens may play a key role in promoting growth of the vaginal membrane and retarding atrophic changes as well as reducing any losses that may have already occurred. The higher androgen and gonadotropin levels may have other benefits. Androgens rather than estrogens may, according to several recent studies, play a key role in maintaining sexual interest both before and after the menopause. And a high level of gonadotropins in sexually active women seems to foster pubic hair growth. In light of all this, it is pretty clear that intercourse has just about everything going for it—should anyone have entertained any doubts on the subject.

Men's Changes

These follow a subtler and more varied course, and one that is very closely linked to a man's overall level of health and fitness. Older men who keep in good physical shape can apparently maintain their output of sex hormones at the levels of young men. This recent finding casts doubt on earlier reports indicating that testosterone declines and female hormones rise as men get older. There is also a direct correlation between testosterone and sexual activity, potent evidence that the use-it-or-lose-it principle holds for men as well as women. Men in their seventies and eighties who are sexually active have stepped-up levels of testosterone; they show no drop whatever in concentrations of the hormone as a result of age. They ejaculate as many sperm as twenty-year-olds, the one difference being that the proportion of immature sperm seems to increase with advancing years. In spite of this, male fertility can continue into extreme old age. Men in their nineties have fathered children.

While most healthy men continue to be sexually active decade after decade, some do lose interest and as it were get out of practice. Contrary to general opinion, however, studies now indicate that such factors as marital adjustment, attractiveness of one's partner, and age do not necessarily affect the sexual functioning of healthy older men all that much. In at least a third of the cases in which an older man reports little sexual activity or none at all, there is no hormonal cause and no sense of sexual deprivation. Physiological changes in the central nervous system that reduce the erotic effect of visual stimuli, normally of great importance to men, are what seem to be involved. Disuse may have a good deal to do with this decline. The ageproofing message for men is emphatically: Use it.

The brain plays an important part in regulating sex hormone activity at any age. The dynamic balance between the numerous hormones and transmitters has far more significant psychological and physiological effects than this or that hormone by itself. Keeping your body in good shape can have a beneficial influence on these hormonal and neural interactions and the cascades of enzymes that facilitate them and so help you have a good sex life.

Immune System

The immune system is responsible for your body's self-defense, protecting every organ, tissue, and cell against danger from without or within. As powerful as it is complex, this remarkable system can deal swiftly and surely with foreign bacteria, viruses, and fungi and also with aberrant cells that arise within the body's own tissues and threaten its integrity and well-being.

As people grow older, this defense system tends to become less efficient. The loss of immune vigor predisposes them to infections, chronic diseases such as cardiovascular disease, and autoimmune disorders like rheumatoid arthritis. Immunological decline over the decades varies a good deal from one person to the next. There are plenty of men and women in their sixties and seventies whose immune response is virtually indistinguishable from that of men and women in their twenties and thirties. Only the progressive atrophy of the thymus, a small gland located just below the breastbone and a key component in immune function, seems to be more or less invariably linked to advancing age. As a matter of fact, the gland starts to decline in size and output of thymic hormones between the ages of eleven and fifteen, and continues to wind down from then on. Among many people in their later decades the immune response has dwindled to no more than 5 percent of its youthful peak value, and this of course can have highly disabling effects. It is not surprising that the thymus gland is often called the aging clock of the immune system.

Is this immunological decline inevitable? There is increasing evidence to the contrary. Scientists are now finding that it may be possible to maintain your immune defenses throughout your entire lifetime by means of some very simple changes in your diet and exercise habits, and without recourse to drugs of any kind.

The suggested dietary shift involves a reduction in total calories—cutting down very gradually until a person has reached a weight somewhat lower than what is known in life-insurance circles as the desirable level—while keeping the nutrient content of the diet high. Such "undernutrition without malnutrition" has been shown in animal studies to keep the immune system younger for a longer period of time. There is even evidence that it can increase the lifespan significantly.

Although it is still too early to spell out just how and to what extent exercise can improve your immune status, experts are finding that regular, vigorous physical activity can both stimulate and help maintain good immune function. Studies now under way indicate that exercise can have a very positive influence on the body's response to antigens, or foreign substances. Looking at it from the opposite angle, Russian researchers have demonstrated the deleterious effects that lack of physical activity has on immune competence. If volunteers are subjected to a long period of bedrest a series of immunological deficiencies occur. They can, however, be reversed by a daily program of exercise. Even routines done in bed are enough to offset the decline of the body's defenses.

White Blood Cells. Exercise of any kind increases the circulation's white blood cell count. This is important because white blood cells provide a wide variety of immune surveillance mechanisms and act as a first line of defense against disease. Their rise during exercise is extraordinarily rapid. From a basal level of 5,000 to 8,000 per cubic millimeter of blood they soar to as many as 35,000 after a quarter-mile sprint lasting only a minute. The greater the amount of exercise stress, the more the white blood cells multiply.

This dramatic increase may bolster your body's defense against infection not only by counterattacking antigens but also through another and quite unexpected mechanism. Fascinating new research suggests there is a link between this surge and the rise in body temperature that occurs during strenuous exercise—the temperature goes up to anywhere from 100 to 104 degrees Fahrenheit, and it remains above normal for as much as an hour after the exercise has stopped. Called jogger's fever, the elevated temperature is produced by the same substance in your blood that brings on a fever when you have the flu or some other infection. It is released by the white blood cells as you exercise. The more the white blood cell population is stepped up, the more this substance—known technically as endogenous pyrogen —is too. So as exercise becomes more intense, the temperature rise becomes more marked. Like a mild fever at the start of an infection, the one you experience during such periods of vigorous exercise can help you ward off illness by inducing physiological changes hostile to viral or bacterial growth.

Red Blood Cells. Intriguing as these recent findings about the link between the white blood cells' defense operation and exercise are, an even more unexpected and very powerful link may exist between the red blood cells and exercise. Until recently it was simply assumed that there was a clear-cut division of labor between white blood cells and red blood cells. In contrast to the white cells' many-faceted immunological action in defending the body against invaders, red cells were believed to function mainly as highly specialized carriers, delivering oxygen and other nutrients to the tissues throughout the body and carrying away carbon dioxide and a mix of other waste products. Now, however, provocative discoveries point to a key immunological role for red blood cells as well.

The new evidence indicates that red blood cells participate quite actively in immune function and that their hitherto overlooked contributions are as diverse as they are important. They can destroy foreign organisms either directly, by means of a lethal enzyme called perioxidase, or indirectly, by bringing killer white cells together with the invaders for a head-on confrontation. Either way, infectious agents are five hundred to a thousand times more likely to be attacked by a red blood cell than by a white one. The red blood cells are also the primary agents for clearing away what remains of enemy forces after each onslaught, in this way preventing any potentially harmful caches from being deposited in susceptible areas. A quite formidable performance.

How does the red blood cells' immunological role tie in with exercise's protective effects against infection? One of the body's automatic adaptations to any program of regular and sufficiently vigorous exercise is a conspicuous and lasting rise in the number of red blood cells as part of an overall increase in blood volume. This boost in red blood cells steps up the immune system's capacity to respond to invaders. The more red blood cells, the more protection.

One thing is certain. People who are in good physical shape rid themselves of, say, a respiratory infection much faster than those who are not. Higher rates of infection are noted in people who have a low red blood cell count. Exercising regularly and vigorously increases the immune response substantially, experts stress, as long as you do not go to extremes. If you exercise to the point of exhaustion continually, your immune response is decreased. In other words, too much exercise can be too much of a good thing.

A program of regular, vigorous exercise, together with a nutritionally balanced diet that cuts calories to a healthy level, can help you keep your body's defense system in fighting shape over the years.

Nervous System

The nervous system, with the brain at its center, governs the workings of every cell, tissue, and organ in your body, guided by the ceaseless flow of information it receives and processes from without and within through the various senses. What happens to this immeasurably complex intelligence and control system over the years is obviously of crucial importance to you.

Your brain controls or influences your body's functions directly and swiftly through the nerves, more slowly and indirectly through circulating hormones. Neural and hormonal regulatory changes occur during every period of your life. There does not seem to be such a thing as a "steady state." As nerve and hormone shifts take place, the brain may respond by introducing still others. Change is the one constant. Body functions are in an ever-shifting dynamic balance at every phase of life.

Brain

The brain itself undergoes certain changes over the years. The most obvious one is loss of weight. After reaching a maximum between twenty-five and thirty-five, weight slowly decreases until by eighty or eighty-five it has dropped by 10 to 20 percent. Neuron, or nerve cell, atrophy accounts for most of the reduction, which is not uniform. In some parts of the brain there is no decline at all. In others there is a marked decline, especially in the cerebral cortex, the mantle of extremely developed gray matter that surrounds the two hemispheres of the cerebrum and is considered the site of the higher mental activities. In some of these cortical areas, neuron loss accelerates from age fifty on, with as much as a 50 percent reduction by age ninety. Beneath the cerebrum lies the cerebellum, which processes movement and sensory information. Its cortical nerve cells may decrease by 25 percent over a lifetime, with stepped-up losses after age fifty. Then comes the brainstem, which lies against the cerebellum at the top of the spinal column. It sorts out information going to the higher regions of the brain and carries out a number of coordinating functions. Sizeable neuron losses occur in a few specific areas of the brainstem, but there is little overall decline.

Not only are neuron losses selective in region and timing but smaller nerve cells are eliminated in greater number than larger ones, the smaller cells being younger and at an earlier stage of development. Nerve cells follow the rule, "Last in, first out."

Adaptation. The decline in neurons does not entail any corresponding decline in mental ability, you will be glad to hear. For one thing, there is a very generous margin of redundancy in the brain: you have many more brain cells than you need. For another, it has now been shown that in individuals who are fit and healthy the dendrites—branches of the neurons which serve as communication lines to other neurons and are therefore vitally important—continue to grow and multiply and reach out to form masses of new connections during all of life.

This new finding indicates that there is much more adaptability in the brain as the years go by than anybody had realized. Dendritic growth may be part of a lifelong process of development, but it may also be one way in which the brain compensates for neuron loss. And there is the intriguing possibility that a link exists between extensive dendritic sprouting and the stimulation a mentally and physically active lifestyle provides—what researchers call an enriched environment in contrast to a deprived one. In the absence of disease, brain impairment may simply be due to lower mental and physical levels of activity. The less brain structures are used, the more the dendrites are apt to wither away.

A spectacular new technique shows vividly that brain activity levels do not decline with the years. Using radioactive tracers, it measures how much glucose is being metabolized and where, and produces a color-keyed chart displaying the results—a sort of cerebral weather map. Readings disclose that glucose utilization, and therefore brain activity, rises during a person's growing years and then remains constant throughout life.

What this means, actually, is that the metabolism of each neuron is higher in an older person's brain than in a younger one's and that the older brain simply has to work a bit harder in order to maintain the same level of functioning as the younger one.

Fitness. The value of physical exercise for mental well-being and fitness is being recognized more and more. The stimulus it provides may help protect against the loss of what psychologists call fluid intelligence as opposed to crystallized intelligence. Crystallized intelligence, which depends on experience and knowledge and verbal ability, increases with age. Fluid intelligence, which depends on rapidity of responsiveness, memory, and alertness, is said to decline somewhat with age. As people get older, adaptive responses that depend on fluid intelligence tend to slow down. This process is related to a very complex interplay among various hormones, each being subject to age-related alterations in its regulation. The time required to make these adaptive responses is directly proportional to a person's age as a rule. It is, however, entirely possible that a regular program of vigorous exercise can do a great deal to counter such tendencies.

An important question is whether an older person's brain is able to respond as well as a younger person's when challenged by a stressful situation. In the brain as in other parts of the body, it may be the response to a stress challenge rather than functioning under routine conditions that becomes an increasing problem with age. But if you keep your brain in the best possible shape from day to day—with the conditioning that vigorous physical as well as mental activity provides—it remains primed for stressful levels of activity. Physical activity and mental activity enhance each other's effects. Mental demands have a significant physical dimension—there is a pronounced increase in blood flow and delivery of oxygen and glucose to the brain. And if you keep your brain in good physical shape through physical exertion, this can help you deal more effectively with mental stress, just as keeping your body in top physical condition helps.

Sight

People's eyes change in various and quite predictable ways through all of life. And from about age forty on, just about every component of the visual system seems to undergo some deterioration. Although much of this change has long been assumed to be due to true aging changes, the link between aging and visual loss may not be as strong as people think.

One very familiar deteriorative change is presbyopia, which means "sight of the old." The condition is one in which the lens, the eye's adjustable focusing structure, fails to accommodate to near vision. This is the reason you see so many old people holding their reading matter at arm's length as they try to zero in on the print. It has long been believed that presbyopia results from increasing rigidity of the lens with age. But the problem, according to the latest research, is not so much with the lens itself as with the muscles and ligaments controlling it and also with those regulating the size of the pupil, the opening through which light enters the eye.

For close vision the pupillary muscles contract to increase the depth of focus, and the lens muscles work to provide the greatest possible curvature for the lens. With time, however, changes in the strength and elasticity of these muscles account for the decreased ability to focus on very near objects. But recent studies show that there is more plasticity in the muscles of the eye than has been realized. It may be possible to retain focusing power by exercising these muscles and thereby increasing their strength and flexibility. Although this has not yet been demonstrated in humans, it has been convincingly shown in monkeys.

Light. The most important changes that occur in the visual system as people get older have to do with the transmission and reception of light. In order to stimulate sight, a certain optimal range of light must reach and be absorbed by the photoreceptor, or light-receiving, cells of the retina at the back of the eye.

The pupil plays a very significant role in light transmission because it controls, by its constant dilations and contractions, the amount of light admitted into the eye. After reaching its maximum dilation capability between ages twelve and fifteen, the pupil becomes much smaller over the years until by age fifty there is a 50 percent reduction in diameter. This decline, which makes a noticeable difference in visual capacity, is due to atrophy of the muscles that control dilation. One day in the forseeable future, however, a way may be found to prevent the atrophy of these muscles.

The pupil is not the only part of the eye that undergoes changes affecting light transmission. There are more extensive ones in the lens. Besides focusing, another thing the lens does is to absorb light energy and so protect the retina from damaging radiation. Absorption increases dramatically after age forty. One reason is that the lens continues to grow in size throughout a person's lifetime, and the larger it becomes, the more light it absorbs. Particularly damaging are the ultraviolet, or UV, wavelengths. They lead in due course to an increasingly opaque yellow coloration of the lens and a concomitant decrease in the amount of visible light that gets through.

The cumulative effect of decades of exposure to UV radiation can be very harmful to the lens. Evidence from a number of countries indicates an extremely strong link between chronic sunlight exposure, and one type of cataract, the brownish cataract. Even though other factors—which include nutrition, metabolism, and biological aging factors —may be involved in cataract formation, the link between a deepening opaque color of the lens and chronic UV exposure is an important one.

The decline in light transmission caused by changes in the pupil and the lens from decade to decade can have a progressively noticeable effect. By age sixty only a third as much light may reach the retina as at age twenty, and the retina itself may become less efficient. The result is a loss of acuity—the ability to distinguish fine detail—and of image resolution. There are, however, surprisingly easy ways in which you can protect your eyes against the insidious damage caused by UV radiation, as you will see in Chapter Four.

Hearing

As people grow older, their ability to hear well usually declines significantly. The term used to describe this age-related impairment, presbycusis, means literally "old hearing." One change is quantitative: faint sounds like a whisper are harder to detect. Another change is qualitative: high-pitch sounds are not picked up as easily.

The quantitative change is due to loss of elasticity in the part of the auditory system known as the middle ear. The eardrum may thicken and stiffen. And the ligaments connecting the minute bones of the middle ear to one another may become less flexible, thus muffling vibrations transmitted to the shell-shaped organ of the inner ear called the cochlea. Such conditions usually reflect a poor blood supply resulting from heart disease, high blood pressure, or other cardiovascular disturbances. They are not to be blamed on aging as such.

Noise. The qualitative impairment comes from irreversible damage to the inner ear, specifically, the cochlea, with its vulnerable little sound-sensing hairs. Especially marked is the loss of sensitivity to higher frequencies. But here again, there is no reason to believe that the damage is due to inherent aging processes, as is commonly thought. Most often it is the result of prolonged exposure to loud noise. This overwhelms and flattens the tiny cochlea hairs, knocking some of them temporarily out of operation and—if the noise is sustained long enough—some permanently. The level of sound and duration of exposure are the two key factors. Industrial noise has been one big hazard in the past but is now increasingly regulated. Disco music, another hazard, is unfortunately not.

There is growing concern that lower levels of chronic noise exposure may in the long run be almost as damaging as exposure to shorter bursts of very loud sound. Experts think that years of exposure to such everyday sources of noise as vacuum cleaners, dishwashers, lawn mowers, hair dryers, city traffic, and stereo sets, can be an insidious cause of hearing loss. And it may be that the cassette earphones so many people now wear as they jog, roller skate, or just walk down the street are particularly hazardous.

Hearing loss is becoming increasing prevalent today. Altogether, between sixteen and seventeen million people in the western world are either totally deaf or significantly hard of hearing. In all this, however, one thing is quite clear: presbycusis is not primarily due to aging, if at all. There are societies in the world, the Mabaan people of the Sudan, for example, where presbycusis does not exist. Both the men and women of this remote Sudanese tribe have excellent hearing in old age—in fact, an eighty-year-old Mabaan tribesman's hearing is better than the average thirty-year-old American's. The environment in which the Mabaans live is exceptionally quiet by Western standards. Also, they do not suffer from heart disease, hypertension, or any of the other chronic diseases that affect so many people in industrialized countries during their later years.

So presbycusis is a misnomer. "Old hearing" results not from getting old but rather from a lifetime of abusive exposure to noise, together with the subtle effects of chronic, degenerative disease—all things that you can do a great deal to prevent.

CHAPTER 3

Preventing the "Diseases of Aging"

The way to keep your body in good working order decade after decade is to use it well day after day. You do not want to let any part fall into disuse. You do not want to subject any part to abuse.

Your body has innumerable kinds of repair mechanisms and fail-safe devices to cope with problems arising from disuse or abuse. But these safety systems work only up to a point. They are not infallible. You have to do your share, too. If you do not respect your body and give it a chance to work the way it is meant to, this can trigger a whole cascade of deteriorative changes and lead to one or more of the chronic diseases that take such a high toll of health and life each year. Coronary heart disease, stroke, high blood pressure, obesity, diabetes, osteoporosis, osteoarthritis, and cancer are the main ones.

It is extremely important to begin protecting yourself against these so-called diseases of aging as early as possible.

One reason is that they get under way surprisingly early, often while people are still in their twenties or thirties, and sometimes even before. The sooner you start to take preventive action, the greater the amount of protection you can count on.

Another reason is that most of these diseases do their damage insidiously for many years before surfacing and being recognized, by which time serious and perhaps lethal harm may have been done.

A third reason is that these chronic degenerative diseases

are very complex in origin. They do not have a single, identifiable cause like the bacteria or viruses responsible for infectious diseases, which can most often be warded off with
a vaccine or knocked out with an antibiotic. Treatment is
generally difficult and the outcome, uncertain. So it is all the
more important for you to reduce your risk of getting these
diseases in the first place.

As one of today's most perceptive health experts says
emphatically, there is no drug or medical treatment on the
market, or even on the horizon, that holds the promise simple everyday preventive measures do against these major
cripplers and killers.

Coronary Heart Disease

Cardiovascular disease, which includes various disorders of
the heart and blood vessels, kills more people in the western
world than all other causes of death combined. The annual
toll, in Great Britain alone, at the last count was over three
hundred thousand. And literally millions suffer from one or
more forms of cardiovascular disease, the three major ones
being coronary heart disease, stroke, and hypertension. It is
important to know what you can do to ageproof your health
against each of these three lethal threats, so they are taken
up individually here and in the two sections that follow.

Within the cardiovascular group, coronary heart disease is
the number one killer and also a leading cause of disability
among both men and women. The heart attacks it is responsible for result in about 180,000 deaths a year in the United
Kingdom. There are far, far more non-fatal heart coronaries.
In the United States the statistics show that three people get
a heart attack each minute.

No age category is spared. Coronary heart disease accounts for a third of all deaths among people between thirty-
five and sixty-four, although up until the menopause women
are far less vulnerable than men. Among men twenty-five to
forty-four and women forty-five to sixty-four it is the second
leading cause of death. And among men over forty-five and

women over sixty-five it is the leading cause of death. Rates for black and white men are approximately the same. Black women, however, have significantly higher rates than white women, and this holds true at every age.

Coronary Heart Disease Risk Factors

All told, some thirty-seven risk factors have been implicated in the development of coronary heart disease, but the important thing is to know the main ones. There are a few, such as being a male or having a family history of cardiovascular disease, that it is obviously impossible to do anything about. But four key factors are ones that you have it well within your power to control: high blood levels of cholesterol, high blood pressure, smoking, and diabetes. There are in addition two other important factors that you should be aware of: obesity and lack of physical exercise. Your aim should be at least to reduce and preferably to eliminate any of these risk factors that you have. The more you are able to do this, the better off you are.

The risk factors have a multiplying effect on each other in increasing your chance of getting a heart attack. It is much more than a matter of one risk simply being added to another. If you have one of the four big risk factors, according to a recent and very thorough survey, you are twice as likely to have a heart attack as if you had none. If you have two, you are five times as likely to have a heart attack. And if you have three, your heart attack risk is at least eight times greater.

Smoking. Of the six key risk factors, smoking calls for the most unqualified advice: do not smoke. If you do smoke, stop. If you do not smoke, do not start. Smoking can hook you very quickly as you will see in Your Ageproofing Anti-Smoking Guidelines in Part Two. Smoking devastates your health in many ways, and most of all by endangering your heart. One fatal heart attack out of every four is directly caused by cigarettes.

Chronic Diseases. Three other risk factors—high blood pressure, diabetes, and obesity—are themselves chronic, degenerative diseases. What you need to know in order to protect yourself against them is spelled out for you a little further on in this chapter, each of the diseases being taken up in turn.

Inactivity. Lack of exercise has numerous detrimental effects on your health, as noted throughout my book, and those relating to the heart are of course of special importance.

Cholesterol. High blood cholesterol is a very big risk because it is intimately linked with a condition called atherosclerosis, which is the underlying cause of coronary heart disease and is characterized by a progressive clogging of the arteries. Atherosclerosis used to be thought of, by and large, as an inevitable and irrevocable result of biological aging processes. But it is now quite clear that the disorder can be prevented or, if already present, halted and even partially reversed. The amount of regression depends on the extent of the arterial obstruction and how long it has been building up.

Atherosclerosis often starts in childhood, and the clogging of the arteries can already be quite extensive by the mid-twenties. What happens is that deposits of cholesterol—a whitish fatty compound—along with other fats, a clotting factor called fibrin, cellular debris, and various other substances accumulate at spots along the lining of the arteries where a slight injury may have left the surface somewhat rough. Plaques then form at these sites and with time increase in size as more and more deposits adhere to the artery wall. With each new deposit the passageway through each affected vessel becomes narrower. Blood flow is impeded, often to the point where it is no more than a trickle. This makes it easy for a clot to close off what little space remains, thereby blocking the channel and leading to the death of the surrounding tissue, deprived as it is of oxygen and other nutrients. When this whole process takes place in the arteries of the heart, the result is coronary heart disease and a heart attack.

The link between high blood levels of cholesterol, atherosclerosis, and coronary heart disease is very strong. This does not mean, however, that you would want to entirely eliminate cholesterol from your blood. Cholesterol is essential to body tissues and systems. A moderate level of cholesterol traffic in your blood is necessary in order to take care of daily metabolic needs. But your body manufactures sufficient amounts of the compound on its own, so any dietary intake of it simply creates a surplus. The foods that contain cholesterol are of animal origin: meat, poultry, fish, eggs, milk, and other dairy products. People eating the typical American diet every day get much too much cholesterol, especially if they eat eggs and fatty meats regularly. They may absorb as much cholesterol from dietary sources as they produce themselves.

If the body could balance this surplus by making proportionately less cholesterol or by getting rid of larger amounts, there would be no problem. But, unfortunately, it does not seem to adjust very well to the excess cholesterol. The disposal system may simply get overloaded. Cholesterol levels in the blood go up and sooner or later the excess gets deposited in various tissues, the lining of the arteries, in particular. This starts the atherosclerotic process and, once it is underway, sustains it.

Cholesterol does not circulate in the bloodstream in a free state. It is carried in packets known as lipoproteins, so called because they are made up of lipids, or fats, and proteins. The two most important types of lipoproteins are low density lipoproteins (LDL) and high density lipoproteins (HDL). LDL carries far more cholesterol in its packets—about 60 percent of the total amount in the blood—and delivers it to all the tissues of the body that need it. HDL packets carry much less cholesterol. Their job is to remove excess cholesterol from the tissues and cart this surplus to the liver, where it is broken down and then sent on its way for excretion from the body.

The distinction between LDL and HDL is crucial. High levels of LDL cholesterol increase the risk of atherosclerosis and coronary heart disease. High levels of HDL cholesterol are on the other hand protective, and the higher the levels, the lower the heart risk. Interestingly, women usually have more HDL and less LDL than men, and they are also less prone to heart attacks.

The cholesterol measurement that is taken in a routine blood test is for the total amount in your blood. This measurement can be a good indicator of heart risk, because when the total cholesterol level is high, so is the LDL level, as a rule. A desirable range for total cholesterol, as worked out by leading experts, is 160 to 180 milligrams per deciliter (the unit of measurement that is used). Above 190 to 220 the risk tends to rise quite fast, and, as it happens, one half of all the men in this country are in that accelerating risk range. It is very helpful to get a separate reading of your LDL and HDL cholesterol, as noted in Chapter Eight.

Diet Against Coronary Heart Disease

The type of fat that people eat can, like dietary cholesterol, have a very important effect on their blood cholesterol level. Saturated fat, found mainly in animal products, raises it. Polyunsaturated fat, found mainly in vegetables and fish, lowers it. Monounsaturated fat, found especially in olive oil, does nothing one way or the other. The mechanism by which the fat you eat affects your blood cholesterol levels has not yet been completely figured out, but it is known that fat of any kind facilitates cholesterol absorption. Also, polyunsaturated fat steps up cholesterol excretion from the body and may even reduce the ability of LDL packets to carry around so much. You will find out more about all this in Chapter Five.

Different fatty acids present in different fats may increase the risk of coronary heart disease and a heart attack in different ways, according to some fascinating new research. Certain saturated fatty acids, such as those in coconut oil, seem strongly atherogenic, meaning that they foster the buildup of deposits along the lining of the arteries. They do not greatly affect the blood's thrombotic, or clotting, tendency. The clotting tendency is increased particularly by the saturated fatty acids found in animal fat. In contrast, polyunsaturated fatty acids, especially those found in fatty fish like salmon, reduce the clotting tendency. This is why moderate amounts of fatty fish, along with the leaner varieties, can be such a healthy component of your diet.

If you keep to a diet low in cholesterol and saturated fat and are able to maintain a desirable blood level of cholesterol from year to year and decade to decade, no significant atherosclerosis is likely to occur during your lifetime. This is one of the main reasons why Your Ageproofing Diet Plan can be so helpful in protecting you against this disorder. The diet also provides you with other foods that have been shown to be protective. Special emphasis is placed on fruits and vegetables and whole grains, the fresh fiber foods that help guard against coronary heart disease. If you like a glass or two of wine with your meals, this may give you an additional edge in countering atherosclerotic buildup, though the reasons for this protection are not at all clear. Intake should of course be kept moderate, because alcohol can be very harmful to your health in other ways.

Exercise Against Coronary Heart Disease

Vigorous physical activity is as important as diet in ageproofing your health against coronary heart disease. People who get sufficient amounts of exercise have less than half the heart attack risk that physically inactive people do, and their death rate from coronaries is but a third that of sedentary individuals.

For one thing, vigorous exercise impedes the development of atherosclerosis by improving blood fat levels, lowering LDL cholesterol, and raising HDL cholesterol. While diet may be more effective in bringing LDL levels down, exercise can be more effective in sending HDL levels up. Endurance runners, for example, have extremely high readings of this protective lipoprotein.

The conditioning you get from a program of exercise that meets aerobic requirements for intensity, duration, and frequency can also help protect blood vessels against the stickiness of the little blood particles called platelets and therefore the aggregation and adhesion so closely linked to the whole atherosclerotic process. This reduces the risk of thrombus, or clot, formation, which is so often the immediate cause of coronary thrombosis. Exercise protects against thrombus formation in two ways. If sufficiently vigorous and sustained, exercise can increase the fluid, or plasma, volume of the blood enough to thin it and make it less viscous. Exercise can also inhibit the formation and accumulation of fibrin, a key component of clots present in the blood, so that excess clotting is less likely. This is of particular significance to women on the pill, because there is mounting evidence that heart attacks due to oral contraceptives are very apt to be thrombotic in origin. Fibrin accumulation at arterial deposit spots is stimulated by oral contraceptive use.

Because exercise, among its many benefits, reduces the percentage of body fat, it can indirectly help protect against high blood pressure, diabetes, and of course obesity, three of the most important risk factors for coronary heart disease. Exercise has a direct lowering effect on resting blood pressure. There is in addition evidence that the mechanical action of the increased blood flow and the flexing of the arteries that automatically occurs with any exertion help prevent plaque formation. Exercise even tones and strengthens the muscular artery walls, increasing their elasticity and widening the diameter of the channel they form.

By strengthening the heart muscle, exercise enhances the heart's functioning in several ways. There is a marked increase in blood volume, a more effective return of blood to the heart from outlying parts of the body, and a slower heart rate—both at any given level of exertion and at rest—which allows more time for the heart to fill with blood between contractions. The increased stroke volume improves oxygen uptake and therefore makes for greater work capacity and endurance. Further reduction in heart rate results from certain skeletal muscle changes and also decreased respiratory demands. All this not only improves cardiovascular efficiency but also reduces the risk of coronary heart disease.

Stroke

There were, according to the latest statistics, seventy eight and a half thousand deaths from stroke in the United Kingdom during one year. At least three times as many will have suffered from strokes, many of whom will be severely incapacitated. A devastating mental and physical crippler as well as a killer, stroke involves the blood vessels that supply oxygen and other nutrients to the brain. It occurs when the blood flow is interrupted by either a clot or a hemorrhage and results in brain impairment of varying degrees of severity.

Two Kinds of Stroke

Between 85 and 90 percent of all strokes are caused by a clot, or thrombus, that blocks an artery feeding the brain. The affected artery need not itself be located in the brain; a stroke can be triggered by blockage in one of the arteries of the neck. There are two distinct types of thrombotic stroke. In the more common one, known as cerebral thrombosis, a clot big enough to completely plug up the arterial passageway is formed right on the spot. This is especially apt to occur in an artery that is already clogged by heavy atherosclerotic buildup. The other type of thrombotic stroke is a cerebral embolism: a circulating clot called an embolus, carried along in the bloodstream, gets wedged in one of the arteries nourishing the brain and stops the blood flow.

Some 10 to 15 percent of all strokes are hemorrhagic—that is, they are caused by bleeding from a ruptured artery. Hemorrhagic strokes, while far less common than thrombotic strokes, are much more likely to be fatal. They take place when a defective artery in the brain bursts, flooding the surrounding tissue with blood. The spill deprives brain cells in the region of oxygen and other nutrients, making it impossible for them to continue functioning. The accumulation of blood from the burst artery puts pressure on the inundated tissue, and this too may interfere with brain func-

tion. In some instances the hemorrhage is caused by a ruptured aneurysm—a ballooning out from a weak spot in an
artery wall. The development of an aneurysm is often linked
to high blood pressure, which is the major risk factor for
stroke. It can occur anywhere in the body and in some areas
does not cause serious trouble. But in a cerebral artery it is
potentially very dangerous.

Even though over 60 percent of stroke victims survive
each year, they may be severely handicapped mentally and
physically for the rest of their life. So preventing a stroke is
obviously of the utmost importance. And the way to go
about protecting yourself against any kind of stroke is to
reduce the risk factors most closely linked to it.

Stroke Risk Factors

Two of these risk factors are genetic and cannot be changed.
The first is sex, with men at slightly greater risk than
women. The second is race, with Blacks at greater risk than
Whites. But there are four major factors that can be
changed: high blood pressure, atherosclerosis, diabetes, and
a high red blood cell count. Whatever your genetic back-
ground, you can lower your overall chance of having a
stroke by protecting yourself against these four conditions.

High Blood Pressure is the most important risk factor for
stroke. It is even more strongly linked to cerebrovascular
disease—hemorrhagic strokes, in particular—than it is to
coronary heart disease. The fact that Blacks are more likely
to develop hypertension than Whites has a lot to do with
their being more prone to stroke. Preventing high blood
pressure or, if it is already present, lowering it to within the
normal range, can greatly reduce the chance of a stroke. As
you will see in the pages immediately following this section,
you can do much to avoid or correct high blood pressure
simply by making sure that you exercise right and eat right.

Atherosclerosis increases the chance of a stroke because
it is so heavily implicated in the artery clogging and clot
forming responsible for thrombotic strokes. Here again, getting a good amount of exercise on a regular basis and eating

the right kind of food every day can make a vital difference. The same exercise principles and dietary guidelines that work to guard against a heart attack also work to guard against a brain attack, which is what a stroke is.

Adult Diabetes, along with the obesity that usually triggers it, is another important risk factor for stroke. It too can be successfully countered; weight control is the main thing. The food you eat and the exercise you get are what really count if you are genetically predisposed to diabetes and are conspicuously overweight. Juvenile diabetes requires special medical care.

High Red Blood Cell Count, the fourth major risk factor for stroke, is one of the most serious of all, and yet very few people are even aware of it. There is nothing wrong with having a good supply of red blood cells. They are essential to life and health. For one thing, they deliver vital oxygen to every cell in the body. If you do not have enough red blood cells, you are anemic. But people can have too much of a good thing. If they gain an excess amount of weight, the red blood cell count increases to a disproportionate degree in comparison with the amount of plasma, or fluid portion of the blood. This upsets the balance between the two, making the blood thicker and its flow slower. The sluggish circulation allows clotting factors to accumulate in one place and foster clot formation, especially if atherosclerotic buildup is present to further slow the flow.

Exercise on a regular basis, if sufficiently vigorous, can counter clot formation. It boosts the production of chemical activators that prevent unwanted clotting. It also leads to a greater blood volume with a proportionately larger increase in the fluid portion of the blood than in the solid red cell portion. Because such thinning makes the blood flow more freely, clotting risk is reduced and oxygen delivery to the tissues is enhanced.

The thinning effect that exercise has on the blood is something which every woman on the pill would do well to remember, because oral contraceptives increase the risk for thrombotic stroke. By exercising regularly and vigorously for at least a half hour at a time, she can reduce the risk of clot formation and therefore of thrombotic stroke. While it is not yet known if exercise can entirely eliminate the danger of blood clots, indications are that it is strongly protective. And by keeping or getting the blood pressure healthily low, women on the pill can guard against both kinds of stroke, hemorrhagic as well as thrombotic.

In order to protect yourself against stroke in every way possible, keep in mind the point stressed in the preceding section about the anti-thrombotic effects of certain foods, especially fatty fish such as salmon, tuna, bluefish, and mackerel. There is very strong evidence that the type of polyunsaturated fat in these fish counters clotting tendencies most effectively.

High Blood Pressure

Many million people in the western world have high blood pressure, or hypertension, often by age thirty-five or even earlier. And the number of people affected by this pervasive disease is increasing every year. Hypertension is a serious concern in itself. It is also, as previously noted, one of the major factors in the large number of strokes that take such a devastating annual toll in this country and a leading contributor to the hundreds of thousands of heart attacks. Kidney failure is still another life-threatening consequence to be reckoned with. High blood pressure is particularly insidious because there are almost never any warning signals until the condition is so far advanced that it has already done considerable harm. This is why it is known as the silent killer. The only way you can tell if your blood pressure is too high is to have it checked at regular intervals. Once a year is the usual recommendation, but if your blood pressure is found to be even slightly on the high side, more frequent checks are advised.

Pressure Ups and Downs

In order to understand why hypertension is such a threat to your health and what you can do to counter it, you need to have a clear idea of how blood pressure works, what makes it go up too high, and what you can do to bring it down. Blood pressure is determined by two things. One is the regular pulsing contractions of the heart muscle—the heartbeats that you can feel through your chest wall—which send the blood coursing through the body's many miles of vessels. The other is the amount of resistance that the arteries provide in order to regulate the blood's flow. Blood pressure rises and falls rhythmically with each heartbeat. It is higher during the contractions, when the blood is being squeezed out of the heart. This is the phase of the two-part cycle known as the systole. The pressure is lower during the pause between the contractions, when the heart is filling with blood. This is the phase known as the diastole. The heart's strong contractions send the blood out into the arteries in great gushes. The arteries, with their powerful muscular walls, which constrict or dilate as needed, temper the force of these rapid bursts in order to maintain a smooth and steady rate of blood flow.

If for one reason or another the artery walls are forced to constrict too much for too long, the condition can become chronic and lead to unremitting pressure. The turbulent flow that results as blood is propelled through the narrowed passageways at mounting speed batters the arterial walls, especially in the regions where arteries branch, and this injures their lining. The more sustained the pressure, the more it contributes to atherosclerotic buildup at roughly repaired sites of injury. As the artery walls get coated with layer upon layer of plaque, they become less flexible. They are no longer able to constrict and dilate as readily as they should in adaptive response to pressure changes. At the same time the blood thickens, and the increasing viscosity is accompanied by a greater tendency to clot. All this makes for stepped-up resistance in the very small outlying vessels, a key event in the development of hypertension. In what soon becomes a vicious circle, these changes trigger further rises in blood pressure, leading in turn to further thickening of the artery walls and the blood.

Taking Your Blood Pressure

Each time you have your blood pressure checked, the doctor takes two measurements: the pressure during the systole, called systolic pressure, and the pressure during the diastole, called diastolic pressure. Systolic pressure may vary somewhat with age, but 140 is usually taken as the dividing line between a normal measurement and a high one. As for diastolic pressure, a measurement of 65 to 85 is considered normal, 85 to 89 is high normal, 90 to 104 is borderline or mild hypertension, 105 to 114 is moderate hypertension, and 115 or above is severe hypertension.

The diastolic measurement is in most instances considered much more significant than the systolic reading, and blood pressure evaluations are usually based on it, as you can see from the ranges given above. About forty million men and women in the United States—a fifth of the adult population and two-thirds of all hypertensives—have a diastolic pressure between 90 and 104. This puts them in the so-called gray zone of borderline or mild hypertension. Their blood pressure can often be brought down to normal by exercise and diet. If these do not work by themselves, medication is available. Doctors agree that medication should definitely be used if the diastolic pressure remains at 95 or above.

Risk Factors for High Blood Pressure

In about 10 percent of all hypertension the cause is an identifiable defect that can usually be corrected. In the other 90 percent, which falls into the catchall category referred to as essential hypertension, the basic cause remains something of a medical mystery. But the main risk factors are known. Two are genetic: a family history of hypertension and a racial susceptibility, Blacks being more likely to have high blood pressure than Whites and to be hit by it sooner and harder. People who are in one or both of these groups should make a special point of having their blood pressure checked at frequent intervals. This way, they can take steps to counter any escalating tendencies right at the outset before the condition becomes chronic.

Overweight and Underexercise. Two of the other major risk factors are things most everyone can control. One is being overweight; this may in fact be the main reason for hypertension. The other is being underexercised. It is especially important for the men and women who have borderline or mild hypertension to be aware of these two interacting factors and realize that by exercising and losing weight they can often bring their blood pressure down to normal levels simply and safely without recourse to drugs. This means that a large proportion of the people in this country who have essential hypertension may be able to avoid medication and whatever side effects might have to be incurred as treatment tradeoffs during a lifetime of prescription drugs.

The relation between overweight and hypertension is indirect rather than direct. The elevated blood pressure is due not to excess body fat as such but to certain conditions that accompany obesity—higher levels of insulin, glucose, or blood sugar, and the fats called triglycerides. There appears to be a particularly strong association between insulin levels and blood pressure. Insulin promotes reabsorption of sodium by the kidneys, and abnormal retention of sodium is an important factor in raising blood pressure.

Exercise and Diet to Control High Blood Pressure

Weight loss is often all that is required to correct these conditions and bring mildly elevated blood pressure down. The weight reduction need not be more than 5 or 6 percent of total weight to cause a significant drop in both systolic and diastolic pressure. Interestingly, the drop occurs in people whose blood pressure is normal as well as in those whose pressure is raised. Losing weight can be achieved by cutting calories—probably the most important nutritional guideline for blood pressure control—or exercise or a combination of the two. The best approach is a good exercise program together with moderate calorie reduction. Aside from the key role that exercise plays in bringing down weight, it has a direct lowering effect on the blood levels of insulin, glucose, and triglycerides.

Exercise. The protective value of exercise extends well beyond its ability to lower weight and modify these metabolic conditions. Much of the benefit has to do with the fact that it tones and strengthens all three kinds of muscle, cardiac and smooth muscle as well as skeletal muscle. By strengthening the heart muscle, exercise leads to a lower heart rate at rest and at every level of exertion. A lower heart rate is linked to lower blood pressure. Exercise also has conditioning effects on the smooth-muscle walls of the arteries. It makes for greater elasticity in the blood vessels. When the muscle walls are toned and flexible and able to maintain their pulsatile contractions, several improvements occur. A normal rate of pressure is exerted by the vessels, the blood flow is properly regulated, and atherosclerotic buildup is curbed and perhaps even reversed.

The great potential of exercise as a powerful physiological means of preventing and reversing high blood pressure— and therefore as a way of sparing millions of people a lifetime of hypertension medication—is at last being recognized. Already there is considerable evidence to show that people who are active have lower blood pressure than those who are inactive. In one study a 4.5 percent drop in diastolic pressure and a 2.4 percent drop in systolic pressure was seen in a matter of weeks. In another study systolic pressure dropped an average of twelve points and diastolic an average of thirteen. Surveys of the health histories of decades of college alumni make it clear that vigorous exercise on a regular basis can effectively lower diastolic and systolic pressure. Non-exercisers are 50 percent more likely to develop hypertension than those who remain active in the years after college.

Important as these findings are for everyone who is at risk for hypertension, they have a special meaning for the people with borderline or mild hypertension. Lowering blood pressure with medication may be very effective in preventing such complications as hemorrhagic stroke, renal failure, and congestive heart failure. But it does not do much to counter atherosclerotic complications, such as coronary heart disease, in borderline or mild hypertension. And coronary heart disease is, after all, the major complication of hypertension. So the fact that regular, vigorous exercise has such a positive conditioning influence on muscular fitness—and against the plaque buildup and the clotting tendencies that link high blood pressure to coronary heart disease—is of crucial importance for every man or woman who has borderline or mild hypertension.

Diet. The exercise prescription is becoming increasingly attractive for another and quite different reason—the fact that there is some uncertainty about the effectiveness of dietary modification other than calorie reduction. The biggest question in everyone's mind is: what role does salt—sodium chloride—play? Does high salt consumption cause hypertension? Does cutting down on salt lower blood pressure? Does a more moderate salt intake prevent hypertension from developing in people at risk? The belief that dietary sodium is a key factor in raising the blood pressure to unhealthy levels and sustaining those levels is by now so ingrained that the United States Food and Drug Administration, with processed foods in mind, has recommended an across-the-board reduction in salt intake. But some of the country's leading authorities on hypertension feel that there is not yet sufficient evidence to warrant such a sweeping recommendation. Nobody doubts that sodium in the diet can contribute to hypertension in some way or that a low-sodium diet can sometimes help relieve it. But, one expert aptly notes, what is forgotten is the word "sometimes." A low-sodium diet has been shown to lower blood pressure in those hypertensive individuals who are salt-sensitive—about 30 percent of all the men and women with high blood pressure. In a much larger portion of the hypertensive population, however, a low-sodium diet seems to have no beneficial effect whatever.

More important than sodium as such in the development of hypertension may be the interactions between sodium and three other essential minerals in the diet: potassium, calcium, and magnesium. A careful but complex balance usually exists between these four vital nutrients, called electrolytes because they conduct electricity when in solution. Abnormalities in the intercellular relationships between any two of them—sodium and potassium, say, or sodium and calcium, or calcium and magnesium—may have a great deal to do with the increased resistance in the outlying blood vessels that plays such a key role in hypertension.

Chloride, the other half of the sodium compound you know as table salt, is another possible factor—and one almost entirely overlooked until now. Recent evidence indicates that it too may be implicated in blood pressure elevation.

One other dietary component to be considered is protein. Excessive consumption on a regular basis can damage the kidneys and accelerate renal vascular disease, thereby increasing the risk of hypertension caused by this defect.

In contrast, new research suggests that certain polyunsaturated fatty acids from vegetable and fish sources may have a protective effect on blood pressure. The mechanism is not direct. It is thought to work through several of the prostaglandins, a group of potent regulating compounds that circulate in the blood. The way these particular prostaglandins help is by enhancing the kidneys' excretion of sodium.

Trace elements in the diet, such as zinc, copper, chromium, manganese, selenium, and cobalt, are starting to come under close scrutiny. They appear to have vital backup roles in many biochemical processes underlying vascular health. And vitamins are also crucial in this area.

What all this actually tells you is that the relationship between nutrition and blood pressure is extremely complex and involves a lot more than whether or not you use the salt shaker. There is no point in singling out any one component of the diet as *the* nutritional factor to avoid or go overboard on in order to curb hypertension. Many different nutritional factors and the innumerable subtle interactions between them come into play. So a varied diet is the way in which nutrition can best help guard against this disease of regulation, as hypertension is often called. Variety is the key to making sure you get sufficient amounts of the nutrients you need and avoid imbalances and extremes. Your Ageproofing Diet Plan provides this for you. Together with Your Ageproofing Exercise Plan, Your Ageproofing Diet Plan works to ensure that all of the nutrients are used optimally and that the cells, tissues, and organ systems all function well, even in response to very stressful situations.

Stress and High Blood Pressure

The relation between stress and high blood pressure, which has been suspected for some time, is suddenly turning out to be quite close. It is a well-known fact that stress raises blood pressure. This is one way in which the body gets ready to meet a possible emergency. After the stress is over, the blood pressure normally goes down. But now there is growing evidence that stress can, if it becomes chronic, be a major contributor to hypertension, and some of the mechanisms by which this occurs are at last beginning to be figured out.

The stress response is started up by alerting stimuli from the external surroundings. These set off chemical messages that nerve cells relay to the hypothalamus, a main control center in the brain. The hypothalamus responds by secreting a neurohormone called corticotropin releasing factor (CRF). This is the substance that triggers the body's cascade of reactions to the outside signal.

One thing that CRF does is send messages from the brainstem down along the spinal cord to the core of the adrenals, a pair of glands right above the kidneys that produce a number of very important hormones. In response to the messages the adrenal glands release norepinephrine into the blood. This powerful hormone makes the heart beat faster. It raises blood pressure. It signals the kidneys to retain sodium and fluid rather than excrete them. All of this means the body is revving itself up to deal with a potential threat. Sodium is husbanded in the process because it is essential to vital body functions.

Stress-Salt Link. For people who are salt-sensitive and

either have hypertension or are at risk for it, this obviously spells trouble, because for them salt has stressful effects. A chain reaction of stress-linked events takes place. The kidneys alert the hypothalamus that salt is being reabsorbed, the hypothalamus releases CRF, blood levels of norepinephrine go up, blood pressure also rises, and more salt is reabsorbed as a result of the increase in norepinephrine. The stress-sodium-stress process works in a vicious circle and keeps feeding on itself.

There are two ways in which salt-sensitive people can deal with this problem. One way is to cut salt intake and so help counter increased salt reabsorption by the kidneys, and therefore the brain alert, the release of CRF, and the norepinephrine action that follow. The other way is to exercise regularly and vigorously enough to become really fit, as physical conditioning and the fitness that results bring about a decrease in the effect of norepinephrine. Why? Because exercise steps up the amount of norepinephrine and other catecholamines circulating in the blood, but in people who are in good physical condition a feedback control mechanism then lowers the response to them. This is the body's way of preventing chronic catecholamine stimulation.

Besides the route that CRF takes to the core of the adrenal glands, there is another, much shorter one that it can travel as well when responding to a stress stimulus. This route goes from the hypothalamus to the pituitary gland at the base of the brain, where CRF triggers the release of a special stress hormone called adrenocorticotropin (ACTH). ACTH affects the outer layer of the adrenals, which in turn discharges its main stress hormone, cortisol. This hormone raises blood sugar levels and speeds up body metabolism, all of which makes sense as part of the stress response. Excessive levels of cortisol lead, however, to the buildup of atherosclerotic plaque in the blood vessels. This seems to be a key mechanism in the link between atherosclerosis and coronary heart disease on the one hand and hypertension and cerebral thrombosis on the other. So here, too, there is a very clear message for salt-sensitive men and women who are at risk for hypertension: hold off on salt.

Obesity

Obesity is the western world's most prevalent health problem, and it is becoming more widespread every year inspite of the apparent enthusiasm for health and fitness. There is no question that obesity in itself causes considerable physical discomfort and even disability. Of far greater concern is the fact that it puts a large percentage of the population seriously at risk for major diseases and disorders associated with it and contributes significantly to the annual mortality rate. In the United States alone 15–20 percent of all deaths are indirectly caused by it.

There is a very strong link between obesity and coronary heart disease, stroke, hypertension, cancer, diabetes, and osteoarthritis—that is, almost all of the big cripplers and killers rampant today. It is also associated with liver disease, kidney failure, and gallbladder disease. Obesity has recently been recognized as an important independent risk factor for cardiovascular disease in both men and women, especially during their twenties and thirties, and for thrombotic stroke in women. Certain forms of cancer are also found to be much more common in people who are noticeably overweight. A large American Cancer Society study shows positive correlations between excess weight and cancer of the breast, endometrium, cervix, ovary, prostate, colon and rectum, kidney, gallbladder, and other sites.

Obesity does not mean a few pounds overweight. To qualify as obese a person must weigh at least twenty percent more than he or she should. This is the definition set by health statistics surveys, and it is alarming how high a percentage of the population falls into this category. Racial variations exist along with sex variations. More white men than black men are obese and more black women than white women are. The steady weight gain seen among young men and women in their twenties and thirties carries a special risk, because increases during these decades can have the most significant effect on the development of cardiovascular disease, much more so than obesity occurring after forty. For anyone who is between 10 and 20 percent overweight there is already a greater risk of disease, but when weight rises above the 20 percent mark, the threat can become serious.

Overfat

Obese means too fat, not unusually heavy. This is an important distinction. When you say that someone is overweight, you really mean overfat. The ratio of fat tissue to lean mass, or muscle, in your body is a much more meaningful gauge of how fit and healthy you are than your total weight. After all, a rugger player who stands 5' 10" and weighs 15 stone is well over the average weight for his height as given in the standard insurance tables, but he is not obese. A small-boned woman who is 5' 4" tall, weighs 10 stone 5 pounds, and has a sedentary job may, on the other hand, very easily be obese.

Fat-Lean Ratio. The amount of fat that is necessary simply to maintain life—what is called essential fat—probably does not exceed 3 percent of total weight. In men any additional fat is known as storage fat. In women, however, allowance must be made for between 9 and 12 percent sex-specific fat over and above the essential 3 percent, bringing the basic female quota to a total of 12 to 15 percent before storage fat deposits can be taken into account. This means that a woman's ratio of fat tissue to lean mass is typically higher than a man's. The ideal standards worked out by experts reflect this difference. A man's fatty tissue should not exceed 14 to 15 percent of his total weight, a woman's should not exceed 20 to 22 percent.

Living the kind of sedentary existence characteristic of the Western industrialized nations today, most of the people in this country store more and more fat with each succeeding year. So their ratio of fat to lean mass tends to rise as a matter of course from one decade to the next. Men in their thirties average about 18 percent fat; in their forties, about 22 percent fat; in their fifties, about 24 percent fat. Women in their thirties average about 29 percent fat; in their forties, about 32 percent fat; in their fifties, about 34 percent fat. Almost all of this increase is the result of lifestyle factors—

eating too much and exercising too little. Interestingly, in primitive tribes, very little weight change is seen during a person's lifetime. Fat increase is not some inexorable aspect of biological aging processes. It is all a person's own doing, as a rule, or to be more accurate, lack of doing.

Most men and women fail to realize the full extent of the deteriorative shift in the ratio of fat to lean mass that so often takes place day after day and year after year because of eating too much and exercising too little. Eating too much causes fatty tissue to increase. Exercising too little causes lean mass to decrease. Statistics indicate that after the age of twenty-five the average person starts losing lean mass at the rate of 3 to 5 percent each decade. That soon and that fast! If they do not lose fat at the same rate, obviously they are going to end up being fatter. By age sixty men and women who weigh the same amount they did at twenty are likely to be as much as 12 to 15 percent overfat. What you want to do is maintain a high level of lean muscle mass and avoid increase in fat.

Diet and Exercise Against Obesity

There are three basic ways you can go about guarding yourself against obesity—diet, exercise, or a combination of both. Experts pretty much agree that a balanced diet with only a slight modification in calories and a program of regular, vigorous exercise can combine synergistically to provide lasting benefits beyond anything that can be achieved by diet or exercise alone.

Diet. Whether you are merely trying to avoid any weight gain or are striving for actual weight loss, what you eat and how much are obviously important. You want to be sure to get the variety and amount of nutrients that your body needs in order to function well. Diets that are unbalanced do not succeed, even though they may appear to at first. To prevent weight gain your energy intake in the form of food calories must not exceed your energy output in the form of physical activity. To achieve weight loss a very moderate reduction in calories works best for most overweight people. The reason for such moderation in calorie cutbacks is that your body is geared to maintain a certain fat level. If you try to lose weight by diet alone, you will find that your body has ways of holding firm at that level, regardless of how low the calorie intake is. That is why crash diets are never the answer. Somehow the body seems to sense when current fat levels are not up to par. No sooner do fat stores fall below a given level than the body responds by means of three control mechanisms. Appetite increases. Physical activity decreases. And the metabolic rate drops, with the result that the rate at which calories are being consumed in the processes vital to life is low enough to conserve fat stores.

Because of these three basic control mechanisms, dieting rarely results in more than a very temporary weight loss unless it is combined with a regular and vigorous exercise program. Few dieters realize much actual weight loss while dieting. Even fewer are able to keep off whatever pounds they do manage to shed. Worse still, the loss usually includes lean mass as well as fat, whereas the regain at the end of the diet period is apt to be only fat. And the fat regain often involves such a rebound effect that more pounds go back on than were taken off in the first place. This means that a person may end up with a larger amount of fat than the combined amount of lean mass and fat lost during the diet.

Exercise. The contribution that exercise can make in preventing weight gain is truly remarkable. Besides burning calories, exercise has a regulating effect on food intake, adjusting it to the body's actual needs. It is therefore extremely helpful in controlling weight. If activity falls below a basic level of intensity, duration, and frequency, the control is weakened or lost. This may lead to excessive hunger and overweight. But if activity is sufficiently intense and frequent, normal appetite regulation remains in effect, and this helps prevent any excess weight gain. The way weight can be controlled most effectively therefore is to maintain a certain intensity, duration, and frequency of exercise along with sufficiently moderate levels of calorie intake so that there is a daily energy balance at all times.

People often think that the calories expended in exercise are too few to be of any real value in preventing weight gain or achieving weight loss. Nothing could be further from the truth. Exercise that meets aerobic requirements for intensity, duration, and frequency has very important effects on body composition.

One is that exercise promotes the breakdown of the body's fat stores. The more fit a person becomes in the course of an aerobic exercise program, the more fat mobilization is stepped up. This is partly due to an increased secretion of norepinephrine and other stimulating hormones. Fat stored in adipose tissue, the fat depots of the body, is released into the blood in the form of free fatty acids. These energy-rich particles are then used by working muscles as a source of fuel.

Another effect exercise has on body composition has to do with the muscles themselves. The more they are worked, the more they increase in mass and strength. The result is an increase in the body's basic metabolic requirements, because muscle, even at rest, uses more calories than fat tissue does. Amazing as it may seem, 90 percent of the calories burned in your body are consumed by your muscles, even when you are just sitting still. So the more muscle you have in relation to fatty tissue, the higher the rate at which your body consumes calories every minute of the day.

There is another quite fascinating aspect of fat mobilization that few people are, as yet, aware of. The extra calories expended during, say, a thirty-minute stint of vigorous aerobic exercise do not account for the total expenditure of calories that occurs. Energy expenditure of course goes up during the exercise itself. But there is also an aftereffect lasting as long as forty-eight hours. During this period, the body's basic metabolic rate is as much as 10 percent above what it would have been without the exercise session. Obviously this adds conspicuously to the energy cost of the exercise. All told, you can easily burn as many calories in the course of the two days that follow a single thirty-minute session of, for example, racquetball as you can during the half hour you are moving about the court. The free fatty acids that circulate in your bloodstream for such a long time after the exercise stint provide enough fuel to meet energy requirements for the length of the overshoot effect.

In addition to the protracted one- or two-day increases in basal metabolism, there is some evidence of another beneficial energy-squandering mechanism: the thermogenic, or heat-producing, effect that is associated with regular, vigorous exercise. Here again, the extra energy expenditure may be triggered by hormone stimulation. But this time, some of the free fatty acid overspill is burned off in the form of body heat. New research shows that exercise right after a meal—whether breakfast, lunch, or supper—is especially apt to increase weight loss by the thermogenic route, a generous portion of calories being gotten rid of as heat at these times.

Exercise does more, however, to keep weight at a fit and healthy level than merely squander calories. The physical conditioning that comes with exercising vigorously on a regular basis seems to have a quite pervasive effect, acting through the brain to provide you with a tremendous sense of energy and vitality, so that you can do a lot more in the course of the day without getting fatigued. This is a key point for every man and woman who is overweight to keep well in mind. If there is one important difference between people who are overweight and those who are not, it is that overweight people tend to be less active physically than those on the thinner side. People who exercise regularly have the vitality to stand more and sit less, walk more and ride less, choose more active forms of recreation and less passive forms of relaxation.

Diabetes

Diabetes is becoming an increasingly serious health problem in the western world. This complex disorder, in which the body is unable to convert sugar into energy the way it normally does, now affects one out of every twenty people. In Great Britain alone, during 1981 it was directly responsible for five and a half thousand deaths. Not surprisingly, it is this country's third leading cause of death. It also indirectly accounts for thousands more, brought on by its devastating complications. Intensified atherosclerosis leading to coronary heart disease and stroke is the main complication: this alone accounts for three-quarters of all diabetic mortality. Among the many other complications, some of the most common are kidney disease, gangrene, nerve impairment, and blindness. But just about any tissue or organ of the body can be affected.

Prevention of this protean disease is of special importance and should start as early as possible. By far the most widespread kind of diabetes can most often be avoided and even reversed if it is already under way by a combined program of diet and exercise.

In diabetes, the levels of glucose, the form in which sugar circulates in the blood and is used as nourishment by the various tissues and organs, tend to get too high. These glucose levels are monitored and controlled by two complementary hormones, insulin and glucagon, which are manufactured in the pancreas and operate in tandem. Insulin lowers blood glucose. Glucagon raises it. If this carefully balanced mechanism is thrown out of kilter, the stage is set for diabetes.

Main Kinds of Diabetes

There are two main types of diabetes. Type I, or insulin-dependent, diabetes, usually develops before a person reaches twenty and is often referred to as juvenile-onset diabetes. It involves an insulin deficiency. The pancreatic cells that make insulin seem to be defective in some way, so there is not enough insulin circulating in the blood. Type I diabetes accounts for less than 10 percent of all cases, but it is by far the most severe form of the disease and must be controlled by regular injections of insulin in combination with a special diet and exercise regime prescribed by a person's doctor.

Type II, or insulin-independent, diabetes is likely to develop some time after age forty and is frequently called adult-onset diabetes. The problem here is not a shortage of insulin but a defect in functioning. Normally the insulin in the blood influences glucose metabolism by binding to special receptors on the surface of cells that use sugar, signaling them that more glucose is available. But in adult-onset diabetes the insulin is not able to bind because a mechanism is not working properly, so no signal gets through to the cells and the glucose is not used. As a result both insulin and glucose accumulate in the bloodstream. Once they rise above a certain level, the condition is described as hyperinsulinemia, meaning too much insulin, and hyperglycemia, meaning too much glucose. Type II diabetes is much more prevalent than any other kind of diabetes, accounting for close to 90 percent of all cases.

Obesity Risk. Four-fifths of the people who have or are at risk for Type II diabetes are considerably overweight. Excessive weight as such is linked to an increase in what is called insulin resistance and glucose intolerance, which is another way of saying an inability to bind insulin and use glucose. Overweight is therefore a major risk factor for this adult form of the disease. As a matter of fact, someone who is more than 20 percent overweight and has a high percentage of body fat is four times more likely to get diabetes than someone who is thin. If you have let yourself put on too many pounds, there is one key question you must be sure to ask your doctor: "Is my blood glucose level too high?" If it is, then you must certainly make a point of lowering it right away, and the surest way is to start on a program of regular, vigorous exercise.

Exercise Against Diabetes

There is a tremendous surge of interest in how much exercise can do to protect people from getting adult diabetes. Exercise is not only the best way to lose weight but, as noted in the preceding section, it has a direct lowering effect on blood levels of insulin and glucose. Fat cells and skeletal muscle become highly sensitive to insulin as a result of exercise and take up and use glucose with alacrity. Even a

single exercise session can be noticeably beneficial—
enough to keep insulin and glucose levels low for several
days. What all this means is that exercise can maintain low
levels of the three factors that count most in guarding
against this potentially lethal disease: weight, blood insulin,
and blood glucose.

Interestingly, inactivity can, by itself, lead directly to diabetic symptoms, regardless of weight or insulin and glucose
levels. Astronauts returning from confining space trips, for
instance, have very high levels. If volunteers are subjected
to a period of bed rest, they begin to develop high blood
levels of insulin and glucose within as little as three days of
inactivity, according to a recent study. So the crucial role
that exercise plays in protecting people against diabetic tendencies is clearly apparent.

Diet Against Diabetes

The right kind of diet compounds the benefits of exercise in
preventing excess weight gain and adult diabetes. This is a
key point and extremely important for people in their twenties and thirties to bear in mind because, as noted earlier,
men and women tend to start putting on weight as they go
through these decades. The process may be gradual and the
gain from one year to the next not too noticeable, but each
extra pound adds to the threat of obesity and diabetes later
on. A diet that maintains a healthy balance of fresh fruits
and vegetables, whole grains, milk and milk products, and
other good sources of nutrients, along with a sensible limit
on calories, can go far to forestall this, particularly when
combined with a program of regular, vigorous exercise.

The most important dietary objective, as far as preventing
adult diabetes goes, is to avoid excess calories leading to
excess pounds. That is, without question, the one basic rule.
Where there is a question is in the whole matter of carbohydrates—sugars and starches—and how different ones affect blood glucose levels. In the past, traditional diabetic
diets restricted carbohydrate foods on the ground that carbohydrate tended to raise the level of glucose in the blood,

but this approach has now been largely abandoned. Most authorities currently favor a diet that is generous in complex carbohydrates, like as those provided by fresh fruits, vegetables, and whole grains, and low in simple carbohydrates like table sugar.

Complex carbohydrate foods are frequently high in fiber, which may curb the rise in blood glucose and insulin as well as provide other health benefits. And as they are usually absorbed more slowly than simple carbohydrate foods, they may help avoid a sudden, sharp rise in blood glucose after meals. Recent tests show, however, that there are quite a few exceptions to this general rule. A white potato, it appears, makes blood glucose go up as rapidly as a dose of pure glucose, whereas a sweet potato has no effect whatever. Rice leaves blood glucose levels flat. The effect of bread and corn is somewhere in between white potatoes and rice. The simple sugars, too, hold some surprises. Lactose, the sugar present in milk and various milk products, has little effect. The same goes for fructose, a sugar found in many fruits. Sucrose, or table sugar, makes blood glucose go up a certain amount. And dietary glucose makes it go up fast. In primitive societies, one leading authority on diabetes remarks, people tend to eat the kinds of carbohydrate foods that give a slow rise in blood glucose and insulin levels, and they have very little incidence of diabetes or for that matter heart disease. He wonders if the widespread shift seen in industrialized nations during this century to the typical Western diet is not largely responsible for the prevalence of diabetes today.

These unexpected effects of various carbohydrates, indicated by a series of recent tests, are certainly provocative. The American Diabetes Association is in touch with the researchers doing this work, and at a later date some revisions in diabetic dietary guidelines may be considered, but not until more complete information becomes available and both short-term and long-term studies have been done. People who have diabetes and who have to be on medically supervised diets should check with their doctor about any further developments.

Anyone who is really overweight is, as one expert puts it, a candidate for diabetes. Diabetes, like atherosclerosis, is far more apt to occur in people who eat too much and exercise too little. If you have a weight problem, the sooner you get started on Your Ageproofing Program for Looks, Health, and Fitness, the better you can protect yourself against the risk of diabetes later in life.

Osteoporosis

Osteoporosis is an insidious disease in which bones become drastically weakened because of mineral losses over the years and decades. As they get more porous and brittle, bones are increasingly apt to crumble or break under very slight stress. These fractures, which heal poorly, if at all, can be disfiguring and crippling, and even fatal because of the complications that follow. Osteoporosis is now a major problem in the western world, affecting more than fifteen million people in the United States alone.

Although people usually assume that osteoporosis is part of inevitable aging processes, it is not. This is a point that cannot be emphasized too often or too much. It is a disorder that you can largely prevent or, if it is already under way, halt and even partially reverse. Remember that bone is dynamic and is constantly being torn down and rebuilt to meet your body's ever-changing needs. The tearing-down phase, which is known as resorption, is both normal and necessary. It is supposed to be balanced by the building-up phase, which is known as adsorption. When, however, there is more tearing down than building up for a long period of time, osteoporosis can develop. Three factors contribute to this chronic condition. One is lack of dietary calcium. One is lack of exercise. And one, seen in older women, is lack of estrogen after the menopause.

Early Bone Loss

Osteoporosis can affect every bone in your body. With the kind of life that people in this country lead today, bone mineral losses usually begin quite early—as soon, in fact, as the bones have reached their adult peak. In trabecular bone, the main kind present in the spinal vertebrae, this usually occurs in the mid-twenties. For cortical bone, the kind that predominates in the long bones of your arms and legs, it happens between thirty and thirty-five. This explains why the spinal vertebrae, one of the two prime target areas for osteoporotic damage, are the first to be affected and why the upper-thigh bone, the other prime target, is affected about a decade later, as a rule.

There are never any early symptoms to warn that bone mineral losses are under way, and there is usually no pain until a bone breaks. If loss of height is seen, this is obviously a sign that one or more fractures have already occurred in the spine. Often the way a person is alerted to the presence of the disease is from a medical X ray taken for some other purpose entirely. By the time that the condition is diagnosed, therefore, a great deal of bone may have been lost. Far too many people mistakenly think of osteoporosis as a disease that only older people need be concerned about— little realizing how early and insidiously the process of bone demineralization can get under way. The fact is, though, that the earlier you start to take action against such losses, the better your chances of countering osteoporotic change will be.

Who Is Most at Risk

Right from the start women tend to lose bone faster than men. During their reproductive years the rate may be about 1 percent annually. At the time a woman passes the menopause, however, her yearly losses increase to 2 or 3 percent. Among those women who have had their ovaries removed the loss is even greater. An annual 7 to 9 percent is common, and rates as high as 15 to 20 percent are not unknown. About three years after the menopause the bone loss slows down again, but the deficit is never made up. All told, a woman may lose as much as a third or even a half of her total skeletal bone by the time she reaches seventy or eighty years of age.

Men fare a great deal better. Their bone mass is almost always greater than women's to begin with; they may have about a 25 percent edge at the time of the adult growth peak. Men are more muscular than women, too, which means that their bones are stronger, a bone being only as strong as the muscles that work it. Men also lose bone mineral much more slowly than women until the mid-fifties, and even after that point their losses are still comparatively less. This is why osteoporosis seldom gets to be a problem for men before they are in their eighties and sometimes not even then. So it is no wonder that there are as many as eight times as many women as men affected by osteoporosis, with at least one out of every four women disabled to some extent by it in her later decades.

There are racial as well as sex differences in vulnerability to osteoporosis. Blacks are at much lower risk than Whites and Orientals, because their bones are much denser. It is the slender, small-boned Caucasian women who are usually the most susceptible, and among Caucasians those of Northern stock with blond hair, blue eyes, and transparently thin skin—Celtic women, in particular—are far more likely to be affected than the darker-skinned women of Mediterranean countries. It almost seems, in fact, as if there is a correlation between the latitude to which a people have adapted over the millennia and their protection against osteoporosis.

Common Fractures

Hip fractures occur in the neck of the femur, or upper-thigh bone, and are the most critical type of fracture, as a rule. There are tens of thousands of osteoporotic hip fractures in this country every year, and at least ten percent of the victims die of complications within six months. Women are far more likely to suffer this type of fracture in later years than men. By age fifty-five the yearly hip-fracture rate among women is already seven times greater than it was at age forty. And by seventy it has soared to fifty times higher.

Crush fractures of the spinal vertebrae, although less serious that hip fractures, are far more frequent. They affect millions of people in the western world, women in particular. What happens is that vertebrae crumble, causing a loss of height—as much as 6 to 8 inches in some instances—and also an abnormal forward curvature of the upper spine. The reason for this deformity is that each of the fractured vertebrae assumes a wedge shape, and they become aligned like pieces of a pie in a pie dish instead of like neatly stacked cylinders in a column. The condition, known medically as kyphosis and more commonly as dowager's hump, can be as painful as it is unsightly if a nerve is pinched in the process or if the overloaded back muscles go into chronic spasm. Eventually, as the curvature becomes more extreme, it can affect a person's whole bearing and even the breathing.

Broken wrists are another type of fracture frequently seen among people with osteoporosis. Like spinal fractures, they are likely to occur during the early sixties.

Treatment of osteoporosis is difficult at best, and this is why ageproofing is so important. Fortunately it is a very simple matter when you come right down to it. The two things that count most are diet and exercise. You want to make sure you get the right kind and amount of both food and exercise. The aim of these two key preventive measures is to maintain your bone mineral mass at its peak level or as close to it as possible. If you have already lost a certain amount of mineral, you want to try to reverse the process and work back to as high a level as you can.

Exercise Against Osteoporosis

Experts stress the importance of physical activity in protecting against osteoporosis. A decline in exercise, as one noted authority states emphatically, is probably the main reason for the loss of bone mineral mass in both women and men. Inactivity has an immediate and drastic effect. If you are confined to bed for even as little as a day or two, you start losing mineral mass right away.

What kinds of physical activity are most effective in protecting you against osteoporosis? The key thing is using your muscles in such a way that they put plenty of mechanical stress on your bones. This triggers the osteoblasts, or bone-making cells, and bone mass accrues. Some new evidence suggests that the best results are obtained when your bones are stressed diversely as well as vigorously. According to these studies, the stimulating effect that exercise has on bone is very localized, and any one small area does not have to be stressed long at all—no more than a minute or two. The idea is to keep stressing different areas and doing so from different angles. The more diverse the muscular action, the better the overall response. Your Basic Ageproofing Exercise Plan has been worked out expressly to meet your bone-stressing needs.

Weight-bearing activity is also essential to bone health. Simply being on your feet and moving about, whether outdoors or in, for a total of four hours a day is very helpful in guarding against mineral loss. Even when you are just straphanging in a bus or subway or waiting for an elevator to come or for street lights to change, your body is working against gravity and your muscles are exerting a tug on your bones in order to keep you erect and enable you to maintain your balance.

Diet Against Osteoporosis

Working together with exercise, diet—specifically, one that provides sufficient calcium—plays a vital role in protecting bone mass and preventing osteoporosis. Milk and milk products are by far the main source of dietary calcium. Unfortunately too many people adhere to the myth that you outgrow your need for milk upon reaching adulthood, and so they drastically reduce their consumption or even eliminate milk altogether. Sometimes they do so still earlier, while they are in their teens. They are making a serious mistake.

One reason is that adequate calcium is needed throughout life in order to safeguard bone mass. Another is that although bones stop growing in length by age twenty or thereabouts, they continue to grow in density—in other words, in mass and strength—during the next fifteen years. So it is doubly important to make sure that you get enough calcium during this period. The amount of bone mass you have at the time of your adult growth peak affects your risk of developing osteoporosis later on. If you have good strong bones at this time, it gives you a valuable margin of safety, regardless of whether or not you lose a certain amount of bone mineral in later years. If, however, your bone mass is already below par at age thirty-five, the deficiency is difficult to overcome completely in the years that follow, and any later loss will simply be that much more deleterious.

Because women are particularly vulnerable, they should make a special point of getting enough calcium on a regular basis. Surveys show that the average western woman has far too low an intake—about 450 to 500 milligrams a day. This is not much more than half the recommended dietary allowance of 800 milligrams a day, which, as noted in Your Ageproofing Diet Plan, is already considered too low by many experts. An intake of 450 to 500 milligrams daily can put a woman in what is called negative calcium balance, with net losses of some 40 milligrams a day. Forty milligrams may not sound like much, but over a long period of time the cumulative effect of such ongoing losses can be a severe deficiency.

In one study of premenopausal women a daily intake of 990 milligrams of calcium was required in order to keep them in zero calcium balance—that is, neither losing nor gaining calcium. There is much greater concern about postmenopausal women, because no sooner do the ovaries shut down their estrogen production than women start excreting more calcium and absorbing less. Many authorities now advise women to step up their daily calcium intake to 1000 milligrams before menopause and to 1500 milligrams after it. The effectiveness of a higher calcium intake has been shown in a recent Yugoslav study. Thirty-year-old women from one part of the country, whose traditional diet contained about 1000 milligrams of calcium a day, were found to have stronger, healthier bones than women from another region, whose habitual calcium intake was no more than 450 milligrams a day.

In Your Ageproofing Diet Plan in Part Two, you will see just how you can get the calcium you need from the food you eat. If there is a special problem, a doctor may of course prescribe calcium supplements, but in general, dietary sources such as fortified skim milk or low-fat yogurt can provide ample supplies of calcium.

The warp and woof of bone consists mainly of protein, and so adequate protein in the diet is needed for bone health. Unlike calcium, however, protein is plentiful in the typical western diet. So this requirement is not something you have to worry about, as a rule. An important point in this connection is that the phosphorous content of most protein foods helps the body retain calcium, according to the latest findings and contrary to earlier opinion.

While phosphorous does not usually affect calcium balance adversely, there are other dietary substances that do. Alcohol definitely promotes calcium loss—another important reason to drink only moderately if at all. A high intake of coffee can also increase calcium losses. Aluminum-containing antacids are further cause for concern, as they have been shown to interfere markedly with calcium absorption.

There is one vitamin that has a special significance in connection with calcium intake, and that is vitamin D. This vitamin not only helps you absorb the calcium you eat but may also have a direct influence on the process of bone mineralization. In the absence of vitamin D bone does not get properly mineralized. New findings indicate, interestingly enough, that your vitamin D status is determined primarily by exposure to sunlight. In adults it seems that dietary sources of vitamin D have little worth except when the body's reserves are low. The vitamin D that is formed in the skin as a result of exposure to sun maintains a steadier and more effective level in the blood than the vitamin D in fortified foods. So you should make a point of getting some sunshine on a regular basis, without, of course, going overboard on exposure and harming your skin. Incidentally, do not take vitamin D supplements except under a doctor's orders—they can be dangerous.

Early Protective Measures

Because osteoporosis is asymptomatic until the chronically degenerative process has reached a point where the density and strength of the bone is undermined, it is essential for everyone, and especially those at greatest risk, to start precautionary measures as early in life as possible. The greater the amount of bone mineral mass a woman has at forty-five or fifty, when she reaches the menopause, and a man has at fifty-five, when his bone losses often start to mount, the better they can avoid osteoporotic calamities in the years to come.

Osteoarthritis

Two out of every three people over sixty-five in Great Britain have some degree of osteoarthritis, at least enough to show up on X rays. So it is not surprising that almost everyone thinks of this degenerative disease as just part of getting older. But even though there is still much to be learned about how and why osteoarthritis develops, it is already quite clear that both abuse and disuse are major factors. There is a great deal you can do to prevent or delay its onset or, if it is aleady under way, mitigate and even help reverse its effects by using your joints properly and regularly.

What exactly is osteoarthritis? The main thing it involves is a gradual breakdown and erosion of the cartilage that caps the ends of the bones and enables them to move with gliding smoothness over one another in a joint. The cartilage softens. Fissures, pitting, and fraying appear, and elasticity is lost. In reaction to such deteriorative changes, the underlying bone often thickens, and there is an abnormal growth of bone around the end of the joint. The first thing a person may notice is a slight pain or an inability to move the joint through its full range of motion. In contrast to rheumatoid arthritis, which is an inflammatory disease striking not only the joints but also many other parts of the body, osteoarthritis affects only the joints and the tissues immediately around them.

Osteoarthritis is the most common form of joint disorder there is. Over five million people in Britain are affected. Up to the mid-forties it occurs more often in men than in women. From then on it is twice as common in women. But even though there are rarely any symptoms in either men or women until the end of the thirties, you should be aware of the fact that the disease can get under way in the twenties or even earlier.

Joints at Risk

Weight-bearing joints—specifically, the knee, the hip, and the spine—are the ones most susceptible to osteoarthritis. The knee is very apt to be affected. But although deterioration can be extensive and cause a good deal of enlargement, a surprising amount of mobility is maintained as a rule. With osteoarthritis of the hip, in contrast, movement is noticeably curtailed—hence the small steps that mark the walk of someone who is seriously affected. In the spine osteoarthritis can affect either the vertebrae themselves or the shock-absorbing discs between them. In the lumbar vertebrae—those in the middle back—spiny outgrowths of bone can put pressure on the nerves, causing severe pain. In the cervical vertebrae—those at the base of the neck—they can lead to headaches as well and even impair the circulation to the brain.

Most of the joints that do not bear weight are much less affected. The disorder is, for instance, seldom found in the shoulder, the elbow, or the wrist unless they have been injured. There is, however, one special type of osteoarthritis that forms nodules on the terminal joint of the fingers, and occasionally on the middle joint as well, at some point during the forties or fifties. These bumps develop ten times more frequently among women than men and seem to be an inherited trait. Some people who have them never incur joint pain or disability in any other part of the body.

Avoiding Abuse

Osteoarthritis may develop as a result of injury or abnormal stress over a period of time. The cause need not be anything as traumatic as a fracture. Years or decades of minute, repetitive damage—the pounding, say, of excessive jogging—may set the degenerative process in motion. Even joints that are not ordinarily vulnerable may be affected by strenuous, unusual, and prolonged stress, as is seen frequently in a ballet dancer's ankle or a pitcher's arm.

So the first rule in ageproofing your joints against osteoarthritis is: do not abuse your joints. Use your body correctly. Bad form simply augments the stress. Listen to your body and pay heed to its pain messages. If a movement really hurts, do not do it. If the pain continues, see a doctor. Avoid over-compressing your joints or twisting them into unnatural positions. Be sure your shoes are well cushioned, especially if you jog or run. Remember that the main function of a shoe is to cushion. The good running shoes on the market are designed to do just this.

Exercise Against Osteoarthritis

Abuse is one thing. Proper regular use is something else again. As long as it is not abused, cartilage can remain whole and undamaged, even after decades of hard physical work. Studies of occupations that are very demanding physically show no above-average incidence of osteoarthritis. Mechanical stress is not in itself a bad thing—in fact, the latest research shows that the reverse is probably true. The healthy stress that regular, vigorous exercise places on your joints can enhance their functioning in ways that are lastingly beneficial. The right kind of exercise can help stave off osteoarthritis or, if you do get a touch of it, keep it in check, so that it remains nothing more than a very minor affliction.

There are several ways in which exercise can benefit your

joints. First of all, it is good for the cartilage. Not only does exercise thicken the cartilage but it also keeps the synovial fluid viscous so that it can provide the nourishment cartilage needs. And the very motion of the joints themselves during exercise facilitates delivery of oxygen into the tissue and removal of waste products.

Joints of course involve much more than cartilage. There are the bones that are joined to form the joint, the ligaments that bind them together, and the tendons and muscles that work them. By keeping the various parts of this complex unit operating at their peak, you can do a lot to avoid the imbalances and abnormal stresses that are otherwise such major factors in triggering osteoarthritis. What you want is to maintain flexibility and a full range of movement and also the highest possible level of strength. Flexibility means, in particular, keeping your muscles well stretched and toned, because tight muscles inhibit movement, and putting your joints through their full range of motion, but without trying to force them beyond their natural mechanical limits. As to strength, exercise makes your ligaments tighter and thicker and so better able to provide support for the joint. It also increases bone density; weak bones contribute to osteoarthritis by failing to supply a solid enough base for the cartilage.

Far too few people are aware of the insidious effects of disuse on the joints. But the fact is that the sedentary lifestyle so characteristic of the industrialized countries of the western world is a key factor in the osteoarthritic damage that most people's joints eventually undergo. Your Ageproofing Law—Use it or lose it—holds for maintaining joint integrity just as it does for every other part of your body.

Besides abuse and disuse, there is a third thing that you want to avoid in order to guard against osteoarthritis: overweight. If you are too heavy, you are putting unnecessary and harmful stress on the weight-bearing joints, and this contributes to the degenerative process. Another deleterious effect of excess poundage is that the ligaments and tendons get separated by fat deposits and their mechanical action is not as smooth and balanced as it would normally be. This too can affect the functional integrity of a joint and over the long run contribute to its impairment. Keeping weight within healthy limits is essential in order to protect your joints against osteoarthritis throughout life.

Cancer

Cancer kills more men and women in Britain today than any other disorder except heart disease. At the last count, in England and Wales alone, cancer was diagnosed in 0.75 percent of the entire population during one year. Out of every million people, over 5,000 died from it during 1982. What few people realize is that many if not most of these cancers and the deaths they bring about could have been avoided by simple, timely changes in things people do every day.

Smoking alone accounts for a third of all the deaths from cancer. Another third is linked—by growing if not conclusive evidence—to certain dietary habits. As a matter of fact, the cancers that can be linked to diet may be even more numerous than those ascribed to smoking. Forty percent of the total for men and almost 60 percent of the total for women are the estimates of one leading group of experts, and an overall maximum of 70 percent is not impossible. Whatever the ratio turns out to be as research progresses, it is definitely substantial, and on the basis of what is already known a number of easy modifications in the typical American diet are called for. Besides cigarettes and diet, other cancer risks that are under people's direct control are obesity, heavy drinking, and too much sun.

Cancer is actually not a single disease but a group of diseases characterized by uncontrolled growth and spread of abnormal cells. Normally cells that make up the tissues of the body reproduce themselves in an orderly manner. They grow, get repaired, and are replaced in line with the basic genetic plan. Occasionally, however, certain cells undergo an abnormal change and begin a process of nonstop growth and spreading. They may accumulate to the point where they form masses of tissue, or tumors, which are either benign or malignant. The danger of a malignant tumor, or cancer, is that it invades and destroys healthy, normal tissue. Although at the beginning the cancerous cells remain localized in one spot, some of the cells will usually extend into neighboring tissues sooner or later. If tumorous cells become detached and are carried to other parts of the body by the circulating blood or lymph system, the cancer is said to metastasize. Left untreated, a malignancy is very apt to spread through the entire body and at some point result in death. As treatment of cancer tends to be difficult and its outcome often uncertain, it is all the more important to do everything you possibly can to prevent it.

The Smoking Risk

If there is one single thing that would dramatically reduce the number of cancer deaths, it is getting people to quit cigarette smoking. The biggest drop would be in deaths from lung cancer, which by the time people reach fifty is more than ten times more common in cigarette smokers than in nonsmokers. In 1980—the most recent statistics available—145 new cases of lung cancer were diagnosed per 100,000 of the population in England and Wales. Most of these will have died—there are few survivors of lung cancer—and about 90% of these deaths were caused by cigarette smoking.

Cigarettes are also a major cause of cancer of the upper respiratory and digestive tracts—the mouth, pharynx, larynx, and esophagus—and are implicated in cancer of the bladder, pancreas, kidney, and perhaps stomach and cervix. Of course, the ravages of smoking are not limited to cancer. You saw earlier the heavy toll smoking takes through heart disease, and there are other deadly chronic afflictions, such as emphysema, for which it is responsible. There is simply no such thing as a safe cigarette, as pointed out in Your Ageproofing Anti-Smoking Guidelines. Switching does not get you off the hook. The only way is to quit. Sometimes people who have been smoking a long time feel that it is too late to get any benefits from quitting. What they have to realize is that it is never too late. As soon as they stop smoking, their cancer risk starts to go down—and may with time go as low as that of someone who never smoked.

The passive effects of smoking on nonsmokers—and on the smokers themselves, for that matter—are cause for a great deal of concern. It will probably be a while before their full extent is known, however, because the risk depends so much on length of exposure, and research in this area is comparatively recent. One important finding that has already come out of these studies is that a lifetime of passive exposure beginning in childhood may have something like four times the effect that limited exposure during adult life has. While not smoking yourself is the key thing, it is obviously also important to steer clear of other people's smoke as much as possible.

The Alcohol Risk

The interaction between smoking and alcohol presents a special risk. Each one increases the carcinogenic potency of the other. And, as it happens, heavy drinking and smoking are apt to go together. Alcohol seems to compound the effects of tobacco on cancers of the mouth, pharynx, larynx, and esophagus, alcohol being more closely linked to esophageal cancer and smoking to cancers of the mouth and throat. In smokers who drink a lot, these cancers account for 7 percent of all cancer deaths in men and 3 percent of all those in women.

Alcohol unaccompanied by smoking contributes to cancer at certain sites. Excessive drinking over the years, for instance, is a cause of liver damage, leading to cirrhosis and from there, to liver cancer. It is directly associated with cancer of two other organs along the digestive tract—the pancreas and the stomach. In the respiratory tract, too, there is a small but definite increase in cancer risk among drinkers, quite apart from the effect smoking has.

Certain strong regional beverages, such as the apple brandies of Normandy, seem to increase the likelihood of esophageal cancer above what might be expected from the alcohol content alone. In a number of countries, including the

United States, Great Britain, Ireland, and Norway, a link has been found between heavy beer-drinking and cancer of the colon and rectum. Such findings suggest that different carcinogenic compounds may be present in different alcoholic beverages. There are of course many compelling reasons to stress moderation in drinking, and the cancer risk, whether due to the alcohol itself or to some other ingredient, is certainly an important one.

The Dietary Risk

The effects of diet on cancer risk are complex, but there is an increasing agreement on what some of the most important ones are. Several types of diet and several dietary components—diets high in fat, for instance, and smoked or salt-cured foods—are known to increase the risk of cancer. Other types of diet and dietary components—diets low in fat and high in fresh fruits, vegetables, and grains—are known to decrease the risk of cancer.

Of all the substances in the diet that have been looked at so far, the evidence is strongest for a cause-and-effect relation between fat intake and cancer. High levels of dietary fat go with high incidence of cancer at certain sites—the breast and colon, in particular, and also the prostate gland. In contrast to heart disease, it is the total amount of fat that counts rather than the kind of fat. In other words, "Eat less fat" is the main rule for cutting cancer risk and "Eat less saturated fat" is the main rule for cutting heart risk. Both rules can of course be combined easily and well, as they are in the guidelines for Your Ageproofing Diet Plan.

A very high protein intake may increase the risk of certain cancers, but the association is by no means as clear as it is for fat. Because fat and protein are so closely linked in the typical western diet, with its emphasis on fatty meats, it is sometimes difficult to disentangle their separate effects. Fat does, however, seem to be the primary cause for concern.

The other main component of the diet, besides fat and protein, is carbohydrate—in other words, sugars, starches, and fiber. Sugars and starches do not seem to have any effect to speak of on cancer risk. But what about fiber, the indigestible carbohydrate found in fruits, vegetables, and grains? Studies suggest that it may help guard against cancer of the colon and rectum. If there is indeed a protective effect, it is probably due to one specific type of fiber called the pentosan fraction, which is abundant in whole grains, rather than to fiber in general.

Several of the nutrients you take in very small amounts are thought to be helpful in preventing cancer. Vitamin A is one. Foods containing the vitamin itself or its precursors, the carotenes—which are plentiful in yellow and dark green vegetables—seem to lessen the risk of chemically induced cancers of the lung, breast, bladder, and skin. This does not mean that vitamin A supplements should be taken. Quite the contrary. What it does indicate is that you should get a healthy amount of the vegetables rich in carotene in your diet. These do not present any danger of toxicity, as vitamin A supplements do.

Vitamin C appears to help. It inhibits the formation of some carcinogens, at least in laboratory studies. And populations that get lots of foods rich in vitamin C, like citrus fruits, have lower rates of cancer of the esophagus, stomach, and some other areas.

Among the trace elements, selenium may offer protection against cancer risk. The amount needed seems to be present in any balanced diet however, and authorities warn against dosing yourself with supplements, since too much selenium can be toxic. Iron may also play an anti-cancer role; iron deficiency has been linked to cancer of the upper alimentary tract and stomach. Interestingly, vitamin C enhances iron absorption when it is present—even as little as a squirt or two of lemon juice—in the same meal.

There is another anti-cancer group of nutrients that has stirred a lot of interest: the so-called cruciferous vegetables, which include cabbage, broccoli, Brussels sprouts, and cauliflower. Their consumption is linked to lower rates of several kinds of cancer, although it is not known which of their ingredients may be responsible for this.

Are there any particular foods that promote cancer?

Smoked and salt-cured products are one type of food that is believed to do so. In countries like Japan and Iceland, where the diet is high in such products, there are also high levels of stomach and esophageal cancer. Certain methods of smoking and pickling food seem to produce chemicals that cause cancer in animals and are suspected of doing so in human beings too.

An intriguing question has to do with the effect on cancer risk of the total amount of calories in the diet as distinct from its various components. There are striking results from laboratory tests in which animals kept on low-calorie diets have fewer cancers and live much longer than those allowed to eat as much as they please. The situation is not as clear for human beings, on whom lifelong austerity tests are obviously impossible. But there is certainly a lot to be said for moderate calorie reduction.

The Obesity Risk

Of course, one conspicuous result of a high calorie intake, unless offset by a lot of exercise, is overweight. And overweight is a risk factor for cancer as well as other chronic disease. It is linked specifically to cancer of the breast, endometrium, cervix, ovary, prostate, gallbladder, colon and rectum, kidney, and other sites. This finding has recently been confirmed by a massive American Cancer Society study. Among women there is a consistent trend toward increased total risk with increased weight. Among men the trend is less clear, except for prostate cancer.

The relationship between obesity and cancer of the endometrium among postmenopausal women is especially strong. Endometrial cancer can develop because of the influence of estrogens. Unless a woman is on estrogen therapy, the estrogens to which she is exposed after the menopause are those produced by adrenal hormones in her adipose, or fat, tissue. So the level of estrogens in the blood is directly proportional to the amount of fat in her body. The risk of endometrial cancer in any very overweight woman is estimated to be ten times higher than in women of normal weight.

The link between obesity and breast cancer is much more complex than that between obesity and endometrial cancer. But leading authorities stress that there is an elevated risk of breast cancer throughout life for women who are extremely overweight.

Diet Against Cancer

All told, there is certainly strong evidence that what and how much you eat has a very definite influence on the risk of your developing various kinds of cancer. And even though it is not yet possible to identify the exact mechanisms that induce or inhibit tumor formation, there are some practical guidelines that it is good for you to go by. Recently set forth by an expert panel of the National Research Council and endorsed by the American Cancer Society, they are:

- Reduce fat consumption from the present American average of 40 percent. A good maximum to aim at is the one used in Your Ageproofing Diet Plan: 25 percent.
- Eat plenty of fresh fruits and vegetables and whole grains. Of special importance are citrus fruits, the carotene-rich yellow and deep green vegetables, and cruciferous vegetables like broccoli, cauliflower, cabbage, and Brussels sprouts.
- Go as easy as possible on smoked and salt-cured foods.

Here again, you see, a diet that is high in fresh fruits, vegetables, and whole grains and low in fat helps you guard against a major chronic degenerative disease.

Exercise Against Cancer

What about exercise, you may ask? Is cancer the only one among the nation's top killers and cripplers that takes its toll regardless of whether or not people are physically active? In other words, does exercise have a protective effect? The fact is that exercise can actually do a lot more to help prevent cancer than most people realize. It is the best antidote there is to overweight. Vigorous exercise on a regular basis is the one sure way to bring weight down to healthy levels and keep it there. A key point for any woman approaching or past menopause to keep in mind is the one made above in connection with cancer's hormonal links: estrogens involved in endometrial and perhaps breast cancer development are produced in a woman's adipose tissue after her ovaries have shut down estrogen production. So the protective effect of exercise may be all the more vital at this time, as it is the most effective way of taking off fat and keeping it off. The less fat tissue there is, the less estrogen the body can make.

Sun Protection Against Cancer

For many men and women, especially those of Celtic origin —the Irish, like myself, the Welsh, Scots, and Bretons— who have very light, sun-sensitive skin, there is one ubiquitous environmental factor that should be guarded against: sunlight. Chronic sun exposure severely damages the skin over the years. But although almost everyone is aware of the fact that skin cancer, as well as wrinkling, sagging, and mottling, can result from sun injury, the link between sun and the one truly lethal form of skin cancer, malignant melanoma, has not been as clear. Now, however, it appears very likely that this killer is associated with occasional severe blasts of sun on parts of the body not usually exposed. Of special concern to cancer experts is the rapid increase in malignant melanoma that has been seen in just the last few decades. One of the world's foremost authorities on melanoma describes the increase as terrifying. It has become a very serious problem all over the world, even in northern European countries with little sun. Also it is being diagnosed in younger and younger people—men and women still in their early twenties. The advice from the best dermatologists is to use a high-potency sunscreen regularly as a precautionary measure, regardless of the season and whether your skin is light or dark, untanned or tanned. This, of course, particularly applies to people who live in parts of the world where the sun shines frequently.

You Against Cancer

The most important thing to bear in mind about cancer risk is that it is largely something you can protect yourself against by what you yourself do. Too many people have fallen for the myth that the main cancer threat comes from an external environment allegedly shot through with man-made carcinogenic pollutants over which they have no control. It is a convenient alibi, because of course it implies that there is little point in their trying to do anything themselves. But in fact the latest and most authoritative estimate allots only 2 percent of total cancer mortality to the industrial pollution of air, water, and food. And most of that 2 percent is hypothetical. It is attributed to by-products in city air of the combustion of coal, oil, and gas, the effects of which are described as uncertain.

Early detection of cancer, if it does occur, is obviously crucial, as it greatly enhances the chances of successful treatment. You will find a list of the various checks you should have at various ages in Your Ageproofing Health-Check Guidelines. They are an essential part of protection against cancer in every period of your life.

PART TWO

Your Ageproofing Program for Looks, Health, and Fitness

CHAPTER 4

Ageproofing Your Looks—the Simple Things That Count the Most

People speak about "looking your age." They say things like, "She looks years younger than her age." Or, "To look at him, you would never guess his age." Or, "There are days when I feel I look twice my age." You hear people talk this way all the time. But when you come right down to it, such talk is quite misleading.

Your looks have very little to do with your chronological age. They depend much more on what you do to avoid or provoke the degenerative changes so commonly mistaken for true aging. How you look at twenty-five or forty or sixty-five or even eighty is largely the result of what you do or do not do on a regular ongoing basis—day after day, week after week, month after month—before you get to be twenty-five or forty or sixty-five or eighty.

There is nothing that you or anybody else can do about having one more birthday each year. But a birthday is an arbitrary milestone. Think a moment—what does it signify? Only that the earth has made another orbit around the sun. In other words, all that getting a year older means is that the solar system has—fortunately—continued going through its usual cycles. There is no reason why your looks have to deteriorate at some predetermined annual rate merely because the earth has chalked up one more round trip. You can get older without automatically "aging" by a proportionate amount.

True biological aging is, of course, a fact of life. But as

you can see throughout this book, most of the deterioration that people take to be biological aging is actually something they themselves are responsible for. If you do not use your body the way it is meant to be used, and the amount it is meant to be used, this can have a conspicuous and devastating effect on your looks. And what goes for your looks also goes for your health—abuse and disuse take a heavy toll of both over the years.

The simple daily things you can do make a tremendous difference in your looks and health—for better or worse. So why not do things for the better? Starting now is what counts, whether you are in your twenties and thirties or sixties and seventies or beyond. It is never too early or too late to begin.

The following sections about ageproofing your looks start with skin and hair—major concerns for just about everybody, given their high visibility. Then comes how to ageproof your face—eyes, nose, mouth, teeth, ears, and neck as well as the all-important contours. Next, your overall body shape. And, continuing downward in sequence, you find out just what it takes to ageproof your back, breasts, arms, hands, nails, waist, buttocks, thighs, calves, and feet.

Of course, these sections will not be of equal importance to you. The thing to do is concentrate on those where you have a special problem, and use the other sections for basic daily-care advice and pointers that can help you ageproof yourself in every way from head to toe. Although this chapter zeroes in on looks, you will find a great deal of useful information that has to do with fitness and health—the three are, after all, very closely linked.

Ageproofing Your Skin

People go by appearances in judging your age. Smooth, clear, firm skin says "young" to them right away, even though you may be sixty. Wrinkled, sagging, and blotchy skin says "old" to them instantly, even though you may be barely thirty. So how young or old you look really depends to a very large extent on how young or old your skin looks. If you take good care of it and give it the protection it needs, it will look young and so will you. If you do not care for it properly, it will look old and you will too.

When I was about forty, I went to see a world-famous skin doctor. I thought I had arrived at an age where I had better heed all the night-cream ads and start revitalizing my skin, and I wondered which course of action would work best for me. The doctor studied my skin carefully under his piercingly bright laboratory lights. After peering—and even pinching and pulling—for several minutes, he asked gruffly, "What do you use on your skin?" Embarrassed at having to face up to the truth, I replied rather meekly, "Nothing—just soap and water." A wide smile spread over his face, and he said, "No wonder you have such good skin."

I tell you this in order to stress a key point about caring for and protecting your skin: it takes very little to give your skin what it needs and thrives on day after day and year after year. The more closely you stick to a few daily basics, the better off you are. The two things that count most in ageproofing your skin are cleaning it gently every day and protecting it adequately every day.

If there is one thing that is really good for your skin, it is water. The key ingredient in your daily skin routines is water—water to cleanse, water to moisturize. Water is vital to every cell in your body, and your skin cells are no exception.

Cleansing

When you cleanse your skin, use water that is warm or cool but never really hot. Excessive heat damages the skin. Washing with soap and water is fine as long as it is done gently. Be sure the soap you use is mild and, if your skin is particularly sensitive, unperfumed. Listed below are mild soaps, suitable for delicate skins, which can also be used on your face.

1. Simple
2. Neutrogena
3. Cuticura
4. Camay

5. Droyt's Glycerine
6. Boots' Skin Care
7. Vichy Cleansing Bar
8. Roc

The above are readily available in chemists and department stores. If you are prepared to spend more, most of the leading cosmetic manufacturers make soap which they consider mild enough for use on your face.

Avoid loofahs, buffers, and stiff brushes of any kind. Friction can be traumatizing. You do not even need a wash cloth. Just make a soapy lather in your hands, smooth the lather lightly over your skin, and rinse. A mild soap that lathers well can double as a shaving cream for men to use on their beard and women on their underarms and legs.

Moisturizing

A moisturizer does not provide any moisture on its own. Its job is to sit on the surface of the skin and seal in whatever moisture is already there. So you want to moisturize your skin with water first. The best way to do this is to get the bathroom good and steamy before you take your bath or shower. Soak or shower for at least fifteen minutes in order to let the water seep well into your skin. When you come out of the water, towel yourself almost, but not quite, dry. Smooth a moisturizer on all the areas that are likely to be exposed during the day.

Petrolatum, a pure example of which is Vaseline, is the most effective moisturizing substance, because it is so occlusive. Pure petrolatum is of course quite impractical for daily use, but there are a number of excellent moisturizers on the market that contain petrolatum as a main ingredient, and the higher the word appears on the product's list of ingredients, the more petrolatum that particular moisturizer contains. It is best to experiment with different kinds of moisturizers until you find the formulation that has sufficient petrolatum and yet is comfortable to use.

Humidity. Skin is highly sensitive to the amount of moisture in the surrounding air, but most people ignore the need to keep the air indoors adequately moist. Central heating in homes and offices can dry out the air and therefore your skin in no time at all. Air conditioning can be almost as dehydrating as steam heat. This applies not only to the air-conditioned buildings that people live and work in but also to the various means of air-conditioned transportation they use regularly: cars, trains, buses, and especially the pressurized cabins of commercial planes.

A very practical and inexpensive way to keep the air at home moist enough, and one that I find works wonderfully in our apartment, is to fill an eight-quart spaghetti pot with water and let it simmer ever so gently on a back burner of the stove all day or even around the clock. Refill it when the water level gets low. The moisture spreads through the other rooms in a matter of seconds.

Another effective tack is to invest in a portable humidifier. Keep it watered and operating at home whenever the steam heat or the air-conditioning is on. If you work and have an office with a door you can close, a humidifier can be used to good effect there too, but if your desk is in a sectioned-off area of a very large space, a humidifier is of no avail because the moisture is instantly dissipated through thousands of cubic feet of air.

The ideal humidity range to aim for indoors is that of a clear spring or autumn day when the air sparkles and, as the song goes, you can see forever, the kind of day on which there is about 35 or 40 percent humidity. You will see a beautiful difference in your skin and also sense a difference in your nose, sinuses, throat, and respiratory system as a whole.

Such simple measures are really all you need, whether you are in your twenties or thirties or in your sixties or seventies, in order to keep your skin adequately moist. If you make a point of moisturizing your skin in these ways, you will find that it is far less likely to develop lines than skin that is low on protective moisture. And "dry skin" is much less likely to become—or remain—a problem.

Sun Protection

Almost all aging skin changes are simply the result of chronic sun damage. An effective sunscreen is an absolute must, no matter how light or dark your natural skin color is, what age you are, or which part of the country you live in. You should use a sunscreen on all sun-exposed areas of your body whenever you are going to be out in the sun for more than a few minutes. And you should apply it before, not after, your moisturizer—this is a key point few people are aware of. The reason is that sunscreens are usually formulated to penetrate the skin in contrast to moisturizers, which provide a surface film.

For day-to-day protection outdoors you can use a sunscreen with a lower sun-protection factor (SPF) than when you are out in bright sun a lot. But do not forget that almost two-thirds of the sun people get throughout the year is apt to be during routine daily exposure.

Whenever you plan to be outdoors in bright sunlight for any length of time, switch to a high-potency sunscreen, preferably one with an SPF of 15 or higher. An SPF-15 sunscreen, incidentally, does not block out all the sun's rays; it takes fifteen times as long for the sun to produce a slight redness when you have an SPF-15 sunscreen on as it would if you did not have a sunscreen on.

The SPF guide to a product's protective ability is actually somewhat misleading, because the SPF number officially indicates only the amount of protection that the product provides against the more energetic band of ultraviolet radiation, UV-B rays. The longer and somewhat less energetic ultraviolet rays, the UV-A wavelengths, are by no means innocuous. They penetrate further into the skin and are in fact responsible for most of the aging changes seen after chronic sun exposure. Even a high-SPF product gives only a moderate amount of protection against UV-A while shielding you very well against UV-B. Even visible light plays some role in skin damage. Infrared radiation (IR), which is perceived as heat, must be taken into consideration as well. In other words, the SPF of a sunscreen does not give you a clear idea of how much protection you are actually getting against all the wavelengths of solar radiation that reach your skin.

If you insist on getting a tan, the wisest way to do so is very gradually, using a high-potency sunscreen. Remember, though, that even the barest tinge of a tan is a response to injury. You pay a price for each and every photon of sunlight that penetrates your skin.

At sixty-two, my skin is smooth, clear, and firm, even though it is the thinnest, most fragile, and least durable type of skin genetically—that of Irish and Scottish people and others of Celtic origin. But until I was twenty, I spent every moment I could at the beach soaking up sun, with the result that at the end of every summer I looked like a photographic negative of myself, with very dark suntanned skin and very light sun-bleached blond hair. Had I gone on this way, I could have passed for a century-old peasant woman by the time I reached thirty!

If you hold your looks at all dear and do not want to let your skin suffer the "aging" changes that chronic sun exposure causes, do as dermatologists urge you to these days: put on your tan—by applying a bronzer in whatever shade you wish. It is the only ageproof way.

Bear in mind that water transmits UV radiation. This means you can easily get a sunburn when you are swimming outdoors—faster, in fact, in fresh water than in saltwater. The more completely hydrated your skin becomes, the greater the amount of UV radiation that can be transmitted through it. What is true of swimming is also true of sweating, though to a lesser degree. For this reason waterproof or water-resistant sunscreens are a good idea, no matter whether you are swimming, jogging, playing tennis, or participating in any other outdoor sport. Any kind of friction, however, such as toweling yourself dry or mopping up sweat, removes even the most waterproof formulations and makes it necessary to reapply the sunscreen.

Although IR rays are not as energetic as UV rays, they can cause considerable damage over a period of time. The damage is cumulative. This is true whether the IR rays are beating down on you from an August sky, toasting you at the fireside or in front of a space heater, or providing you with a dry roast in a sauna.

A special caution is in order for fitness buffs who do the solarium-sauna circuit at health clubs; the heat of IR sauna lamps in the wake of a solarium stint augments the UV damage to the skin caused by the solarium lamps. Solariums should simply be avoided, period. To the extent it is possible sauna IR lamps should probably be avoided as well. Even the IR lamps now being used four at a time in hair salons to dry hair give quite a blast of heat.

Skin Exercise

There is increasing evidence that physical exercise, if sufficiently vigorous, can have a noticeably beneficial effect as far as ageproofing the skin goes. For one thing, exercise acts as a stimulus for opening up the millions of tiny blood vessels that permeate the skin. Over a period of weeks it also increases the total volume of blood circulating through those vessels and the number of red blood cells carrying oxygen and other nutrients to the tissues. This can of course do a great deal of good to all the skin cells as well as to the body as a whole.

Another significant effect of vigorous physical exercise is the accompanying rise in the temperature of the skin. It goes from around 86 to 90 degrees F to almost 98.6 degrees F— the normal reading when a healthy person's temperature is taken by mouth with a thermometer. This moderate internally caused rise—as distinct from one induced by excessive external heat—can be good for the skin in several ways. The rate at which collagen, the mainstay of the skin's supporting structure, is produced is apparently temperature-dependent. When a rise occurs, the new collagen is churned out faster, as are other components of the underlying dermis. The result is that this layer increases in both thickness and strength, and therefore so does the skin as a whole. It even weighs more.

There is a noticeable improvement in the elastic quality of

the skin among people who exercise regularly and vigorously. The skin has greater resiliency and snap. Interestingly, the reason for this improvement has to do with Your Ageproofing Law: Use it or lose it. Skin is meant to move. Its plasticity is essential for its function. The rate of formation of new elastic tissue is influenced not only by a rise in skin temperature with exercise but also by the skin's mobility—the degree to which the skin expands and contracts with each movement. In other words the fibroblasts, the cells that produce the elastic fibers, recognize the need to produce more of them when they are subjected to sufficient stress. How much you lift and lower your arm, for instance, can have a lot to do with how much the skin's elastic-fiber-making cells in that particular area function.

As studies of age-matched pairs of athletic and sedentary people show, there is a most conspicuous difference in skin tone and texture between the two. The skin of those who exercise looks smoother and more supple, with fewer wrinkles and a much better color. Even the bags often seen under the eyes seem to disappear as people get in better condition with exercise.

Ageproofing Your Hair

Hair has a very special significance for most men and women. At the first sign of graying or thinning or conspicuous new growth in inappropriate places, reason often goes right out the window. Some people make a rash rush to try every new hair treatment and product as they come on the market. And men are usually even more agitated than women.

Most of the trauma and drama over hair changes is unnecessary. Of the various true biological aging changes, those affecting hair are the ones you can deal with the most effectively. Simple, safe ways of keeping hair color at its peak as the years go by—and for that matter subtly improving on what you had to begin with—are within easy reach if you choose not to go gray. And very successful ways of coping with hair loss and hair excess have been developed and are widely and readily available.

Countering Gray Hair

If there is one thing that men and women certainly do not have to put up with if they do not want to, it is graying. The corner drugstore or neighborhood supermarket can always provide an easy solution. There is a wide range of excellent and inexpensive hair-color products on the market now, and all the major firms have toll-free numbers you can call for advice about shades and techniques. If you prefer to let a hairdresser handle the coloring, all sorts of special effects can be worked out by salon colorists that add subtle dimensions of shading and enhance the natural look of color-treated hair.

There are basically three types of color products to choose from. Each process involves a somewhat different type of chemistry and produces a somewhat different effect, in this way meeting an extremely broad range of needs. In order to help you know exactly what each kind of process does and how it differs from each of the others, here is a quick rundown.

Temporary Hair-Color Process. These products blend the gray with the natural color as the hair starts to turn. The solutions are available in a number of shades and work by laying down a very sheer layer of color on the cuticle, or outermost portion, of the hair, without penetrating the hair shaft. The product is poured through the hair like a final rinse after a shampoo but is not washed out. The best way to dry the hair after tinting with this process is to set the hair on rollers while wet or use a blow dryer.

Semi-Permanent Hair-Color Process. The products in this category are used to mask either graying or completely gray hair. The best effects are achieved when the shade used is the same as the natural color of the hair rather than a lighter or a darker tone, because the products are formulated to enhance, not change, the natural shade. These products do penetrate the hair shaft, and the colors last through four or five shampoos as a rule. They are usually combined with a shampoo in a single easy-to-apply preparation. The mixture is washed into the full length of hair and left on for about twenty minutes. Then it is rinsed out, and the hair is ready to be dried with a towel or dryer.

Permanent Hair-Color Process. This technique is the most versatile. You can use it to go as dark as you like or as light as you like. Oxidation by hydrogen peroxide is what makes the range of lighter shades possible. Such products are colorfast—and last through countless shampoos with little or no fading, because the color particles in the formula expand within the hair shaft and remain trapped there. After the initial coloring with this technique, all that is needed is a touch-up every three or four weeks so the new hair growing in is the same shade.

Men are now using hair-color products almost as unhesitatingly as women, especially if they feel that hiding the gray is a must for their career. Many even go to the same hairdresser as their wife or girlfriend. And lots of couples often go together.

Body-Hair Coloring. Hair-color options have begun to open up in other ways too, and coloring no longer stops at the traditional hairline. If brows are graying or lashes fading, they can be colored at the same time as the scalp-hair roots. Products to color your lashes at home are now widely available and quite easy to use. They claim to last for five or six weeks. Dyeing the eyelashes makes sense, as it is then not necessary to wear mascara all the time. If mascara is not worn, it need not be removed and removing eye make-up encourages lines in the particularly delicate skin in that area.

Although not yet widely-known, it is now possible to color body-hair also. It makes good sense for a woman to color her pubic hair if it is beginning to turn gray and she is self-conscious about it. It is suggested that you consult the colorist at your own hairdressing salon for advice on where to have this done. It is available in this country, but not as readily as in America, where it is now accepted practice in many beauty salons. Body-hair coloring also makes good sense for men. If they are already covering up the gray at temples and sideburns, they may want to color their chest hair as it starts coming in white during their fifties. In other words, hair-color products can and do go the limit these days in order to counter hair-color loss.

Special Hair-Coloring Pointers. Here are three key tips you should keep in mind if you decide to use hair-color products to deal with graying.

- Avoid going darker than your natural hair color, because a dark shade tends to make you look older. This is increasingly true with each decade. A lighter shade is softer, and it usually does much more for your appearance.
- Remember that the natural color of your hair is a mix of many shades; there are likely to be thirty or more tones in, say, a single head of blond hair. That is why natural hair color never has the flat, poster-paint look that poorly bleached or dyed hair has. One way to get this natural effect is to lighten the hair around the face with a scattering of very fine "sun streaks," as they are called. Hairdressers are very adept at this, and even if you want to do your own hair-coloring at home, it is a good idea to have a hairdresser put the streaks in at the start so that you have a pattern to follow. If you have a few gray streaks at the temples, they can provide a gradation in tone when covered lightly but not entirely with color—this is where a temporary hair-color product can be particularly enhancing.
- Make a plan and stick to it. Figure out how often you are going to need coloring in order to keep the roots covered and the tint uniformly fresh. Surprising as it may seem, hair in need of a touch-up gives you an older look than untouched gray hair does.

Countering Hair Loss

Hair loss is for most people a far more unwelcome sign of aging than going gray, and it is not as easy to deal with.

Products for Men's Hair Loss. There is an unending quest for some magical lotion capable of preventing or curing the balding process. One of the latest in a succession of offerings is a product called Formula MJS. It has been given an official green light in Canada after being clinically tested and approved by the Canadian Health Protection Branch, but doctors in other countries seriously question whether MJS can actually grow hair. Their doubt is based on the fact that hair follicles programmed for loss on a balding scalp undergo such a complete and seemingly irrevocable change. In any balding area, however, follicles at all stages of transition are to be found. Even in a scalp that is almost totally bald and sprouting fine, unpigmented hairs, some few follicles remain that are capable of growing thicker, pigmented hairs. They may be quiescent, but they can be stimulated to regrow. It is this that raises so many false hopes of a cure. Maybe limited and sporadic growth is all that can come of MJS, despite the fact that 77 percent of the men who tried the formula are said by the Canadian authorities to have experienced a significant thickening of hair.

In the United States a number of effective anti-androgens that successfully block the activity of dehydrotestosterone, the male hormone mainly responsible for baldness, are being tested. But manipulating the body's hormones, particularly the sex hormones, is both complex and risky, and so clearance of these anti-androgenic products, should it occur, is still a long way off. Laboratory studies and animal experiments must provide convincing proof of the products' safety and effectiveness before trials with human volunteers, the final step in such testing, could be done.

In the meantime there have been some intriguing findings in America with minoxidil, which is a drug used in the control of hypertension, and which promotes hair growth in the bargain. Animal tests are under way, and the first results of topical application on the stumptail macaque, a monkey whose balding patterns are very like those of human beings, are encouraging. But here again only if further tests with animals determine that the treatment is safe and effective could experiments with humans start.

Surgery For Men's Hair Loss. Surgical treatment of balding in men has been shown to produce very good results in instances where a noticeable amount of hair loss has occurred. Grafting is one technique. It takes advantage of the characteristic pattern of male baldness. Tiny plugs of scalp tissue that contain functioning hair follicles are transplanted to the bald areas from unaffected areas on the back and sides of the head. The process is tedious and calls for a great deal of skill, all of which makes it expensive, but it usually works very well. Hair grows just about as thickly in the new sites as in those from which the plugs were taken. Another approach, called scalp reduction, is being used by quite a few plastic surgeons. This technique involves removing skin from balding areas in the front of the head and drawing up flaps of hair-bearing skin on either side in such a way that hair covers most of the previously bald area.

Products for Hair Loss. Balding is rare in women. The pattern of hair loss affecting them is most often diffuse, and concentrated in an area that extends back over the crown of the head from about an inch behind the hairline. The shedding is not really conspicuous until 50 percent of the scalp hair has been lost. And even then a woman can usually mask the condition by wearing her hair quite short and curled.

A prescription lotion containing as its active ingredient an infinitesimally small amount of estradiol, a potent female hormone, has already been cleared for use in the United States. When it is applied topically to the scalp, it reduces hair shedding. This means that it can help women have the same kind of abundance that is usual during pregnancy, even though it cannot actually reverse hair loss.

There is one other change that is typical of hair loss in women: reduction in the diameter of the hairs, even those in non-shedding regions. This may give older women's hair a wispy appearance. The reason is obvious. If each hair thins from, say, .08 millimeter in diameter to .04 millimeter, the loss in collective bulk is bound to be sizeable when multiplied by the close to 100,000 hairs present on a woman's head.

Topical products called thickeners attempt to deal with this problem. They can be helpful up to a point, but there is a trade-off—the hair is eventually weakened by the buildup of the thickening agents and so becomes more fragile than before. Some shampoos are formulated so as to help bulk up fine, wispy hair. Proteins present in the shampoo temporarily coat the hair, and the thickening they provide lasts just until the next shampoo. Light "body" permanents also give the hair an air of thickness. Another helpful measure is keeping the hair short. Long hair makes for a straggly, skimpy look, because the weight makes it appear less buoyant. As one who was born with tons of wispy hair—so wispy, in fact, that there was no conceivable way it could get any wispier over the years—I can tell you that the best item on the market I have found is a shampoo for oily hair, even though my hair is not oily. The shampoo is formulated to dry out each hair a trifle and in so doing provides my hair with a look of real bulk. Just be sure to avoid any rinses or conditioners as a finishing flourish. They counter the drying-out effect.

If a woman's hair loss progresses to the point where thickeners, body permanents, short cuts, and oily-hair shampoos fail to conceal the fallout, then a hairpiece or wig is worth considering. The choice of sizes and shades and styles is excellent, and the look can be absolutely natural. What's more, the health of the hair, contrary to what people generally believe, is not affected in any way by wearing a hairpiece or a wig.

Body-Hair Loss. Hair loss in the underarms and pubic areas, which occurs much sooner in women than in men, can be a very traumatic experience. Eventually, many women will be glad to hear, there may well be a means of dealing with the problem. Topical testosterone has produced good results experimentally in the pubic area. And pubic hair transplants using the same grafting technique that was developed to treat baldness in men are already being performed successfully. The plugs of hair are taken from the back of the head near the baseline, a region that can easily be concealed by a woman's hairstyle.

Countering Excess Hair

Of just as great concern to women as loss of scalp hair are the inappropriate growths of facial hair so characteristic of the postmenopausal years. Unfortunately, few women realize how simply and how well the problem can be dealt with.

Shaving with a razor once a day is a quick and easy answer. It does not in any way irritate the skin. Nor does it cause new hair to grow in thicker or coarser, as so many people mistakenly believe.

Waxing. Excess hair can also be removed with a waxing technique. The method will, incidentally, discourage growth if done regularly over a long enough period of time.

Chemical dissolution of the superfluous hairs with any of the hair-removal creams commercially available is yet another effective choice. However, dermatologists caution against possible complications, such as contact dermatitis, if the skin happens to be at all sensitive to the active ingredients in these creams.

Bleaching with hydrogen peroxide solution can help make the hairs less conspicuous, and this approach is used by a large number of women to mask the down on their upper lip. Unfortunately, in strong light—indoors or out—the bleached hairs tend to stand out.

Electrolysis, if done by a qualified professional, can be a highly successful means of getting rid of unwanted hair once and for all, although the procedure is admittedly painful, laborious, and costly. It involves permanent destruction of the hair bulb, the vital portion of the hair follicle responsible for growth. No more than thirty or forty hairs can be treated at one session, and allowance has to be made for regrowth in a certain proportion of those treated, as not all hair bulbs can be completely destroyed the first time around. Where there are dense, fine hairs, as on the upper lip, electrolysis may not produce as good a cosmetic result as it does in an area like the chin where there are coarse, stubbly hairs. Electrolysis often triggers keloids, and as Blacks are prone to keloid formation, electrolysis may not be advisable for a large number of black women. Those who are apt to react in this way are better off using another removal method, such as shaving or just snipping the hairs with a pair of manicure scissors.

Because hirsutism is caused by high circulating levels of testosterone in the blood, research on substances that block testosterone is now going on. One anti-androgen, a compound called cyproterone acetate, has shown good results in experimental studies, the results being more dramatic in more serious cases. Rebound relapses are common, however, especially during the first few months, and there are certain side effects. So it would seem to make more sense to use one of the simple, self-help methods mentioned above.

Ageproofing Your Face

It is quite astonishing how much you can do, all on your own, to ageproof your face. You can give yourself a very effective face lift—without recourse to nips, tucks, or peels —simply by doing some very quick and easy little exercises every day. I think the results are better and safer than anything cosmetic surgery is able to promise and far more enduring as well.

What counts most in ageproofing your face—and what has never really been considered in facial exercise programs until now—is that most of your facial muscles differ in a very basic and important way from the muscles in other parts of your body. You cannot apply the exercise principles you apply to your muscles elsewhere. This, as a matter of fact, is the main drawback to many anti-wrinkle exercise books currently on the market; they fail to make that fundamental distinction.

The thing that sets facial muscles apart from muscles in other parts of the body is that they are to a large extent involved in conveying expressions rather than performing mechanical actions. For this reason they are attached to the skin, in contrast to the skeletal muscles, which are attached to the bones.

Facial muscles are, moreover, constantly being used. So disuse is not the problem that it is with muscles in so many other areas of the body. Instead, misuse is the problem. In ageproofing your face, therefore, the idea is to make your expressions work for you rather than against you—as they are all too apt to do without your even realizing it.

There are two distinct ways to go about ageproofing your

face, and they work together synergistically to give you a real and lasting lift. The two ways are based on the two types of facial expression you have and on the two types of muscles you use to produce the expressions.

The first type of expression is unconscious. Your unconscious expressions are your reflex reactions—those you make automatically. They occur in response to something you see, hear, touch, taste, smell, feel, or just happen to recall, and involve a group of muscles that are quite aptly called the involuntary muscles. The second type of expression is conscious. Your conscious expressions are your intentional reactions, those you give some thought to and are aware of making. These involve a group of muscles called the voluntary muscles.

In every reflex, or unconscious, reaction, your involuntary muscles always work in exactly the same way time after time. The pattern of muscle fiber movement is unchanging. In any thought-out, or conscious, reaction, the mix of muscle fibers you use is likely to vary from one occasion to the next. The pattern of muscle movement is forever changing, just as your thought-out responses are constantly changing. This is a key difference between the two types of muscles and the expressions they produce.

In order to prevent unwanted lines from forming and smooth out wrinkles already there, you need to get at the involuntary muscles that you use in your reflex responses. And, in order to firm the contours of your face, you need to get at the voluntary muscles you bring into play for thought-out expressions. Your Ageproofing Face Lift shows you how to get at both kinds of muscles and how to make them do their separate jobs in ways that make for lasting enhancement—the first part helps you smooth out lines and wrinkles, and the second part helps you firm contours.

Smoothing Out Lines and Wrinkles

Your Ageproofing Face Lift begins by helping you make changes in your reflex reactions to all sorts of sensory signals produced by things you see, hear, touch, taste, smell.

The idea is to be able to recognize what reflex muscle activity is going on in your face and where. Then it is very easy to zero in on the particular batch of muscle fibers involved and relax the minispasm responsible for a specific wrinkle— a frown line, for example. What you want to do is get a feel for the muscles that are used in a reflex reaction associated with a certain contraction so that you can get right to the bottom of the matter—the muscle fibers causing the contraction.

YOUR AGEPROOFING
ANTI-WRINKLE EXERCISES

You can do this set of four exercises right after your bath or shower every day. Use the medicine cabinet mirror in your bathroom to guide you. These four quickies can help you smooth out areas that are starting to show frown or laugh lines or miscellaneous puckers. Even if the wrinkles are as yet only fleeting indications of what is ahead, you can stave them off by beginning the exercises now. If you wait until the lines are all but indelible, they will simply be far harder to remove.

The key areas are forehead, eyes, nose, and mouth. Work on as many of them as you feel you need to.

• *Forehead.* Place the middle and index fingers of your right hand very lightly against any part of your forehead where lines are visible. This not only helps you identify the area you want to concentrate on but also gives you a feel for the muscle fibers you want to get at.

Your fingers should graze the skin just enough to help you sense where the muscle fibers have formed the contraction you want to work on. Then you can tell when you have succeeded in switching off the sensory input responsible for the contraction and are able to maintain the muscle fibers in a relaxed position long enough to counter the contraction.

Now close your mind, and your eyes, to everything except the kind of sensation capable of triggering the frown lines you want to get rid of. Try to visualize in your mind the muscle fibers involved in these frown lines, and then see if you can "unfrown" mentally. Can you feel the muscle fibers relaxing as you do this? See if you can hold the unfrowning state of mind for a count of 10 or 12; you need to hold it long enough to counter the contraction.

Work up to 3 repetitions, resting 5 seconds between each. After you feel you have the hang of it, hold the unfrowns to a count of 15.

- *Eyes*. Repeat the procedure you use for the forehead area in order to get at the laugh and squint lines around the eyes.
- *Nose*. Repeat the procedure again, this time in order to get at the nasolabial fold, which runs from the side of the nostril down past the corner of the mouth. Interestingly, this is usually the dominant expression line in the face, and it is one that cosmetic surgery is unable to correct. A supplementary procedure such as dermabrasion or chemical peeling is usually needed in order to help get at the deep line. And even these procedures are only partially successful. The crease does, however, respond to this special ageproofing anti-wrinkle technique.
- *Mouth*. Repeat the procedure once more, in order to help efface the downturning lines and pouchy little folds at the corners of the mouth.

Your anti-wrinkle exercises end literally on an upnote. Holding two fingers first at the left side of your mouth and then at the right side, use the same procedure to sense the muscle fibers that are involved in a reflex smile. Try to recall something that strikes you as funny. As soon as you can feel, even faintly, muscle fibers activated by your expression, hold the position for a count of 15. Repeat. This very "up" expression can make a noticeable difference in ageproofing your whole face.

When you are not doing anti-wrinkle exercises, be sure to keep your hands away from your face. Far too often people lean their chin on a hand, or rest their cheek against a hand, or point a supporting finger alongside an ear. Such seemingly unimportant gestures end up stretching the skin, and in due course they contribute quite conspicuously to sagging contours. If you look around you at the gestures people use to prop up their head, you can see for yourself how they have inadvertently stretched their facial skin.

Firming Contours

Voluntary muscle activity can be helpful in ageproofing your face, though in a quite different way. By getting at this type of muscle, you can help firm and lift the contours of your face, because in working voluntary muscles, you tone and tighten the main areas that underlie the overall shape.

As each of the exercises involve specific facial features—the nose, the mouth, the ears—you will find the directions for doing them spelled out in the sections on the nose, the mouth, and the ears, which follow a little later in this chapter.

Ageproofing Your Eyes

The things that count in ageproofing your eyes have to do not only with the eyes themselves but also with the entire area around them.

Do you realize that the skin around your eyes is thinner and more fragile than that in any other part of your body? This is why you should try to do everything you can to protect the whole area, lids and all, from the effects of even the most routine wear and tear. Friction of any kind, including that which can occur when one is applying or removing eye makeup, squinting or laughing, or being exposed to the elements, all leave their mark on this almost transparent tissue. Here is what you should do about each of these factors.

Avoiding Friction

Even a slight amount of rubbing that would have no effect whatever on the skin in any other part of the body can be enough of a physical stress to injure the skin around the eyes if done often enough. That is why you should make a special point of avoiding one very common habit—rubbing your eyes, the way people so frequently do when they feel tired or sleepy. This seemingly innocuous gesture is enough to produce or aggravate bags under the eyes, because the thin skin stretches at the slightest amount of drag. As a result people who rub their eyes when they are tired end up looking tired even at times when they are not. The delicate skin, once stretched, remains baggy instead of snapping back into its original shape.

Women should realize that certain kinds of eye makeup are another cause of stretching. The skin is almost bound to be pulled, if ever so slightly, when eye shadow or eye liner is applied and when makeup remover is used to take off waterproof mascara, shadow, and liner. Application and removal of concealers, which are used to camouflage bags and dark circles under the eyes, only end up making matters that much worse for the same reason. Cosmetic consultants are careful to advise women to apply makeup with the fourth, or ring, finger, because it is the weakest of the four and so has a relatively light touch. But a pull occurs even so. The best thing is to use only brow pencil and non-waterproof mascara on the eye area, except for special occasions. Neither of these two products involves application of cosmetics to the skin itself or calls for makeup removers. All it takes to get them off at night is a little soap and warm water.

Bags under the eyes and puffiness around the eyes are sometimes due to genetic factors. But it has been shown that exercise can definitely help reduce their occurrence. If sufficiently vigorous, exercise can be a real boon to those who have a long family history of either of these conditions.

Avoiding Crow's Feet

Squinting is a very natural adaptive response. You do it instinctively to protect your eyes from excess light. You also squint in attempts to focus better on things you are not able to see well. What this does is etch in the squint lines. It helps to wear tinted glasses to protect your eyes against bright light outdoors and glasses or contact lenses indoors or out to correct your vision, if need be.

Wraparound sunglasses are especially effective in preventing signs of "aging." Crow's feet are less apt to develop at the outer corners of the eyes until considerably later in life. And the fragile tissue around the eyes keeps its tone and resiliency much better, so the lids do not take on the crepey droop characteristic of sun-damaged lids.

It is a well-known fact that both wind and extremes of temperature compound the damage caused by chronic sun exposure. Wearing glasses can therefore protect still more by providing a barrier against the elements. Even if you prefer contact lenses for general use, keep a pair of tinted or plain glasses handy to put on whenever you go outside, regardless of how good your eyesight is.

Avoiding Eye Damage

Sunglasses can help protect your eyes against radiation damage, if they happen to be the right kind. Very few people realize, however, that there is such a thing as a right kind and a wrong kind. So it is important to explain just what the problem is and why certain types of sunglasses are helpful and some, not.

Among the structures of your eye—and for that matter those of your whole body—the lens is the most susceptible to damage from radiation. And it happens that almost all the ultraviolet radiation that reaches your eye is transmitted clear through the cornea to the lens. The lens absorbs a certain amount of this radiation, more so with each decade. The photochemical damage that results eventually leads to a buildup of pigmented substances. The lens becomes increasingly opaque and transmits less and less light. The pigmentation buildup causes the lens to turn an ever-deepening yellowish brown until in due course it is actually brown. If the photochemical damage progresses beyond a certain point, a brownish cataract is formed. Obviously, one main objective of ageproofing your eyes should be to avoid this.

The development of brownish cataracts can usually be checked or at least slowed considerably by adequate protection of the eyes against too much ultraviolet radiation. Although only a relatively small amount of UV radiation enters the eye under ordinary circumstances, the cumulative effect of many years of exposure can be significant. Brownish cataracts occur at a much higher rate in regions of the United States where there is strong sunlight most of the year. And manmade sources of illumination also contribute to the problem. Even the low level of UV radiation in the fluorescent lights that are used in homes, offices, schools, and gyms should not be altogether discounted.

It is important to protect your eyes against excess radiation indoors and out and particularly against strong sunlight. Maybe you think you are already doing this, but there is every likelihood that you are making matters worse. You probably wear sunglasses whenever you are in blazing sun for any length of time. The glasses cut the glare and make you feel more comfortable. But do they actually protect your eyes against UV radiation? The answer given by leading photobiologists may come as a surprise to you. It is an emphatic no. With few exceptions the sunglasses now on the market increase rather than decrease the risk of sun damage to your eyes.

The reason for this increased risk of damage is that your eyes do not perceive UV radiation. You have natural defense mechanisms, which work very well as long as the UV radiation is accompanied by bright visible light: you look away, your pupils contract, and you squint. Sunglasses lower these natural defenses by reducing the visible light that triggers them. The darker the sunglass lenses, the easier it is to look toward the sun. Your pupils dilate more and you squint less. So the darker the shade of the sunglass lenses, the greater the amount of UV radiation entering your eyes and getting through to the lens. What even very few opticians realize is that the dark hue of the sunglasses, while cutting down on wavelength transmission in the visible light range, has no effect on the transmission of UV radiation.

As to materials, all glass, regardless of tint, stops the more energetic UV-B rays. But all glass transmits the longer, more prevalent UV-A rays. And plastic is an excellent transmitter of both UV-B and UV-A. So the usual type of sunglasses gives you a very false sense of security. Ask the optician to show you the light transmission data on any

pair of sunglasses you are thinking of buying. If he does not
have the information, he can certainly obtain it from the
manufacturer.

Among the makes of sunglasses that provide protection
from UV radiation, there are two which screen UV entirely
and several others which screen it enough for all practical
purposes.

· UV-400 lenses, made by Di-Optic Company and marketed in
this country by Norville Optical, completely block UV, can take
prescriptions and are available at good opticians.

· AmberMatic, a photochromatic type of sunglasses that blocks
out 98 percent of UV radiation, is made by Bausch & Lomb and is
also available at good opticians.

Any polycarbonate lense blocks out UV sufficiently for most
people in non-tropical climates. It is, however, not easy to
know which sunglasses have polycarbonate lenses simply by
asking in the chemist's or department store. Norlight, made
by Norville Optical, are effective and are available at
opticians.

If you wish, your optician can send any prescription
lenses, clear or tinted, to a specialized company that can
coat them with UV-proof film.

Avoiding Eye Irritation

Everybody's eyes become irritated at some time or other.
There are countless reasons why this can happen. Here is a
handy list of some of the most common causes of eye irritation and what to do about them.

• Throughout the day, be sure to blink frequently. Odd as it
  may seem, one common cause of irritation and eye redness is too little blinking. This is often a result of concentrating too hard on something and simply forgetting to
  blink.
• If your eyes are apt to get bloodshot from close work,
  check with your doctor to see if you need glasses. If you
  already wear glasses or contacts, make sure you do not
  need a new prescription.
• The strong overhead fluorescent lighting used in so many
  offices can make your eyes quite bloodshot by the end of

the day. If possible, turn the overhead lighting off for at least a few hours of the day and work by daylight instead.

• If you drink, drink moderately, for the sake of your eyes as well as for your health in general. Alcohol dilates the capillaries everywhere in your body, but most noticeably those in your eyes.

• It is a good idea to avoid eating spicy foods on a regular basis, because these can have much the same effect on your eyes as alcohol has.

• If you swim in a pool, make a point of wearing goggles to keep your eyes from becoming bloodshot.

• Avoid the common habit that people have of using over-the-counter eyedrops to ''whiten'' their eyes whenever they appear bloodshot. If used regularly over a period of time, these drops—which act by constricting the blood vessels of the cornea—may actually irritate the eyes and cause further reddening, which is just the reverse of what you want. It is therefore always best to deal with the problem directly and try to eliminate the cause of the irritation itself if possible.

Ageproofing Your Nose

There is one change that occurs in the look of your nose over the years about which people say you can do nothing. I tend to disagree. There is one other change that without any question you can do something about.

Nose Lift

First, the change that is said to be unavoidable. Studies show that as people get older their noses usually grow a trifle longer. In one very large study of men, nose length averaged 55 millimeters early in the twenties and 58 millimeters late in the sixties, a relatively modest gain of 6 percent over a forty-year period. There was a similar increase in thickness. Even though it is generally agreed that you can do nothing to counter this kind of change—and by way of condolence it is duly noted that a couple of millimeters are not enough to make a noticeable difference in anybody's looks—I see no reason to accept any change as inevitable if it need not be. That runs counter to all ageproofing principles.

There is an exercise I find quite helpful in giving the nose a lift. All you do is place a finger on the cartilage where it divides the nostrils and meets the upper lip and then press gently up so that the cartilage is lifted. With a finger of the other hand try to press the nostrils closed, one at a time, as you take a deep breath. Over a period of a few weeks you should begin to see the lift effect.

Nose Shaper

The other change that occurs in the appearance of the nose over time is a wasting away of the little facial muscles that work the nostrils. Ordinarily these are toned by the simple act of breathing. When you increase your activity and breathe deeply, you do not consciously do anything with your nostrils—they just flare automatically to avoid being pulled shut by the rapid inhalation of air. As people get older, however, and are less physically active, they tend to breathe less deeply. The muscles that expand the nostrils start to atrophy, and the nostrils themselves acquire a collapsed look.

Once again, apply Your Ageproofing Law: Use it or lose it. Exercise has a host of benefits, but you have probably never realized what it can do for the looks of your nose. And all you have to do in the way of nose-conditioning exercise is to take deep breaths whenever you happen to think of it. It is enough to keep your nostrils well toned for life.

Ageproofing Your Mouth

Your upper lip appears to lengthen as you get older, and in so doing it loses its becoming upward curve. Both lips also tend to get thinner. The result is a longer upper lip and a thin, flat lipline from corner to corner. With such a combination of changes, your mouth cannot help but look old.

There are two things you have to do to give your mouth an ageproof appearance, and the sooner you start doing them the better. One is to make the lips themselves thicker. The other is to give your mouth a shapely curve, paying special attention to the upper lip so it rises noticeably in the center and turns up at each corner.

Fuller Lips

The key to making your lips thicker is to use them. It is that simple. Playing a saxophone or clarinet or any kind of wind instrument makes the lips much fuller—and curvier too. Nobody is going to take up the trumpet or flute merely to have a better lipline, of course, but the message is clear: Using your lips—exercising them regularly, in other words —is the thing that counts here, just as it does in the other aspects of ageproofing.

Something as routine as talking helps. So does whistling. Learn to whistle if you do not already know how, and make whistling a daily muscle-toning exercise for your lips. You can practice as you walk down a street, wait for a bus, drive to work. Even more effective as well as more fun is kissing! It is great for getting your lips in shape. Kissing not only helps make lips full but also gives them a decided lift, provided you do enough daily reprises. The upper lip, when well-conditioned by such exercise, will arc up in the center in a very attractive line.

There are also two extremely effective little lip-plumping exercises that you can do each day. They keep the muscles around the mouth good and firm. And they make your lips come together the way they should so you avoid a condition known technically as lip incompetency, in which the lips do not automatically meet when the face is relaxed. If not corrected, lip incompetency can contribute conspicuously to lines around the mouth in later years. So here is a daily double to get started doing now.

LIP TONERS

- *Lip Pop*. Extend your lower lip so that your two lips really hug each other, and then separate your lips with a loud pop. Repeat 25 times.
- *Lip Puff*. Stuff a small wad of facial tissue or cotton into the end of a drinking straw. Try to blow the stuffing out of the straw. As you blow, puff out your cheeks and do not allow the air to escape from your lips. Then release the air with a loud rush. Repeat 25 times.

Shapelier Lips

Everything you do to make your lips full and firm helps give them a curve as well. But there is one specific exercise that can, if done every day, give your mouth a really emphatic curve. What's more, by lifting the upper lip so it forms an attractive arc, this exercise helps shorten the distance between the nostrils and the mouth. Everything has to do with how you breathe—if your nostrils are closed and your breathing is done through your mouth, your upper lip becomes perceptibly shorter and lifted. Here is the exercise that does the trick.

LIP LIFT

- Gently press your nostrils closed and keep them closed while you do this exercise. Make a round, full mouth in the shape of an O and a bit pouty. Through as small an opening as possible in your O-shaped mouth take in all the air you need for one deep breath. You can actually feel the muscles of your lips tightening as you do this. Repeat 25 times at first. Gradually increase to 50 repeats a day.

In ageproofing your mouth, it is also important to give it a lift at the corners. Mona Lisa had the look down pat. That incorrigible little half-smile of hers is exactly the effect you want to strive for. You see a lot of men and women in their early twenties and even some teenagers whose mouth has already taken a downward turn at the corners. A line like that is not specifically a sign of age, but it does become progressively more noticeable as you get older. When it is combined with the other subtle changes taking place in your facial features and contours, even the slightest downward turn of the lips is bound to have an old look. To counter the tendency and get that enigmatic upturn, it also helps to do the exercise for the mouth on page 114.

Ageproofing Your Teeth

Astonishing as it may at first seem, tooth decay and tooth loss affect almost everyone in the western world. It is undoubtedly the most widespread disorder in this country today, except the common cold. The average number of filled teeth in 15-year olds was 4.2 according to a 1983 survey. Happily this figure is an improvement on the 1973 average of 6.0. In the United Kingdom alone a horrifying 27% of the population in the 35–44 year-old age bracket have lost all their natural teeth. In the over-65 age bracket only 15% of the population have *any* of their own teeth left. These statistics are no better in the rest of the western world.

Most people assume that they are bound to lose at least some teeth as they grow older. Nothing could be farther from the truth. A tooth is an extremely durable object, good for at least two hundred years with ordinary wear and tear. Tooth loss is due almost entirely to caries, the familiar decay that results in cavities, until about age thirty-five, by which time the teeth have become more resistant because of an increased fluoride content and a gradual buildup of immunity to decay-causing organisms. After thirty-five, periodontal disease, which progressively degrades the gums, connective tissue, and bone that surround and support the teeth—the word "periodontal" means "around the tooth" —is the main cause of tooth loss. Periodontal disease is so prevalent today that some twenty million people in the United States have lost all their teeth because of it.

Daily Double

Barring some special condition, there is no reason why you cannot keep your teeth for life by giving them the right daily care. Proper cleaning morning and night is basic, starting with careful brushing. Brushing helps remove both food particles and plaque, the sticky, colorless film that forms on the surface of the teeth. When a tooth has not been thoroughly brushed and cleaned, colonies of decay-causing bacteria begin to multiply on its enamel surface, especially near the gum line. These prolific hordes of microscopic organisms are ceaselessly active, converting sugar and other fermentable carbohydrates present in food into organic acids that eat away at the enamel coating of the tooth, despite the fact that enamel is the hardest substance in the entire body. If this plaque buildup, two-thirds of which simply represents the masses of actual bacteria present on the enamel, is not removed regularly, it soon hardens into a substance called calculus, or tartar, a main factor in the development of periodontal disease.

Even with the most careful brushing there are bound to be some places that your toothbrush is not quite able to get to. This is why it is also essential to floss your teeth daily. Flossing is enormously helpful in extricating any food particles that have become lodged between the teeth. Your dentist may suggest a water-irrigating device as well, as this can be useful in flushing out bits of food trapped in hard-to-get-at spots.

It is best to get in the habit of cleaning your teeth the same way every day. Then you will be able to go through the routines quickly and automatically, no matter how rushed or tired you are. Here is a special program that has been worked out by a leading clinical authority.

DAILY DOUBLE TOOTH CARE PLAN

A.M.
- After breakfast, brush your teeth with a fluoridated toothpaste and a soft bristle brush. Brush down from the gums

on the upper teeth and up from the gums on the lower
teeth. Use short strokes. As you brush your teeth, both in
front and in back, pay particular attention to the gumline.
For good measure, brush the roof of your mouth and your
tongue very lightly.

P.M.

• At bedtime, mix a heaping teaspoonful of bicarbonate of
soda in a shot glass with a few drops of hydrogen peroxide, just enough to give the mixture a paste-like consistency. Brush the mixture straight across the gumline front
and back, top and bottom, making certain that it reaches
the areas where the teeth and gums meet.
• Next floss your teeth to remove any remaining food debris
and bacterial growth wedged between the teeth.
• Now fill a glass with warm water and a tablespoonful of
salt. Rinse your mouth well with the solution. If your dentist recommends that you use a water-irrigating device,
this is the time to do so. Fill the container with the salt
solution, set the speed only as fast as the dentist suggests
and no faster, and play the stream of water over all the
teeth, back and front, in order to get at any stubborn particles of debris.
• The last step is to brush your teeth with a fluoridated
toothpaste.

Yearly Double

It is of course essential to see your dentist at regular intervals. The British Dental Association suggests a visit
every six months, with professional cleaning each time to
remove whatever calculus has accumulated in the interim—
a certain amount is bound to, despite your best efforts,
especially just below the gum line. Some people's teeth
need more frequent attention. If your dentist feels that your
teeth call for professional cleaning every four months, he
will suggest this. It is a good idea, too, to check him
from time to time about your brushing and flossing techniques; he may have some advice to give you about
methods or some tips about the kind of brush and dentrifice
to use.

Tooth-Decay Trio

What you eat and do not eat every day can have a significant effect on the looks and health of your teeth. Tooth decay involves three factors: teeth that are susceptible to decay, bacteria that cause acid, foods that contribute to the decay process by fermenting to form acids when acted upon by bacteria. The food that leads to the most trouble is sucrose, otherwise known as sugar. The British eat on average about two pounds of it a week. This accounts for 15 to 20 percent of their total caloric intake, without contributing anything in the way of nutrients. All it does is provide a mouthful of dental problems. You should therefore make every effort to cut down your sucrose consumption in the form of table sugar, candies, cookies, cakes, ice cream, and every other kind of other sugar-rich dessert and snack. Chewing gum and soft drinks are not any help either. If you eat little sugar, the type of bacteria found in dental plaque and involved in at least 90 percent of all cavities—*Streptococcus mutans*—will be able to colonize only in small numbers, since it will lack the kind of food it needs in order to thrive and proliferate.

Sucrose heads a long list of trouble-makers—any food containing acid-forming carbohydrates can cause tooth decay. One unlikely source of trouble is apples. As it now turns out, they contain quite a lot of acid-forming carbohydrate. So, while an apple is a very nutritious food, it does not boast the cleaning properties it was long thought to have. Another unexpected food is potato chips. They, too, contain enough acid-forming carbohydrate to cause cavities.

How often you eat foods containing table sugar or other acid-forming carbohydrates can be even more important than how much of them you eat. There is a direct correlation between the frequency of eating harmful snacks and the incidence of cavities. Each snack break causes a separate acid attack on the surface of the teeth. If, say, you have a box of candies and you eat one every twenty minutes or so during the day, that is worse for your teeth than if you open the box only once and eat as much as you happen to want just at that particular time.

Another thing that matters is the consistency of the snack food. Sticky foods stay in the mouth much longer and are much more cariogenic, or cavity-causing, than those that are swallowed quickly. A caramel, for example, or a piece of salt water toffee, is much more damaging to the teeth than a soft drink.

Good-Teeth Diet

If certain foods are decidedly noxious, other foods can be quite helpful in protecting your teeth and their supporting structures. Recent studies indicate that cheeses do this, especially Gruyere, Emmenthal and mature cheddar. If eaten at the same time as a sweet snack, they reduce the sugary food's cavity-causing potential by cutting down the amount of acid produced. Researchers hope to identify the ingredient responsible for this protective action. If discovered, it might be used as an anti-cavity supplement in sugar-containing foods.

Fresh fruits and vegetables that are potent sources of vitamin C may help prevent plaque formation and periodontal disease by bolstering oral defenses against harmful organisms. This is because some of the body's feistiest fighters against invaders are polymorphonuclear leukocytes (PMNs for short) and they are rich in vitamin C. The way PMNs help is moving swiftly against the bacteria the moment they start to colonize, engulfing and destroying them in no time at all.

Good-Teeth Exercise

The foods you eat can help maintain and even improve the looks and health of your teeth and the supporting bone by forcing you to use your teeth the way they are meant to be used. Your Ageproofing Law is at work here too. Your teeth and jaws are made to bite and grind food into a pulp that you can easily swallow. So it is important to eat a good amount of foods that give them something to chew on, as distinct from soft foods like chopped meat and hamburger rolls that make up so much of the American diet. Crunchy Italian or French loaves of bread are very good, particularly the heel of the loaf. Raw carrots are another way to give your teeth a good workout. Other foods with plenty of bite to them are spring onions, radishes, celeriac, and raw cauliflower or broccoli. Try the skin of a well-baked potato. Excellent 'grinding' greens are the the coarse outer leaves of curly and cos lettuce. The marketplace is full of such chewy foods.

The effect of vigorous chewing on the bony structures that provide support for your teeth is of the greatest importance, because physical stress strengthens bone while lack of stress weakens it. The more you exercise your jaws every day by eating food that requires lots of biting into and grinding up, the more you help them remain strong and healthy.

Interestingly, people who habitually grind their teeth when asleep—a condition known as bruxism—maintain strong, firm bone in their jaws as a result of the constant stress. This does not mean that bruxism is a habit you want to cultivate. Besides the excessive mechanical wear and tear on the teeth, clenching contractions cut their blood supplies and make them much more susceptible to breakdown after a period of time. It is worth noting here, incidentally, that alcohol can increase bruxism. If you happen to be one of the many with this involuntary stress reaction and are used to having a couple of drinks in the course of the evening, it might be helpful to cut out after-dinner drinking, until you are able to break yourself of the teeth-grinding habit. Your dentist can spot early signs of bruxism and alert you to the presence of the condition, which you may have no other way of becoming aware of. Bruxism usually tends to wear down the edges of the canines in the upper jaw—the pair of pointed teeth located third from the front center line. Sometimes one canine may be worn down much more than the other because of more forceful grinding on that particular side.

Bone loss in the jaw often seems to be a first manifestation of osteoporosis, which is such a devastating disease among postmenopausal white women. Recent studies show, in fact, a dramatic link in this group between extensive tooth loss and osteoporotic bone demineralization in other parts of the body. So this is an additional reason for getting plenty of calcium in your diet—dietary calcium and exercise are the two great natural defenses you can use against the disease.

No Gimmicks, No Trade-Offs

The message comes across pretty loud and clear—do all you can to avoid tooth and jawbone loss. Sometimes, as it happens, this may involve not doing things that might otherwise be done in what is assumed to be a person's best interest. Occasionally dentists remove teeth in order to improve the overall dental alignment and avoid the crowding that appears so common—and which may be due in part to a soft rather than a hard diet during the growing years and lack of forceful enough chewing to stimulate optimal breadth in jaw development. If a person has a tendency toward protruding teeth, a dentist may recommend extractions, usually in the upper jaw, in order to help pull back the teeth in front and provide a straighter profile. Occasionally the recommendation is even made when there is no evidence of overcrowding, merely to achieve a straighter and more pleasing cosmetic effect.

This is assumed to be a procedure without trade-offs. Indeed, there are not likely to be any at the time of straightening. But some experts have questioned its advisability from a long-term point of view. By age twenty-five, they say, noticeable wrinkles may appear as a result of the procedure, especially in the area between the nostril and the corner of the mouth, where a deep line known as the nasolabial fold usually forms. The look, these experts believe, is suddenly that of a person at least fifteen years older.

There may be other "aging" effects as well. It is one thing if the teeth conform to the overall shape of the face because they are naturally straight. If, however, they are straightened to form two perfectly even rows, they may be pulled so far back from their original line that they give the appearance of a set of dentures. Denture-wearers have a typical look: a set-back mouth with perfect rows of teeth— and wrinkles.

There is always a certain risk involved in moving teeth around, so it may not be the wisest thing to do this simply for cosmetic reasons. Not only is there a chance that the supporting structures may be weakened and that early wrinkles may occur, but also there is the chance that periodontal disease may do greater damage, leading in due course to an increased risk of tooth loss. If this happens, and if the jawbone in turn becomes weaker and thinner because it is no longer being stressed by the pressure of the teeth in their sockets during chewing, a whole cascade of events may be set in motion within a fairly short time that can adversely affect a person's whole appearance.

Ageproofing Your Ears

When you look at people's faces in the bus or standing in line for a movie or in a crowd anywhere, you note more or less unconsciously which look younger and which look older. One way you sense this, oddly enough, is by how their ears look. Very subtle changes occur in every feature over a period of years, and the ears are no exception.

First of all, people's ears get longer as they get older. Measurements of men's ear length, taken fifty years apart, show an increase from about 66 millimeters, on the average, during a man's twenties, to about 73 millimeters during his seventies. Ear breadth also increases throughout this span of years, from about 36 millimeters to 39 millimeters. The lobe of the ear thickens with age as well.

Avoiding Droop

Women's ears change the same as men's do. There is, however, one further shift that is apt to increase the length of a woman's ears—drooping lobes. This markedly elongated appearance, suggesting statues of Buddha or assorted Indian deities, is actually more the result of heavy earrings than years. Luckily the trend among people in their twenties and thirties today is toward minuscule gold or stone earrings rather than the weighty hoops, pendants, and ball types of earrings. And many women now prefer to wear no earrings at all.

Avoiding Wrinkles

There is another change that contributes subtly but definitely to an old look. It is the gradual formation of a small vertical fold immediately in front of the ear, which often becomes apparent during the forties or early fifties. Although it is highly visible, very few people seem to be consciously aware of its existence. That does not mean that it does not convey its message subliminally.

Certain gestures may contribute to the slackening of skin responsible for this vertical ear fold. When people prop their head against their hand, for example, they stretch the skin in that area a good deal. There is, however, an easy little exercise that helps both prevent and counter such stretching: ear wiggling.

EAR WIGGLE

• If you remember wiggling your ears as a child, practice doing just that. Hold your ears back and up for a count of 15. Then relax for a few seconds and repeat. Gradually work up to 10 repeats.

If you have forgotten how to do the wiggle, stand in front of a mirror and practice it. At first the movement may seem relatively slight, but you can develop it in time. As you do, you will see the toning and tightening effect it has on the skin in that area as well as on the eye and cheek area and also the face as a whole.

Ageproofing Your Neck

I am sure you have often noticed how many people tend to crane their neck forward more and more with the years until it is almost horizontal instead of vertical. I do not think such people are aware that this is happening, because if you suggest to them that they should make an effort to stand up straight—a suggestion that few seem to welcome—they immediately pull their hunched shoulders way back and leave their neck craning forward. Unfortunately, the tendency is already evident in many twenty-year-olds and increasingly pronounced in quite a lot of thirty-year-olds. One way to become aware of the extent to which you may do this—and see exactly what needs correcting—is to look at snapshots of yourself in profile taken on occasions when you were not conscious of how you were standing.

Shaping Up

A dancer's neck is always set well back and aligned with the spinal column. Dancers are taught early to stand in such a way that the base of the skull is in a plumb line with the uppermost vertebra of the spine, and they keep that alignment throughout life. To get a wonderfully ageproof neck line you have to work at it, just as they do. On the following page is the dancer's way for you to try.

LINE-UP

• Stand up tall against a wall, pressing the base of your skull as close to it as you can. Gradually bring the rest of your body in line with the wall, starting with your upper back and continuing down to your lower back. Then try to get your legs and heels as near the wall as you can without losing contact with the wall at any other body points. Hold this posture for 10 counts. Walk away from the wall, keeping the alignment as well as possible. Try to have a mental image of what it feels like. This will help you get back into alignment whenever you catch yourself craning forward during the day.

There is another great exercise you can do to counter the craning tendency and keep your neck in better alignment with your spine. It helps keep your neck set back and erect by strengthening and tightening the trapezius muscles in back, which tend to sag, and stretching the pectoral muscles in front, which tend to be overtight.

SHRUG-UP

• Place a 5-pound wraparound weight over each shoulder. Join the weights across the back and front of your neck so they form a harness. When the harness is securely in place, shrug your shoulders as high as you can for a count of 5. Release. Repeat 10 times.

Activities like dancing and swimming that give you a chance to stretch your back muscles and open out your chest, can be a big help. And if you have the time, the place, and the energy to walk four or five miles at a stretch, you will also find that your body will shed its tension. You will end your walk with a fine natural balance that will align your neck plumb with your spine.

I find that it is a good idea to use a small pillow for sleeping rather than a large one. A baby pillow stuffed with down can be very helpful. If your head is propped up on a heftier pillow for eight hours every night, your neck does not have a chance to extend itself properly.

Sunscreening Up

Although craning is by far the most conspicuous change affecting the neck over the years, there is an entirely different kind of blight to guard against as well: sun damage.

When sunbathers—women, in particular—put on sunscreens they tend to ignore the neck. They overlook the fact that when you are standing up, your head provides your neck a certain amount of protection from the sun whereas if you are lying on the beach, it is very much exposed to the sun's rays. After a decade or two of sun exposure, a crepey "necklace" appears at the base of the neck, because of cumulative injury. Whenever I see women with scarves or beads massed at their throat, I cannot help wondering if this is a camouflage hiding the damage caused by too many summers in the sun. If you are out in the sun for any length of time at all, try to remember to lavish sunscreen on your neck, particularly if you are a woman and have very light skin. The skin in the neck region is more delicate than that in almost any other region except the eyes.

Ageproofing Your Body Shape

The shape of your body at rest and in motion can be a far more telling indicator of how young or old you look than your actual age in years ever can. So what are the things that count most in determining your body shape? In what ways is your body shape apt to undergo deteriorative change? What ageproofing action can you take to get your body into great shape and stay that way?

Insidious Inches

Weight is obviously one thing that counts a lot. When people keep putting on weight over the years, the extra pounds make a conspicuous difference in how young or old they look. And there is a decided tendency for American men and women to gain weight steadily during their thirties, forties, fifties, and sixties because of their sedentary way of life, with women continuing to gain for a decade or so longer. People simply take it for granted that such weight gain is to be more or less expected as they get older—hence the expression "middle-age spread"—and resign themselves to excess poundage as one more unavoidable fact of life.

There are two very important things that most men and women fail to understand about gaining weight decade after decade. The first is that it is entirely avoidable. The second is that much more is involved than merely putting on pounds. People not only overeat but also underexercise, so they not only put on fat but also lose lean tissue, or muscle. The number they see when they step on the bathroom scale is misleading. Take a thirty-five-year-old man who has been leading a fairly inactive, desk-bound life and now weighs twenty pounds more than he did when he was in college. Those twenty pounds of additional weight probably represent twenty-five or thirty pounds of fat gained minus five or ten pounds of muscle lost. That is the way such weight shifts usually work. But they can be prevented and also reversed. There is nothing inevitable about such fat gain and muscle loss.

Fat-Lean Ratio

You can see that, as far as ageproofing your body shape goes, your ratio of fat tissue to lean muscle tissue—or, to put it another way, your ratio of body fat to total body weight—is more significant than your total body weight by itself. Body fat should amount to no more than 14 to 15 percent of a man's total body weight, ideally, and no more than 20 to 22 percent of a woman's total body weight, according to the reckonings of leading sports physiologists. There is a greater body fat allowance for women than men because of sex differences. Men are usually taller and leaner than women to begin with. They tend to have a heftier skeleton, more muscle, and less fatty tissue overall. Women are likely to be somewhat shorter with a slighter frame and a smaller amount of muscle but proportionately more fatty tissue, distributed mainly in the breast and pelvic regions.

Men and women put on fat in different ways over the decades, but there is a long-term redistribution that is basically centripetal for both, with fat being lost earlier and to a greater extent from the extremities while being maintained or increased on the trunk. This tendency is especially conspicuous in men. After reaching maximum thickness by about forty-five, the fat on a man's upper arm and hip areas is likely to decrease, whereas the roll of fat around his waist may continue to increase for thirty years more. In contrast, the fat on a woman's upper arm, hip and abdominal regions, after reaching maximum thickness by the time she is forty-five, changes very little in later years. Fat in her breast and mid-back area, however, goes on accumulating for at least another thirty years. Women simply have a greater percentage of fat deposited in all of the body's fat depots than men, and this is true during every period of life.

How can you gauge your own body fat percentage? How can you figure out just how close to or wide of the ideal it is? Sports physiologists can get pretty reliable estimates by measuring skinfold thickness in various parts of the body with a pair of calipers, which are what you might call professional pinchers. A truly accurate reading requires a more elaborate procedure in specially equipped laboratories—underwater weighing.

Three-Way Fat Check

Fortunately there is a far easier way for you to size things up than by being calipered or dunked. All you have to do is stand in front of a full-length mirror without any clothes on and survey yourself in the flesh. Try to judge what you see as objectively and honestly as possible. If you look too fat, you probably are too fat. And if you look too fat through the trunk, typical long-term weight shifts are probably occurring as well.

I have a quick and easy way of checking on any incipient fat and weight shifts every day, so that I can nip them in the bud before they become a real problem. All I do is take two basic kinds of measurement: inches and pounds. The two measurements counter-check each other. My tape measure shows me where there are slight day-to-day shifts in inches, and therefore fat, at any key point, such as bust, waist, or hips. My bathroom scale shows me where there are slight day-to-day shifts in pounds. I check up on myself at the same time every morning—the first thing on getting up—and adjust my eating and exercise patterns for the day accordingly. I am 5′ 6″ tall in my bare feet and weigh 105 pounds. My measurements at sixty-two are bust 32″, waist 21″, hips 32″. They are the measurements I had in 1940, the summer of my freshman year at college. I happened to be working as a model then and have a written record of my measurements on my model-agency composite—the 8″ by 10″ equivalent of a business card. Interestingly, they are also the measurements I had before and after both my pregnancies—in 1955 and in 1958—even though I gained fifty pounds with each pregnancy and had two beautifully healthy nine-and-a-half-pound babies to show for it. The tape-and-scale measurement technique is a terrific combination,which you can count on any time and under any conditions. You know in a matter of seconds precisely what is going on and where, and get enough advance warning to prevent any unwelcome changes.

But what about the standard tables of desirable weights for men and women of different heights and body frames. They are not much help. For example, the average "desirable" weight for a woman of my height by standard life-insurance reckonings is 128 pounds. Allowing for body-frame differences, this so-called desirable range goes from a minimum of 114 pounds to a maximum of 146 pounds. But I happen to weigh 105 pounds, and I look and feel fit and well at this level. If I were to put on the nine pounds needed to reach the minimum "desirable" level, I would be extremely uncomfortable. I refuse to dwell on what I would look and feel like at even the average "desirable" level, to say nothing of the maximum "desirable" level.

The tables seem to have two main drawbacks. One is that they are skewed toward overweight. The other is that the weight ranges for any given height and build are so broad that they really do not tell you much at all—except, of course, that any person who is over the more than generous maximum is either right tackle on a football team or too fat. Just looking in a full-length mirror provides you with more and better information about yourself than any of these weight-and-height tables can.

Fat Control

What is the best way to deal with excess fat? Keeping your calorie intake heathily low is important. But dieting by itself does not provide lasting results. It can actually be counterproductive, as you saw in Chapter Three, with a rebound overshoot in fat regain after you stop and a sizeable loss of muscle mass. In contrast, a program of regular and vigorous exercise, combined with a moderate calorie intake, can get fat off and keep it off. Together, they can bring your fat percentage down closer to an ideal level and help keep it there, so you avoid the unsightly redistribution of excess fat that is otherwise apt to occur from decade to decade.

Muscle Maintenance

Exercising is absolutely essential in order to ageproof your body shape. It not only gets at excess fat stores by burning calories but also, of course, firms and strengthens muscles. It is in fact *the* means of maintaining the good muscle shape that underlies good body shape. Use it or lose it, your key principle in ageproofing, applies more noticeably to your muscles than it does to any other part of your body. Physical inactivity leads quite rapidly to loss of muscle mass. As the muscles become weaker, they tire more quickly. People then get in the habit of using them less and less. What results is a vicious circle, with weak muscles fostering inactivity and inactivity fostering weak muscles, a situation that nothing short of vigorous exercise can reverse.

Muscles that are not used vigorously on a regular basis suffer even more than a loss of lean tissue; they get infiltrated with fat. This is the human equivalent of the marbling you see in prime beef, an effect that is achieved by keeping cattle penned up and inactive for a certain period before slaughtering. Fat marbling in muscle is a process that is entirely different from other types of fat storage in the body —the accumulation of fat in sex-specific regions, for example, or in the thin layer of cushioning tissue directly beneath the skin. The marbling phenomenon is now coming under careful study, and findings throw new light on the controversial question of whether or not exercise can effect spot reduction.

The going theory among experts has long been that when you exercise, your body draws equally upon fat stores in all parts of your body for use as energy and not preferentially on those in the immediate vicinity of the muscles being worked. This is why they have so long held fast to the view that there is no such thing as spot reduction. But now it is becoming evident that, as exercise firms and strengthens a muscle in the area being worked, it helps prevent the shift from lean mass to fat and the marbling that is otherwise so apt to occur in the muscle tissue. What's more, exercise also helps reverse accumulations of fat after they begin to replace the lean tissue in the actual muscle, dislodging the fat buildup when synthesis of new lean tissue gets under way. This can explain why people who have, say, good abdominal muscles and use them to hold their abdomen flat, do not seem to get flab in that area. In other words, there seems to be such a thing as spot reduction after all. It works not through a reduction of normal fat stores but through a restoration of the muscle's peak level of lean mass, which necessarily does away with fat infiltration.

Strong-Bone Tactics

Good strong bones are as important as good strong muscles in ageproofing your body shape, though their contribution is not immediately obvious. Bones often become weak and fragile over the years through loss of mineral mass and eventually crumble and break under relatively slight stress, as you saw in the section on osteoporosis in Chapter Three. The most conspicuous of the numerous crippling effects of osteoporosis is the humped back and shrinkage in height caused by crush fractures of the spinal vertebrae, a particularly common disability among postmenopausal white women. Bone demineralization can get under way as early as the twenties, so it is important to take preventive action much sooner than people are apt to realize. This means getting plenty of calcium in your diet and exercise in your day.

Joint Action

Besides seeing to it that your fat percentage stays down, your muscles stay firm, and your bones stay strong, there is one further aspect of ageproofing your body shape that you should take care not to ignore: flexibility. You want to do all you possibly can to maintain good flexibility. Loss of joint mobility is actually one of the most pronounced and critical changes that can occur over the years, and it affects even the appearance of the body at rest as well as every movement a person makes. Keeping maximum flexibility by means of regular stretching exercises, such as those provided in Your Ageproofing Racquetball Plan, along with activities like dancing that gently stretch and lengthen the various muscle groups so that the joints can maintain their full range of motion decade after decade, is what make the greatest difference.

Your musculoskeletal system is made up of a series of interconnecting links, each joint being affected by the workings of the other joints above and below and the various muscles and bones involved. In one way or another your joints end up being collectively engaged in practically every movement you make. So it is pretty clear why working them regularly, properly, and in lots of different ways, can be so vital to maintaining good joint function throughout your life.

Vigorous exercise is not in itself harmful to the joints, contrary to what many people believe. It can have a very beneficial effect on the key components of the joint, thickening the cartilage and strengthening the tendons and ligaments, to say nothing of its effect on the muscles and bones brought into play. The one thing you want to be sure to avoid at all times is joint misuse and abuse, as this damages the irreplaceable cartilage, the crux of joint integrity, and leads to degeneration and osteoarthritis.

Ageproofing Your Back

Is it possible to keep your back strong and straight throughout life? The answer is an emphatic yes.

Back Alignment

The first thing you want to do is make sure that you stand properly, because ageproofing your back begins with good alignment. You do not want to be as straight as a board. There ought to be a slight natural curve at the back of your neck and again at the back of your waist. If a plumb line were dropped alongside you, it should go right from your ear lobe past the knob of your shoulder and the middle of your hip, then just slightly behind your kneecap and in front of your ankle bone.

When you stand correctly, all your muscles work together the way they should to keep you holding your own against the pull of gravity. Nothing is askew. This well-balanced interaction tones and strengthens your muscles. Every bone in your body stands to benefit too, because each is being stressed the way it should be by the muscles working it. This stress in turn stimulates the mineralization required to maintain bone mass at a strong, healthy peak.

If people do not stand properly, there is a progressive series of deteriorative changes. The abdominal muscles, which are the most important ones for standing erect, become weak through disuse, and the abdomen protrudes. As the abdominal muscles go lax, an additional load is placed on the small muscles of the lower back, which they are not up to handling. The result is the low-back pain that so many millions of people suffer from.

The misalignment in the lower back, with the abdomen going out and the lower back going in, produces the slouch that is characteristic of people who have let their abdominal muscles go to pot. Early in life all this can be corrected by simply standing up straight. But chronic slouching weakens and overstretches the muscles of the upper back and reduces their ability to keep it in upright alignment. Over time this weakens the vertebrae; they are not being stressed enough by the muscles to maintain good mineralization levels. The bone degradation, in which inadequate dietary calcium also plays a part, can start as early as the twenties and thirties.

Back Exercise

Exercise can help you avoid such bone degradation and its outcome later in life, often involving crush fractures of the vertebrae, conspicuous loss of height, and the disfiguring spinal hump of the upper back known as kyphosis.

The most important exercise for the lower back is sit-ups. If you do them regularly, you are almost bound to maintain strong abdominal muscles. For directions, refer to Sit-Ups in Your Basic Ageproofing Exercise Plan (see page 194). Aim at very gradually increasing the number of repetitions to 25 or 30 a day, and when you are able to do this number of repeats comfortably without letup, increase the speed with which you do each daily set.

If you are at risk for upper-back problems—if, for example, you have been slouching for too long or if osteoporosis runs in your family and there is a possibility that you have inherited a genetic tendency toward it—you will find it very worthwhile to do the special set of exercises below regularly three or four times a week.

BACK-UPS

These exercises are meant to be done in a specific order, beginning with three relaxing and easy routines, working up to slightly more demanding ones, and then repeating the series in reverse order. Do the trio of easy relaxers at the start of the series lying down on an exercise mat or a firm bed.

- Lying on your back, inhale through your nose and blow the air out very slowly through pursed lips. Repeat 3 times.
- Gently roll your head from side to side as you lie on your back, making no muscular effort to hold any one position. Repeat 3 times.
- Bring your shoulders up to your ears. Then let them drop completely. Repeat 3 times.
- Standing up, place your palms on your chest. Pull your shoulders down. Bring your elbows to shoulder height and rotate your arms 3 times clockwise, 3 times counterclockwise.

• Lying on your back, place your hands behind your neck. Bring your elbows down to the surface you are lying on and press down hard. Hold 5 seconds. Relax. Repeat 3 times.

• Put a 1-pound wraparound weight on each elbow. Lie on your stomach, with a pillow underneath. Clasp your hands behind your neck. Lift your elbows high. Hold 5 seconds. Relax. Repeat 3 times.

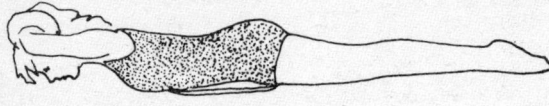

• Now do the exercises in reverse order all the way back to the first one.

One more tip: be sure to try the Line-Up exercise on page 134. It is very helpful not only for your neck but for your back as well.

Ageproofing Your Breasts

There is a great deal that men and women can do to ageproof their breasts, and by very simple means. It should be quite reassuring to know that undesirable changes can be prevented, mitigated, or—if already under way—either partially or entirely reversed.

The main age-related problem for women's breasts is sagging. Of course, the larger the breasts, the greater the problem is apt to be. Women with small breasts have a distinct advantage, but even they should take three basic precautions.

Up Standing

Probably the single most effective measure is standing tall. A woman who slouches is bound to have sagging breasts whether she is seventeen or seventy, whereas if she stands up straight, she is very likely to have attractively lifted breasts until extremely late in life. To cultivate the habit of good posture, use the Line-Up exercise on page 134. There is no simpler way to get the marvelous alignment of a dancer, and nobody stands better or has more beautifully lifted breasts than a dancer does.

Full Support

The second most effective measure is using some means of support. Today, many women feel that in the exuberant surge of fitness and freedom bras should go the way of girdles. They look to Nautilus rather than Maidenform for whatever lift they need. But they may be pushing their luck. For any woman, ageproofing your looks has a great deal to do with figuring out ways to resist gravity's pull decade after decade. Bras are one way. This holds even if a woman has breasts that look as firm as marble and also works out regularly at a gym.

Good Boost

A third effective measure is a rather roundabout one. The breasts themselves have no muscles, but the pectoral muscles that circle around and under them can provide a good boost. It is possible to get a very buoyant lift just by strengthening the pectorals—the breast as a whole becomes increasingly firm in the process. Two specific exercises that help do this are the Push-Ups in Your Basic Ageproofing Exercise Plan (see page 196) and the Beach Ball (see page 149). Swimming, besides being a wonderful all-around activity, is another excellent way to work these muscles—and so help ageproof the breasts. The breast stroke and the back-stroke are particularly beneficial.

Skinny Dips

Men benefit from swimming for quite a different reason. As they get older, they tend to get heavier in the chest region. When this occurs, their breasts may begin to look somewhat overdeveloped, more like a woman's. Swimming is a great antidote, as it gradually effects a redistribution of fat in the body, especially if the water is fairly cool. Cold water stimulates fat shifts so as to better insulate the whole body. Rather than getting stored in spot deposits, the fat tends to spread out smooth and thin, so that it envelops the body entirely, without loopholes in the insulation. Of course, vigorous swimming also promotes fat loss by burning lots of calories, which helps reduce heavy breasts too. But a man really has to do his laps and work up to a good mile at a time at a reasonably good speed in order to get noticeable results. Any man who swims a mile several times a week and is careful to watch excess calorie intake is bound to get his fat redistributed and his weight down.

Ageproofing Your Arms

How much do you use your arms?

This may strike you as rather an odd question. But how young or old your arms look at any point in life has a lot to do with what shape your arm muscles are in. These muscles do not get much of a workout in the course of a typical modern day, certainly not as much as leg muscles. Men's arm muscles tend to hold up better than women's. Men have larger and stronger muscles to begin with, because the male hormone testosterone promotes muscular development, starting at puberty and continuing until quite late in life. A woman's arms often start to lose muscle mass and strength quite early unless she makes a point of toning and conditioning them on a regular basis.

Interestingly, the hormonal shifts occurring as a woman passes the menopause can work in her favor. Just as the loss of mass and strength in her arms—the upper-arm region, in particular—begins to be noticeable, she loses the copious supplies of female hormones that inhibit muscle-building during the reproductive years. So arm-muscle exercises now become more effective, and can help keep her arms firm, without conspicuous loss in size or strength, until late in life.

Flab Free

The arm muscles that men and women, particularly women, have to concentrate on are the triceps and the biceps. The triceps, at the back of the upper arm, is the one that seems to dwindle most noticeably unless you do something about it. But the biceps at the front of the upper arm also requires a certain amount of attention. Push-Ups do a great job for the triceps. Front Curls are the way to get really good results in the biceps area. Both exercises are part of Your Basic Ageproofing Exercise Plan (see pages 196 and 200). Because the triceps is especially important to condition, it is a good idea to work this muscle in more than one way. You do not want to leave an inch unexercised if you can help it. An effective routine to do is this squeeze play:

BEACH BALL

- Extend both arms straight out in front of you, your hands pointing ahead. Curve your arms out at each side, keeping the elbows up, and pretend you are holding an enormous beach ball.
- Clasp your hands and press very hard against the imaginary beach ball, with one hand pushing against the resistance of the other.

• Keep squeezing harder and harder, to a count of 10. Release. Repeat 10 times.

Water Therapy

There is probably no other sport that can do as much for your upper arms as swimming. Swimmers of all ages invariably have a strong, firm triceps. The best stroke you can use to develop the triceps is the freestyle, or crawl, because of the way your arms have to push back the water as you propel yourself along. If you do not like swimming with your head under water—and many people whose eyes are irritated by the chlorine in pools and who feel uncomfortable in goggles prefer not to—the backstroke is also very good for working and toning the triceps area. Although the breast stroke is not quite as effective as either the freestyle or the backstroke, it can still strengthen the area to a considerable degree, especially if you are careful not to bring your arms any further back than your shoulder line before thrusting them forward again.

Ageproofing Your Hands

Most people pay far too little attention to their hands, not realizing how important regular care is in order to keep them looking well over the years. Hands are one of the very first parts of the body to appear old. There are two reasons why. First of all, the skin on the back of the hand is extremely thin. Second, the hands get more rough treatment—everything from strong soaps to strong sun—than any other area. Although the face may be exposed even more of the time, it is likely to be protected to some extent by moisturizers, sunscreens, glasses, and, in the case of women, makeup. It does not come into contact with harsh chemicals in the course of the day, as hands often do.

What counts most in ageproofing your hands is taking a few minutes each day to do a few simple things that make a big difference in the long run.

A woman's hands are much more apt to look old earlier in life than a man's, partly because of the greater fragility of the skin on the back of her hands and partly because of the premature loss of fatty tissue that is so apt to occur there. This localized fat loss is one of the true biological aging changes, occurring as a rule when a woman is in her forties. This section on ageproofing your hands on a regular basis is therefore directed mainly toward women. But the basics of daily care apply to men as well.

YOUR HAND-CARE DAILIES

- When you wash your hands, use warm rather than hot water. Choose a mild soap; a number of well-known brands are listed in order of mildness on page 98. Be sure to dry your hands well after each washing.
- If you have to use harsh soaps or detergents or solvents for any reason—washing dishes, doing laundry or other household chores, or in connection with your work or leisure activities—wear protective gloves whenever possible. Cotton-lined rubber work gloves are excellent for guarding your hands against chemicals and heat. Job-

specific work gloves are available for various other kinds of exposure, gardening, for instance.

- If you are outdoors in cold or windy weather, you should certainly make a point of wearing gloves. Few people understand the extent to which cold and wind compound the skin damage caused by chronic sun exposure. The best types of gloves to wear are made of or lined in a natural material like wool or cotton.
- Moisturizers are essential to good basic daily care for your hands, just as for all the other exposed regions of your body. During the daytime it is helpful to use a light moisturizer on the back of your hands, applying it after you wash them. Any lotion that contains petrolatum as one of its ingredients usually works well.

At night you can use the moisturizer you use during the daytime, if you like. Or try experimenting with heavier ones—especially any of the creams that contain a high percentage of petrolatum. It is worth recalling here, for those who want to give their hands the best possible ageproofing care, that the ideal moisturizer is pure petrolatum: Vaseline. Smooth some on the back of your hands at night and blend it lightly over the skin. Avoid rubbing, because the skin in this area stretches easily. Cover your hands with a pair of cotton night gloves, which you can buy in any drugstore, so that the grease does not rub off on the sheets. Dermatologists suggest that, in addition to being the most effective moisturizer available, pure petrolatum may have an active beneficial effect which works in ways that are not yet understood.

- From day to day and season to season, use a high-potency sunscreen to protect the skin on the back of your hands whenever you are likely to be out in the sun without gloves for any length of time. Most of the "aging" effects that show up in the skin over the years are, as stressed in Ageproofing Your Skin, due to chronic sun exposure. The damage is responsible for some of the thinning the skin undergoes. It also contributes noticeably to the loss of tone and elasticity. And it is the cause of the numerous brownish so-called age spots you see on men's and women's hands, starting while they are still in their forties.

If you plan to be outdoors at some point during the day, apply a waterproof or water-resistant sunscreen a good fifteen or twenty minutes before leaving the house, so that it has time to work into the skin the way it should. Be sure to apply it before you apply a moisturizer, because sunscreens penetrate the skin, as a rule, in contrast to moisturizers, which sit on the surface.

Hand Hype?

You may have heard about cosmetic surgery techniques that are sometimes tried experimentally in seeking ways to counter loss of subcutaneous fat and thinning of the skin. Although some work has been done with silicone, such augmentation is still very much at an experimental stage, as any reputable dermatologist will be quick to tell you. Other "hand lift" procedures are even further over the horizon. In contrast to such experimental manipulations, which many dermatologists consider questionable at best, there is one very simple means of augmenting the thickness of the skin —physical exercise. If sufficiently vigorous, exercise can do a lot to help prevent or reverse the skin's tendency to become thinner with the years.

For additional advice on how to ageproof your hands, see Ageproofing Your Skin on pages 96–103. Those tips apply to skin everywhere on the body.

Ageproofing Your Nails

The changes your nails undergo in the course of time are slight. Some daily nail-care routines are essential, however, in order to keep your nails looking their best.

YOUR NAIL-CARE DAILIES

• Once a day, scrub your nails lightly with a natural bristle nailbrush, mild soap, and warm water. This helps remove any dirt and debris from beneath the free edge of the nails. It also revs up the circulation so that the nails have a good healthy color. And it stimulates nail growth as well, counteracting the slowdown that normally occurs over the years.

- As you dry your hands, use the edge of a soft towel to press back the cuticle of each nail. Water softens the cuticle, so this is the ideal time to coax it back. Do not press too hard, as excess pressure can injure the living portion of the nail directly beneath. If you can get in the habit of cuticle control once a day, you get better results than if you try to force back the cuticle at less frequent intervals. It is not a good idea to resort to sharp instruments or cuticle creams, as they often end up being more trouble than help.
- Healthy nails have a good pink color and a slight natural shine. One of the best ways to give your nails this attractive appearance is to buff them. Buffing stimulates nail growth, as well, because it steps up circulation in the vital germinative, or growing, portion of the nail.

  There is no need to bother about buffing creams or powders. Just use an ordinary chamois-covered buffer. It is the buffing action not the cream or powder that does the job. If you do not have a buffer, the palm of your free hand is an excellent substitute. In some ways it may even be better, because it brings your nails in contact with your skin's natural oils. Simply place the nails of one hand in the palm of the other and buff.
- There is one additional, stimulating daily routine that takes only about a minute to do and can be beneficial to your nails in several ways. All it involves is pinching the tip of each finger from the sides, so you see the blood rushing back under the nail as you release it. This slight action is great for the circulation. But it does something else as well: it prevents the nails from becoming broader and flatter, as they otherwise tend to do in later years. By pinching each nail daily, you can train your nails to become attractively narrow and oval and to taper toward the tip.
- How often you trim your nails depends on how fast they grow. As with hair, there is a wide variation. In general fingernails grow about twice as fast as toe nails and should therefore be trimmed twice as often. If you find it works best to trim your fingernails once a week, then you will probably do well to trim your toenails once every two weeks. In doing your toenails, incidentally, be sure to cut straight across and not too close so as to avoid the risk of ingrown toenails, a painful and serious problem that seems

to afflict people more and more frequently as they get older.
• Brittleness is a common and quite irritating condition, especially among older women, but it is easier to remedy than most people are aware of. If you have brittle nails, all you need to do is soak them in warm water for a few minutes at bedtime. Then smear a little moisturizer over the nail and work it gently and well into the nail and the cuticle. Do not use products that claim to harden the nail. Brittle nails are already too hard, and you need to soften them in order to make them more pliant, not harder.

Polishing Off Problems

The best treatment is almost invariably the simplest, gentlest, and most basic—and the one that aims to get at the actual problem and correct it rather than cover it up. One noticeable exception to this general rule is nail polish.

People usually think of nail polish only in cosmetic terms. Of course, it can be very attractive, but it is also a very practical way of dealing with some of the most annoying and frequent nail problems. Take splitting nails. If nails keep splitting, making it impossible to grow them or even file them properly, a couple of coats of clear polish will reinforce the nails and keep them from constantly breaking. Polish can also be used to cover up some of the unavoidable changes that take place as a result of true biological aging. The longitudinal ridging characteristic of older people's nails can be completely masked with a layer or two of colorless polish. Nail discoloration related to the aging process, which can be an aesthetic concern for an older woman, can be effectively concealed with any shade of polish; even a pale shade is enough to hide the yellowing of the nails.

One common condition for which no effective and lasting solution has yet been found, however, is fungal infection of the toenails. The disorder, which can range from mild to serious and occurs with increasing frequency among older people, defies both topical and systemic treatment. Usually the edge of the nail becomes yellow, thickened, and eroded and there is likely to be a large accumulation of horny debris underneath it. The best that can be done is to bring matters more or less under control with treatment and trims by a good podiatrist, daily sprinkling with powder to keep the area dry, and adequate airing of the feet. Wear stockings or socks that allow the toes to breathe and shoes of natural materials such as leather, and go barefoot or in open sandals whenever practical. A pedicure by an experienced professional can frequently be quite helpful in keeping fungal clutter from getting out of hand, and this goes for men as well as women.

Ageproofing Your Waist

Take a good look at yourself in the mirror without any clothes on. Can you see a definite indentation marking your natural waist? Your waistline or lack of one is often a very good gauge of the kind of shape you are in. Unfortunately most people's waist tends to inch out over the years, as abdominal muscles weaken and fat accumulates, until no indentation remains.

Muscles which are constantly used undergo little or no change in mass or strength from one decade to the next. If you get in the habit of using your abdominal muscles and holding in your waist, you can do a lot to prevent or reverse the loss of lean mass and strength and the replacement of muscle protein by fatty tissue. The more you do to get strong abdominal muscles and keep them strong, the better able you are to pull everything in that area neatly into place and keep it that way.

Shaping In

How? One good way is by simply doing Sit-Ups every day. You will find the directions in Your Basic Ageproofing Exercise Plan (see page 194). The effect that this one exercise can have on your abdominal muscles is remarkable, provided that you do it without fail each day and gradually increase the number of repetitions and the speed with which you do them. If you do the Sit-Ups independently of the exercise plan, gradually increase the repetitions to 25 or 30 at a stint, and when you can do that comfortably, step up the speed. Depending on your girth at the outset, daily Sit-Ups can account for as much as a 3- or 4-inch reduction.

Cinching In

There is an additional and very simple means by which you can help yourself achieve a trim waistline. Surprisingly, it is one that is overlooked by almost everybody. Wear the kind of clothes that encourage you to hold in your abdominal muscles rather than the kind that let them collapse and spill out. Your shape is influenced far more than your realize by the clothing you wear.

Start with a belt. For women this means choosing clothes that call for a belt; a chemise, for example, does not. Make sure that the belt fits well, and that there are enough notches to allow for a gradual decrease in girth. Some belts stretch with time, so it is best to pick ones made of types of fabric or leather that have as little give as possible. Get in the habit of wearing a belt every day. Buckle it as tightly as you can and still feel comfortable. As you become used to the feeling of a snugly belted belt, this will serve as an automatic reminder to hold in your abdominal muscles for longer and longer periods of time. It is the subliminal cue, not the physical constraint, that is important. Any time you feel you can pull your belt one notch tighter, do so. Do not feel bad, however, if you cannot keep it there all day, because your waist measurement is apt to change from hour to hour.

Have you ever noticed how men and women, as they get older and their waists get larger, seem to wear their belt higher in back and lower in front? Young men, on the other hand, seem to wear their belt straight all around. And young women, especially those with a small waist, tend to wear their belt up in front and slightly down in back. Look around and you will see older men with a large paunch whose pants are belted beneath the overhang. You will also see older women with a large shapeless midsection whose belt, held in place by loops on the dress rather than by any natural indentation, sags way down in front from the weight of the buckle. Even if your waist is larger at present than it ought to be, make a point of giving it an ageproof look when you belt it: for men, level all around, and for women, a tinge higher in front and lower in back.

Inch Checking

Keep a tape measure handy—drape it over the towel rack in the bathroom—and check your waist measurement every day after your bath or shower to make sure you are not inching out. Do not cheat and try to pull the tape measure tighter than usual if it reads more inches than it ought to; instead, make sure you do Sit-Ups regularly every day. Get plenty of exercise and pay attention to what you eat. You have Your Ageproofing Program for Looks, Health, and Fitness to guide you so that you can hold the waist line against age.

Ageproofing Your Buttocks

Now that more and more men and women are running or working out in gyms or exercising in some other way, stripped down to very brief sports gear, they and everyone else around them are becoming much more aware of the unshapely changes that can take place in various parts of the body now going public for the first time—the buttocks, in particular. Their present high visibility is even cause for special concern to men and women in their twenties, because the flat-bottomed look can often begin to be a problem quite early, even during that peak period when people are supposed to be in optimal shape. What with office jobs, elevators, cars, telephones, TV, and other non-activities, it is hard to sport the high, round, firm buttocks of a body in top condition.

Well-Rounding Exercise

Really working the buttocks and getting them firm and round is not that easy. The muscle you have to concentrate on is the gluteus maximus. If you are standing, this muscle extends your leg backward; if you are lying facedown, it raises the leg up. The movement is not one that you make much in everyday life. Your ability to raise your leg high in back without bending the knee to any extent is usually lost quite early in life unless you make a determined effort to maintain it. So keeping your buttocks firm depends on a really specific effort.

KICKBACKS

• Lie facedown on an exercise mat or rug or firm bed with a pillow under your hips. Lift your left leg as high as it can go. Hold the position for a count of 10. Release. Repeat with the right leg. Alternate, starting with 3 sets and gradually working up to about 10 sets a day.

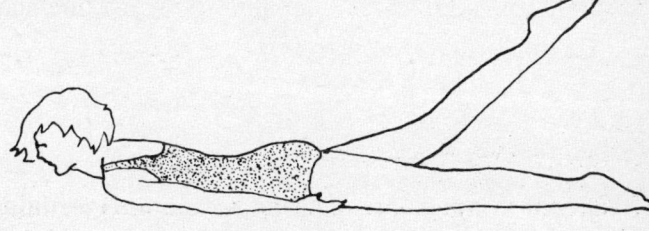

• You can also do this exercise in a standing position. Stand on your left leg and extend your right leg straight back. Gently lift it as far back as possible, which may not be very far at all in the beginning. You may find it helps to do the exercise in an open doorway, holding onto the door frame to steady yourself.

Although this upright version is not as effective as the horizontal version, which has more leverage, it has the advantage of being an easy routine you can do in odd moments—in the kitchen while waiting for the water to boil, or in the office when you feel like taking a break and shaking a leg after too much sitting.

Well-Rounding Sports

Certain sports and activities are particularly helpful for strengthening your buttocks muscles. Walking and running can be good, provided you take long strides. Swimming the crawl is excellent if you emphasize the leg action, and doing laps with a kickboard can really get results. Dancing is of course the best buttocks-toner there is. You will never see a good dancer who does not have good buttocks muscles.

Ageproofing Your Thighs

Just about every man and woman would do well to pay more attention to their thighs. Fortunately, ageproofing this area is not something that is at all hard to do or that takes long to produce results. It is simply a matter of the right kind and amount of exercise. If you just watch people walking down the street, running for a bus, or climbing a flight of stairs, you can easily see that this part of the body is made to work, to move. The thigh bone is the longest and strongest in your entire body. And some of the largest and most powerful muscles you possess are arrayed over it—the quadriceps group curving out in front, the hamstrings group coursing its full length in back. So what you want to do, first of all, is avoid the muscle-poor look that comes of sitting in offices, cars, buses, trains, and in front of TV. That is the basic thigh problem that men and women have to do something about.

Male Losses

For men the special concern is a tendency toward skinny thighs, which becomes more and more apparent as they get older. Whatever fat there is goes off their thighs and onto their middle. The only way a man can counter this tendency is by building up the muscle in his thighs so that they become lean but strong. Swimming, walking, biking, and tennis are among the best ways to really work the legs.

Female Gains

Women often have heavy thighs—just the opposite of the usual male pattern—because female sex hormones not only augment but also protect fat deposits in women's hip and thigh regions. Studies show that women have larger fat cells in this area than men.

Because of the protective hormonal mechanism, the fat cells in a woman's thigh area tend to be less metabolically active. Their response to any call for release of fat-energy stores during, say, periods of vigorous exercise is blunted. In contrast, the fat cells in a woman's abdominal area are usually much more sensitive to changes in energy balance and more responsive to conditions that signal the need for release of fat-energy reserves. What this means in practical terms—and this is an important point for any woman with a weight problem to be clear about—is that a given amount of exercise is more likely to burn off excess fat from her abdomen than from her thighs. As you can now see, whether or not the words spot reduction are used to describe such phenomena, the fact remains that fat deposits are not drawn evenly from each and every part of the body as women expend energy.

Surprise Strategies. How does a woman reduce bulging thighs? There are several effective ways, each of which can get around the protective hormonal fat-deposit tendency. Paradoxical as it may at first seem, one way is to increase the size of the thigh muscles. This strategy has the visual effect of spot reducing because when the layer of subcutaneous fat covering the thighs is stretched over a larger area of muscle, it becomes thinner. The result is a firmer and therefore more slender look, even though the total amount of fat in the region is not necessarily reduced. Stair-climbing is a fine means of stepping up the amount of muscle in this area and providing a smooth, clean thigh line. All it takes is a flight of stairs at home or at work. Go up and down one flight several times, pause to catch your breath, and then repeat. Work toward a ten-minute daily stint, but do not rush. Stair-climbing can be quite a strenuous form of exercise.

Another little-known way of getting at the female thigh problem, which can also produce quite becoming results, is to swim—especially the breast stroke and especially in cool water. Any woman who is intent on having trim thighs should try this. To get noticeable results, a woman does have to swim regularly, increasing the number of laps each week as Your Ageproofing Swim Plan outlines (see page 215). By following the plan and doing the breast stroke with vigorous frog kicks, any woman can do a lot to ageproof her thighs. There are two reasons why swimming provides this special edge. One has to do with the muscular development that occurs. The other is the unique benefit of swimming in cool water: redistribution of fat for insulation purposes. The fat is spread more evenly over all regions of the body rather than being lumped in a few sex-specific areas.

Fat Fallacy. Any woman who sets about ageproofing her thighs in either or both of the ways suggested above is going to have a very hard time finding any trace of what is called cellulite. There is, in fact, no such thing as cellulite. Then how do you explain all that dimpling? What looks like some sort of pathological condition to members of the cellulite cult is, as any physician will tell you, nothing more than the way the excess fat in that area happens to be packaged. Muscle is all it takes to dispel the cellulite myth!

Ageproofing Your Calves

If you have shapely legs, you have a lot going for you. Not only are they attractive but they are proof against a great many of the debilitating changes that take place as people get older. Look at the spindly, sticklike legs of many elderly women you pass on the street. Were it not for the trousers that men wear, you would see a similar wasting in their legs as they get older. Developing good, strong calf muscles literally gives you a leg to stand on in later decades. And your bones are the better for this as well.

Calf Contouring

In shaping up your legs, you want to strike a good balance between an attractive calf line and well-stretched calf muscles. Too tight a calf muscle can lead to inflammation or even a tear of the Achilles tendon. So here is a daily double that you can do to give your calf muscles plenty of shape *and* stretch.

SHAPE AND STRETCH

- *Shape Up*. Rise on your toes. Try to hold the position for a count of 10 without having to support yourself against a wall or piece of furniture. Repeat. Gradually work up to 10 or more repetitions.

- *Stretch Out*. Stand barefoot at arm's length from a wall, with your feet together. Place your forearms vertically against the wall and lean on them. Drop your buttocks so that there is a straight line from the back of your neck to

your ankles. Hold the position for a full minute. Return to
your original position. Rest for a few seconds. Repeat. Do
at least 3 repetitions a day. Step back a little further away
from the wall each week so that you stretch your calves
more and more all the time. When you reach a 3- to 4-foot
distance from the wall (depending on your height and arm
length) you will have reached your maintenance distance.

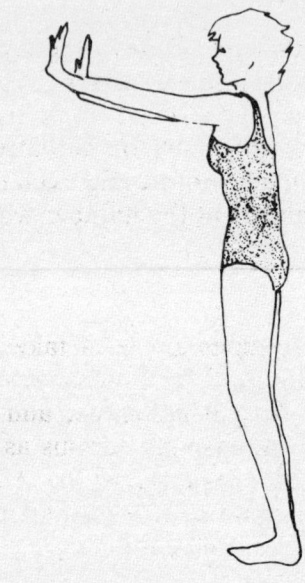

There are two other shape and stretch exercises for the
calves that balance each other well. You can do these from
time to time when you feel like a change of routine. Rope-
jumping is the great calf-shaper. Boxers are inveterate rope
jumpers, and when have you ever seen a photo of a boxer
who did not have shapely legs? The directions for rope-
jumping are given in Your Basic Ageproofing Exercise Plan
(see page 194). If you want to do the exercise independently
on days you are not doing the basic workout, jump for one
minute, get your breath, then jump another minute. Gradually work up to five minutes of jumping, or more if you want,
but always with as many breaks as you need to get your
breath.

Calf Steps, a great stretcher, is the other exercise in this duo. The directions for it are also in Your Basic Ageproofing Exercise Plan. On the days you do skipping independently, do Calf Steps independently also—10 times, with a 10-count hold each time.

Ageproofing Your Feet

Giving your feet good daily care is one of the most essential ageproofing measures of all. It is essential not only for your looks but also for your health and head-to-toe fitness. Look at the way other people walk past on the street and try counting how many are in discomfort and even in pain with each step. You will be amazed at the number who are.

Preventive Care

A few surprisingly easy routines are all it takes to protect your feet against common problems—like excess callus, corns, ingrown toenails, fungal infections, and bunions—which are apt to become increasingly serious as people get older. One noted orthopedic expert says that 90 percent of all the foot ailments that bring people into his office could be avoided with the right kind of simple daily care. Here is what you want to be sure to do.

YOUR FOOT-CARE DAILIES

- Wash your feet well with mild soap when you take your bath or shower each day. Rub pumice stone over the calloused areas, using a circular motion. Do not remove too much callus; callus is basically protective. By rubbing off only a very little each day, you can prevent excess buildup.
- Dry your feet thoroughly after washing, paying special attention to the area between the toes. Moisture in the interdigital spaces is what you want to avoid, as it fosters fungal infections and soft corns.
- Sprinkle talcum powder on your feet before you put on your stockings or socks and shoes. Dust well in the spaces

between your toes; this will help keep the area dry
throughout the day and lessen the chance of fungal infection.
- Besides putting on a fresh pair of socks or stockings every
day, it is a good idea to switch shoes. If you do this, each
pair has a chance to air for at least twenty-four hours and
dry out completely—it can take that long if much moisture
has accumulated during one day's wearing.
- At bedtime rub a small amount of moisturizer on heavily
calloused regions, especially around the rim of the heel, in
order to prevent the cracks and deep fissures that are so
apt to form with chronic callus buildup.
- Check your toenails every ten days or two weeks to see if
they need trimming. Cut them straight across and not too
close, with a good pair of clippers, to avoid ingrown toenails.

Preventive Exercise

Exercise is vital for your feet. It improves the circulation
and keeps everything in good working order. Specific exercises that help you tone and develop the muscles controlling
your feet can be extremely helpful. Having strong, flexible
feet can do a lot to help counter the loss of fatty cushioning
that occurs in later years and maintain a dynamic spring in
your step at all times. These two daily exercises give the
muscles in your feet just the workout they need on a regular
basis.

FIT-FEET FLEXERS

- *Toe Lift*. Stand with your back flat against a wall, keeping
your knees straight and your bare feet about 2 feet from
the wall. Your ankles should be together, and your toes
should be pointing out. Now lift your toes, while your
heels remain firmly on the floor. Lower your toes. Repeat
5 times. Try to do this exercise daily, and increase the
number of repetitions by 5 each week until you can do 25
at a time.

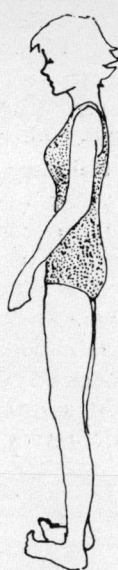

• *Pigeon Toes*. Stand barefoot and pigeon-toed, facing a wall and at arms' length from it. Rise on your toes. Hold for a count of 5. Come back down. Repeat 5 times. Try to do this exercise daily, and increase the number of repetitions by 5 each week until you can do 25 at a time.

There is no better way to exercise your feet than by walking. The more you walk, the more you are going to get your feet as well as the rest of your body in good shape. Feet are made to move. Problems stem from having to stand in one place for hours at a time, as many people have to do during work hours, or from sitting at a desk nine to five. As with every other part of the body, the key word is *use*.

Fit-Feet Shoes

Wear shoes that let you work the muscles of your feet as you walk. The shoes should fit properly, be comfortably roomy in the toe and snug in the heel—with a shoemaker's pad on either side of the heel, if necessary, but never encircling the entire heel area—and provide a generous amount of shock absorption. Shoes should never confine or constrict your feet. That is what causes excessive callus buildup and corns and blisters, as well as aggravating ingrown toenail problems and bunions. Be sure, too, that your shoes are made of a natural material, like leather, that breathes. This can help prevent the moisture retention that triggers and sustains fungal infections.

CHAPTER 5

Your Ageproofing Diet Plan—
Across-the-Board Protection

What you eat, how much you eat, and even when you eat are all important factors in the way your body functions from day to day, year to year, and decade to decade. The type of diet that the body has become adapted to during the thousands and thousands of centuries that it has been evolving is at once simple and varied and well balanced. Based largely on plant foods, it has sustained peoples of widely different cultures in widely different regions of the world since the earliest days of the human race. Only in this present century has a markedly different pattern of eating come to predominate in the United States and other Western industrialized countries.

The typical twentieth-century Western diet has a number of distinctive features, including high fat and meat content and much less food from plant sources than was traditional. It is linked in various ways with the chronic diseases that have reached such epidemic proportions during the same period. Unlike the infectious and deficiency diseases now largely behind us and for each of which there is one specific cause, today's killers and cripplers are complex in origin. They stem not from a single cause but from a number of causes. And diet clearly plays a key role right across the board. What's more, dietary factors known to put people at risk for one of these major chronic diseases are almost invariably those that put them at risk for others as well.

The good news is that, by eating the right kinds of foods

in the right amounts, you can do a great deal to prevent or counter degenerative changes and the chronic diseases they so often lead to. Doing this just means making a few simple switches in daily eating habits. Here is all the information and advice you need about key dietary factors. They are the basis of Your Ageproofing Diet Plan—a way of eating that you will find enjoyable and protective for life.

Your Calorie Intake

Calories count decisively in just about every aspect of age-proofing, and what counts most of all is the balance between how many you take in each day and how many you expend. You want to be sure that your total daily input does not exceed your total daily output for basic metabolic processes and the physical and mental work you do. There is a great deal of variation from one individual to another when it comes to calorie balancing. Differences in size, age, activity, and even the ratio of muscle tissue to fatty tissue in each person's body—muscle tissue burning far more calories at rest than fat tissue—are among the most obvious variables. Others have to do with individual differences in metabolism, but this is an area about which not much is yet known.

Although lots of obese people consume fewer calories per day than lots of skinny people, they tend to be very inactive whereas skinny people tend to be very active. This is not to say that there are not plenty of obese people who overeat as well as underexercise. What's more, those who do, tend to overeat at night. This brings to mind a lean bit of dietary advice: Eat breakfast like a king, lunch like a prince, and dinner like a pauper. Weighty individuals prone to pantry night raids would do well to keep this trim little dictum in mind.

Obesity happens to be the most widespread chronic disease in this country at the present time, and its incidence is increasing every year. It is a cause of real concern not only in itself but also because it increases the risk of other major chronic diseases: coronary heart disease, stroke, hypertension, diabetes, and certain cancers. It can contribute significantly to the loss of immune system integrity as well.

If fat and pounds seem to be inching and ouncing on, as you can easily tell by the tape-and-scale technique mentioned in Ageproofing Your Body Shape, the first thing to do is check if there is some source of empty calories in your diet—such as sugar, fat, or alcohol—that you can cut back on or eliminate. If there is, do so. The second thing is try to find time to get more exercise. Moderate but adequate daily calorie intake together with vigorous daily exercise is by far the best way to take off fat and pounds and keep them off.

Your Fat Intake

The three components of food that provide calories and are therefore sources of energy are fat, carbohydrate, and protein. Fat is the most concentrated source. There are 9 calories in every gram of fat as compared with 4 calories in every gram of carbohydrate or protein.

All fat is mostly made up of fatty acids, which are either saturated or unsaturated, and unsaturated fatty acids are further divided into monounsaturated and polyunsaturated. Here is a simple breakdown:

Saturated means that the fatty acid has as many hydrogen atoms as it has room for.

Monounsaturated means that the fatty acid has a vacant spot that can hold a pair of hydrogen atoms.

Polyunsaturated means that there are two or more such vacant spots.

Most of the time people take a short cut and speak of the fats themselves as being saturated, monounsaturated, or polyunsaturated. But to say that a fat, such as beef or pork fat, is saturated actually means that it contains mainly the saturated type of fatty acids. To say that a vegetable oil, like corn or safflower oil, is polyunsaturated means that it contains mainly polyunsaturated fatty acids. By the same token, a monounsaturated fat—olive oil is a good example—has mostly monounsaturated fatty acids.

Saturated fats are usually solid at room temperature, whereas unsaturated fats are likely to be either soft or liquid. Most animal fats are saturated to some degree or other except for fish oil, which happens to be unsaturated. Practically all plant fats other than coconut oil, palm kernel oil, and cocoa butter, are unsaturated. Unsaturated vegetable oils are, however, often processed by manufacturers in such a way that they become either partly or entirely saturated. The process, which is known as hydrogenation, is used to improve the consistency and shelf-life, of a product.

Controlling what kinds of fats you eat is extremely important because of the different effects different kinds can have on your blood cholesterol. Saturated fat can significantly raise blood cholesterol levels, and this contributes to atherosclerosis, the disorder that underlies cardiovascular disease. Polyunsaturated fat lowers blood cholesterol levels. Monounsaturated fat, in between, does not affect blood cholesterol levels one way or the other.

The typical western diet is high in total fat, which currently accounts for at least 40 percent of daily calorie intake. It is also very high in saturated fat, which contributes 15 to 17 percent of daily calorie intake, largely because of all the fatty meats eaten. Polyunsaturated fat, on the other hand, is present only in relatively low amounts, 4 to 8 percent. This diet, with its high content of total fat and saturated fat, is linked in various ways to the incidence of coronary heart disease, stroke, hypertension, obesity, diabetes, and cancer. Because of this, the American Heart Association has long taken a strong stand on the need to reduce the amount of total fat and saturated fat in the diet and to increase the amount of polyunsaturated fat somewhat in order to have a better ratio of polyunsaturated to saturated fat. Now a report from the National Research Council, commissioned by the National Cancer Institute, also urges a reduction in dietary fat.

Your Ageproofing Diet Plan's aim is to keep total fat at no more than about 25 percent of your daily calorie intake. If you want to eat even less fat each day, there is nothing to stop you from keeping your intake around 20 percent or lower still. The traditional Japanese diet contains between 10 and 15 percent fat and is considered extremely healthy by leading experts who have been studying the links between diet and disease.

Your Ageproofing Diet Plan aims to have polyunsaturated fat intake provide 10 percent of your daily calorie intake, which is more than the typical western diet affords. One reason for not going higher is that the long-term effects of a higher polyunsaturated fat intake are not yet known. Most of the polyunsaturated fat you get is bound to come from plant sources. But some should also come from a newly important source: fatty fish. Fatty fish has been found to be a source of certain fatty acids that are especially effective in lowering blood cholesterol and keeping blood from clotting. So this type of fat is proving to be an extremely valuable one to have regularly.

A quick look at the Fat Chart below shows you which foods are which—saturated, monounsaturated, or polyunsaturated. Use the chart as a guide in choosing foods.

FAT CHART
(measured in grams)

	Amount	Saturated	Monounsaturated	Polyunsaturated
Meat, broiled or roasted:				
Ground beef, regular	3 oz	8	8	Trace
Ground beef, lean	3 oz	5	4	Trace
Ham	3 oz	7	8	2
Lamb, leg	3 oz	9	6	Trace
Veal	3 oz	5	4	Trace
Chicken	3 oz	1	1	1
Tuna, oil-packed	3 oz	2	1	1
Dairy Products:				
Milk, whole	1 cup	5	3	Trace
Milk, low fat	1 cup	3	2	Trace
Milk, skim	1 cup	Trace	Trace	Trace
Cream, light	1 tbsp	2	1	Trace
Butter	1 tbsp	6	4	Trace

FAT CHART
(measured in grams) (*cont.*)

	Amount	Satu-rated	Mono-unsaturated	Poly unsaturated
Cheese, cheddar	1 oz	9	5	3	Trace
Cheese, cream	1 oz	11	6	4	Trace
Egg	1	6	2	3	Trace
Yogurt, low fat	1 cup	4	2	1	Trace
Ice cream	1 cup	14	8	5	Trace

Vegetable fats:

	Amount	Satu-rated	Mono-unsaturated	Poly unsaturated
Margarine, soft (corn oil)	1 tbsp	2	4.5	4.5
Mayonnaise	1 tbsp	2	2	6
Oils				
Safflower	1 tbsp	1	2	10
Corn	1 tbsp	1	4	7
Soybean	1 tbsp	2	3	7
Peanut	1 tbsp	3	7	4
Olive	1 tbsp	2	11	1
Avocado	1	7	17	5
Peanut butter	1 tbsp	2	4	2
Peanuts	½ cup	8	15	10

Your Cholesterol Intake

Saturated fats are not the only dietary component that raises blood cholesterol levels. Dietary sources of cholesterol itself, a fatty substance found only in foods of animal origin, also have this effect. The less cholesterol your daily diet contains, the better. You do not need it; your body makes all the cholesterol that it requires. Try to keep your daily cholesterol intake to no more than 300 milligrams, the maximum recommended by the American Heart Association, rather than around 500 milligrams, which is the current American average. In order to get a good idea of how much cholesterol various kinds of food contain, check the chart below. It can serve as a helpful guide in keeping your daily cholesterol intake within the recommended limits.

CHOLESTEROL CHART

**CHOLESTEROL CONTENT OF COMMON MEASURES
OF SELECTED FOODS**

Food	Amount	Cholesterol, milligrams
Milk, fortified skim or skim	1 cup	5
Milk, whole	1 cup	34
Cream, light	1 oz.	20
Yogurt, low fat	½ cup	10
Cottage cheese, creamed	½ cup	24
Cheese, cheddar	1 oz.	28
Margarine	—	0
Butter	1 tbsp.	35
Ice cream	½ cup	27
Egg, yolk or whole	1	250
Beef or pork	3 oz., cooked	75
Lamb or veal	3 oz., cooked	85
Chicken or turkey	3 oz., cooked	70
Liver, chicken	3 oz., cooked	635
Kidney	3 oz., cooked	680
Salmon	3 oz., cooked	40
Halibut or tuna	3 oz., cooked	55
Shrimp	3 oz., cooked	130

Your Carbohydrate Intake

This component of your daily diet, which is mainly derived from plants, is a far more important one than people usually realize. Carbohydrate is a major source of energy. It supplies the fuel for your brain. It helps you use fat efficiently. It provides power for every movement you make. And it also contributes vital building materials for all of your body's tissues.

One of the things you should be sure to do in order to help ageproof your looks and health and maintain a lastingly high level of fitness is to eat plenty of fresh fruits and vegetables and whole grains, because these carbohydrate foods are such an abundant source of nourishment. The more varied the mix, the more certain you can be that you are getting the vitamins and minerals and other essential nutrients your body needs in optimal amounts and optimal balance. Always try to eat such foods in their most nutritious form, whole, rather than in a refined state as juice or puree. A whole orange, for instance, provides you with the pulp and the pith, both of which are rich in nutrients you do not get when you drink only the juice. By the same token, whole-grain bread furnishes all the valuable nourishment stored in the kernel of the wheat, which even the most advanced fortifying techniques may not be able to restore entirely to refined white flour.

The proportion of carbohydrate in the typical western diet is about 45 percent of the daily calorie intake, only slightly more than the proportion of fat present in the diet and definitely low by historical standards. Your Ageproofing Diet Plan provides you with a healthier proportion of carbohydrate, amounting to a good 60 percent of daily calorie intake. The increase is mainly in fresh fruits and vegetables and whole grains. It is not in refined kinds of carbohydrate such as sucrose, or table sugar, which bulks so large in most westerners' diet—providing at least 15 percent of the daily calories, all of them devoid of nutrients and a source of nothing but unwanted pounds and cavities. You should cut back as much as possible on refined sugar. The sugars present in such natural foods as fruits and milk, on the other hand, come in a package bound up with a whole range of valuable nutrients and can be enjoyed as often as you like.

Among the various carbohydrate foods, Your Ageproofing Diet Plan places a particular emphasis on citrus fruits, on the yellow and dark -green leafy vegetables that are such excellent sources of beta-carotene, the precursor of vitamin A, and on cruciferous vegetables such as broccoli, cabbage, cauliflower, and Brussels sprouts, all of which have been shown to be inversely correlated with the incidence of certain cancers.

Fiber, the non-digestible part of fruits, vegetables, and grains, is usually classed with the complex carbohydrates but provides no calories. There are various kinds of fiber, and good evidence exists that the different types provide quite different benefits. One type, which is found in whole wheat, may reduce the risk of colon cancer. Another type, abundant in certain fruits such as apples, may lower blood levels of cholesterol and, for this reason, be important in protecting against atherosclerosis.

Your Protein Intake

The amount of protein in Your Ageproofing Diet Plan is proportionately the same as in the typical American diet, about 15 percent of daily calorie intake. This provides you with a generous safety margin. There is, however, a distinct difference in the sources of protein in Your Ageproofing Diet Plan and those in the typical western diet. Instead of the heavy preponderance of meat—with its high levels of total fat, saturated fat, and cholesterol—which forms the protein mainstay of the western diet, Your Ageproofing Diet Plan places much more of its emphasis on healthier sources of protein. Take skim milk, for example, especially fortified skim milk. It is low in calories, fat-free, rich in extra calcium, and from every point of view an excellent way to get top-quality protein in your diet every day. Low-fat cheeses and low-fat yogurt, which are fortified with milk solids as well, are other good ways of getting fine quality protein on a daily basis. And egg whites are an absolutely unbeatable low-calorie source of first-rate protein—the best there is, as a matter of fact—as well as an exceptionally versatile means of enhancing the nutrient value of your meals. This is not to imply that Your Ageproofing Diet Plan is a vegetarian pattern of eating. What it does is stress a healthy balance of protein from various sources other than fatty red meat. Lean red meat, poultry without the skin, and fish—fatty fish quite as much as non-fatty varieties—are all basic protein components of a well-balanced way of eating.

A great many people think that boosting their protein intake gives them a special edge on fitness and health. It does not. Muscular activity does not call for an increase in protein intake over normal levels, regardless of how much you exercise, the one possible exception to this general rule being athletes in training, who may require somewhat more protein in their diet during periods of muscle-mass increase. Your protein requirements remain more or less constant from day to day, year to year, and decade to decade, despite changes in work intensity, stress, environmental conditions, and age. Excess protein intake carries no special advantage. It merely ends up being broken down in your body and converted into a form of energy that can be burned as fuel or stored as fat, just like other excess calories. Such excesses can become a genuine concern over a period of time. The reason is that a diet high in protein places too great a load on the kidneys and can be harmful to your health.

Your Vitamin Intake

Vitamins are certain nutritional elements that your body requires in very minute amounts in order to keep functioning the way it should. Because your body is unable to synthesize them in sufficient amounts or at all, they have to be supplied almost entirely by the food you eat, and so they are essential to any proper diet. A baker's dozen have been officially recognized, and additional candidates have been lined up as well. You may be wondering how you can possibly tell whether or not you are getting the vitamins you need in your meals each day. The answer is that if you are in good health and are eating varied, well-balanced meals such as those Your Ageproofing Diet Plan provides, you have all it takes to meet your daily requirements for every vitamin.

It is most important to understand that for the normal person there is no value to vitamin intakes over and above the amounts supplied by a proper diet. In other words, there is no such thing as supernutrition. Dosing the body with megavitamins actually does it harm rather than good and can pose a very serious potential threat to a person's health. If you have a special problem, of course, your doctor may prescribe an appropriate amount of supplementation.

Your Mineral Intake

Of the ninety known elements in nature, twenty-seven are listed as essential for the human body, at last count, and the list is growing all the time. Even though they are needed in extremely small amounts in the daily diet, a distinction is made between the major minerals—calcium, phosphorus, magnesium, sodium, potassium, chlorine, and sulphur— which are required in quantities of 100 milligrams or more a day, and the trace elements—such as iron, zinc, copper, iodine, fluorine, chromium, and selenium—which are required in quantities no greater than a few milligrams a day at the very most. There is also a functional difference between the major minerals and the trace elements, which may be helpful to keep in mind. The major minerals, which are far more abundant in your body, of course, often serve in a structural capacity. A 150-pound man, for example, has about 1200 grams of calcium in his body at any one time, and 99 percent of it is present in his skeletal structure. The trace elements usually perform regulatory roles that have to do with the body's vital metabolic processes.

You do not need to worry about whether or not you are getting all of these numerous macronutrients and micronutrients in the amounts and combinations your body requires, any more than you need to worry about adequate vitamin intake, as long as your diet is varied and well-balanced. A healthy pattern of eating, like the one Your Ageproofing Diet Plan provides, gives you these key nutrients in quantities that fall well within the optimal range, even though the range for some important trace elements, such as selenium, is extremely narrow. In this connection it must be stressed that taking supplementary doses of minerals can be hazardous unless prescribed for a specific purpose by your doctor. The amounts afforded by supplementation may easily reach toxic levels. As a general rule, therefore, it is wise to avoid megaminerals of any kind, just as it is to avoid megavitamins.

There are two key minerals that for entirely different reasons are of special significance in ageproofing yourself. They are calcium and sodium.

Getting enough calcium in your diet throughout life is vital for the prevention of osteoporosis and its disfiguring and disabling effects. As you saw in Chapter 3, this is particularly important for women—especially white women. They are most at risk and yet, on the average, take in not much more than half the recommended dietary allowance of 800 milligrams of calcium a day. And that allowance itself, which is meant to give virtually all adults a good safety margin, may have been set too low. In order to offset progressive calcium loss throughout life and avoid brittle bones in later years, a daily dietary intake of about 1000 milligrams a day, starting at age twenty or even earlier, is probably closer to the actual requirements for both men and women, according to a number of leading authorities. A further increase to 1500 milligrams a day seems indicated for women upon reaching the menopause and during postmenopausal years, when bone loss accelerates.

You can get these amounts of calcium without freaking out on milk or going overboard on daily calories. The fortified skim milk available today can give you about 350 milligrams of dietary calcium per cup at a calorie count of only 100, in contrast to only 290 milligrams of calcium in a cup of whole milk at a calorie count a third higher. Low-fat yogurt has calcium levels comparable to those of fortified skim milk: 415 milligrams of calcium and no more than 145 calories per cup.

If you happen to be lactose-intolerant, as certain peoples of the world are, you can substitute low-fat yogurt for milk and achieve an adequate daily calcium intake quite comfortably. The fermentation process that takes place when yogurt is made reduces the content of lactose in the milk sufficiently to alleviate the problem.

Sodium, the one other mineral that has a special significance in regard to ageproofing, is present in your diet mainly in the form of sodium chloride, or table salt. It is one—and only one—of a number of factors that can contribute to high blood pressure. This is a point that needs to be emphasized, as many people mistakenly believe that it is always a factor. It presents a risk for about 30 percent of all the men and women in this country who have hypertension; the rest of those who have or are at risk for hypertension are not salt-sensitive. Because moderating salt intake somewhat is in keeping with the best current dietary advice about levels of all nutrients, however, it is wise for everyone to try to cut back on salt use at the table, in cooking, and through consumption of processed foods. Someone whose blood pressure readings are normal should consume about four grams of sodium per day. This is the equivalent of two teaspoons of salt. For those with hypertension or who are liable to suffer from it the daily intake should be kept to two grams per day. As the average amount of sodium in a typical western diet is somewhere in the region of ten grams per day this means a considerable reduction.

Your Basic Ageproofing Diet Plan

Your Ageproofing Diet Plan has been worked out to give you all the nutritional benefits your body needs in the simplest way. Your Ageproofing Diet Plan Guidelines stress the key points that you want to keep well in mind at all times. Your Basic Ageproofing Menus help you organize your meals in order to make each one work well for you. Your Basic Ageproofing Foods is an at-a-glance check that you can use in planning your meals, marketing, and eating out. This list is worth keeping close at hand. Your Ageproofing Diet Plan, as you can see, balances specific nutrient advice with the kind of leeway you really have to have today in order to make eating patterns work for you under any and all conditions and meet each and every one of your individual needs. It is a way of eating that is good for life!

YOUR AGEPROOFING DIET PLAN GUIDELINES

• Regulate your total calorie intake by keeping track of your weight and girth. If you are putting on pounds and inches, cut back, especially on empty calories from fat, sugar, and alcohol. And exercise more.

- Curb total fat and go very easy on saturated fat like butter or meat fat.
- Include moderate amounts of polyunsaturated fats or oils in your meals in the form of soft margarine, vegetable oil, or mayonnaise.
- A good limit for meat, poultry, and fish is 4 or 5 ounces a day. Favor fish over poultry, poultry over lean red meat, and lean red meat over fatty red meat. Be sure to include some fatty fish in your diet on a regular basis.
- Limit your intake of egg yolks to three a week. Use other high-cholesterol foods sparingly.
- Have the widest possible assortment of fresh fruits and vegetables. Make a point of including at least one of each of the following every day:
  Vitamin C foods like oranges or tomatoes
  Yellow or dark-green leafy vegetables like carrots and escarole
  Cruciferous vegetables like broccoli, cauliflower, cabbage, or Brussels sprouts
- Cut down on refined sugar, both from the bowl and from processed foods.
- Have three or four cups of skim milk or the equivalent in low-fat milk products every day.
- Reduce your use of salt in cooking and at the table.
- Favor fresh over processed foods whenever possible. Processed foods often contain a good deal of fat, sugar, and salt.
- Have a substantial amount of bread and cereal products daily, especially those made from whole grains.
- Go as easy as you can on smoked and salt-cured meats.

YOUR BASIC AGEPROOFING MENUS

Breakfast

Water—1 glass
Fresh fruit
Bread—2 slices
Margarine—2 teaspoons

Jam, jelly, or marmalade*
Cereal*
Coffee or tea and/or
Skim milk

Break—Morning

Coffee, tea and/or
Skim milk
Fresh fruit*

Lunch

Water—1 glass
Cheese, fish, poultry, or lean meat—2 ounces—or
egg—1 medium or large
Vegetables—raw or cooked
Bread—1 or 2 slices
Margarine—2 teaspoons
Fresh fruit
Coffee or tea and/or
Skim milk

Break—Afternoon

Tea and/or
Skim milk
Fresh fruit*

Dinner

Water—1 glass
Fish, poultry, lean red meat, or cheese—3 ounces
Vegetables—raw or cooked
Bread—1 slice*
Margarine or vegetable oil—2 teaspoons
Fresh fruit
Decaffeinated coffee or tea*

*Optional

Break—Evening

Skim milk—1 cup or
Low-fat yogurt—1 cup
Fresh fruit*

*Optional

YOUR BASIC AGEPROOFING FOODS

Foods to Use	Foods to Avoid or Use Sparingly

Milk

Milk, skim	Milk, whole
Yogurt, low fat	Whole-milk products
	Cream
	Cream products
	Cream substitutes
	Butter

Cheeses

Skim-milk cheeses, such as cottage cheese or continental quark	Whole-milk cheeses, such as Swiss, Camembert, and cheddar
	Cream cheese
	Creamed cottage cheese

Eggs

Egg whites	Egg yolks, no more than 3 a week
	Products made with egg yolks

Fruits

All fresh fruits, especially
citrus fruits, such as
oranges, grapefruits,
berries, melons,
tangerines, papayas,
mangoes, and tomatoes

Frozen and canned fruit,
water-packed

Fruit in syrups or sauces

Vegetables

All fresh vegetables,
especially dark-green
leafy vegetables, yellow
vegetables, and
cruciferous vegetables
such as cabbage,
broccoli, cauliflower,
and Brussels sprouts

Vegetables in butter or cream
sauce

Grains and Cereals

Whole wheat, rye, and
white breads

All cereals, except sugary
ones

Spaghetti, macaroni, and
non-egg noodles

Sweet rolls, commercial
biscuits and muffins,
doughnuts, pancakes,
waffles, French toast, corn
bread, potato chips,
crackers, cakes, cookies,
and pies

Legumes and Nuts

Lima beans, kidney beans,
black beans, lentils,
green peas, split peas,
chick peas

All unsalted nuts

(cont'd)

Foods to Use	Foods to Avoid or Use Sparingly

Fish, Poultry, and Meat

All fish, especially fatty fish like salmon, swordfish, bluefish, tuna, and scallops	Duck and goose
	Fatty meats
	Organ meats
Chicken and turkey without skin	Luncheon meats
	Sausages and frankfurters
Lean, well-trimmed red meat	Bacon

Fats and Oils

Soft margarine	Solid margarine
Mayonnaise	Butter
Vegetable oils, such as safflower, sunflower, corn, olive, sesame seed, soybean, and peanut	Coconut oil, palm kernel oil, and cocoa butter
	Salt pork or suet
	Fatty gravies and sauces

Beverages

Skim milk, coffee, tea, fruit and vegetable juices, mineral waters low in sodium	Whole milk and chocolate drinks

CHAPTER 6

Your Ageproofing Exercise Plan— Five Ways to Peak Fitness

There is nothing like exercise to help you ageproof your looks and health and keep physically and mentally fit every day, year, and decade of your life. Your body and mind are made to be active, to do work. And the more you do, the more you are able to do.

The importance of exercise as a means of looking good, feeling fit, and staying healthy is increasingly recognized by medical and other scientific authorities. Looks and health are so closely linked that, as you saw earlier, your looks are actually a far better indication of your true age than the passage of years and birthdays. If you look young and fit, you are young and fit—physically. If you look old and unfit, you are old and unfit—physically.

Exercise can, to a remarkable extent, counter and even reverse the degenerative changes that so often lead to the major chronic diseases. It can also help maintain the integrity of your immune system. There is no other prescription for protecting your health and preventing disease that is so free of trade-offs and side effects.

The full worth of exercise in ageproofing every aspect of your looks, health, and lifelong fitness is not yet known. But there are intriguing indications that regular, vigorous exercise over the years can avert the age-related decline in the brain's capacity to use oxygen efficiently and so help maintain at a peak level the information processing that goes on in higher cortical regions. And work now being carried out by scientists at the forefront of aging research suggests that vigorous exercise on a regular basis may significantly extend life expectancy. The possibilities that such studies are opening up seem truly extraordinary.

Each of Your Ageproofing Exercise Plans, which follow in the pages ahead, can provide you with the kind of physical activity you need in order to get the greatest ageproofing results. Each can do you good in its own way. You may wonder why there happen to be five, and why these five. Why not running? Why not bicycling? Why not roller-skating or yoga or karate or cross-country skiing? Why not indeed—they are all excellent. The kinds of physical activity that make up Your Ageproofing Exercise Plan are those I happen to find especially helpful, practical, and enjoyable, both in themselves and as a mix. I combine them in every which way, with sometimes more of this one and sometimes more of that, and the variety seems to compound the good I get from any single one. The specific benefits of each mesh very well together.

Your Basic Ageproofing Exercise Plan provides you with a bottom-line exercise program for flexibility, strength, and aerobic endurance. You can use it on its own. Or you can alternate it with one, two, or more of the other plans. Or you can make it your daily base and combine other activities as time allows and opportunity arises.

The Walk Plan could not be better as a program to use either some of the time or all of the time. And walking is of course ideal for people who are just beginning to exercise regularly and get in shape.

The Dance Plan involves various kinds of fundamental, rhythmic movement that can be great fun to do. What's more, you can do the steps just about anytime and anywhere. Dancing gives you flexibility, strength, and endurance, as well as balance and coordination, so it goes far to meet everybody's most important ageproofing needs. Overweight people will find it particularly rewarding as a way to exercise regularly and vigorously without risk of injury.

The Swim Plan is a great way to get started on a lifelong habit—swimming on a regular basis, if sufficiently vigorous, provides lasting benefits of just about every kind. It not only maintains but also restores high levels of vital functions that until quite recently were generally believed to undergo irrevocable age-related decline.

Another suggestion for exercising is to play tennis, although to benefit from it you must play energetic singles. This involves you not only in 'running around' type exercise but also useful stretching. Moreover you get a chance to meet other people who share your interest in the sport, which makes the game a very sociable type of exercise.

Choose any one, two, or more of the exercise plans. You can mix them any way you like. You may want to switch activities with the seasons, alternating a winter choice with a summer choice, or with the days of the week, alternating a weekday activity with a weekend one. Do whatever works best for your mood and your schedule. Together, Your Ageproofing Diet Plan and Your Ageproofing Exercise Plan go far to keep you looking great and feeling great for life.

YOUR AGEPROOFING EXERCISE GUIDELINES

• You want to have a regular program of exercise that develops and maintains your flexibility, strength, and aerobic endurance, and helps protect you against degenerative disorders. Set aside time for this in your weekly schedule so that it is part of your basic lifestyle.

• Your exercise sessions should meet certain requirements of intensity, duration, and frequency, in order to provide the best results.

Intensity. The exercise should be intense enough to raise your heart rate to between 70 and 85 percent of its maximum, although somewhat lower rates can also be beneficial. The way to tell if you have reached your target range is explained at the end of these guidelines.

Duration. The exercise should usually last at least twenty minutes at target-rate intensity.

Frequency. You should count on a minimum of three exercise sessions a week, with no more than two days between each stint.

- Any strenuous exercise session should be preceded by a few minutes of warm-up and followed by a similar cool-down period to avoid injury to muscles and joints and to keep your cardiovascular system working smoothly. These opening and closing periods should always include some form of stretching. Muscles which are used strenuously should also be stretched.
- Try a combination of activities to give variety to your weekly exercise schedule. Draw upon the five plans that follow in any way you like.
- Supplement your regular exercise program by stepping up your level of activity as you go your daily rounds. Walk instead of ride whenever you can, stand instead of sit as often as possible, and choose active rather than passive types of relaxation each chance you get.
- If you have been leading an extremely sedentary life, start your exercise program slowly and gradually build up your pace over the weeks and months. Never feel that you have to rush matters. The cardinal rule is to listen to your body. Heed any pain warning of overstressed muscles and joints. If you have symptoms of possible heart trouble, such as a pain in the chest, an irregular pulse, or nausea, stop exercising right away and check with your doctor. If you have a medical problem, be sure to check with your doctor before starting on this or any other program. A medical check is also wise for anyone over thirty-five.

YOUR TARGET RANGE FINDER

- You can figure out what your maximum heart rate is, more or less, by a simple rule of thumb: subtract your age from 220. If, for instance, you are twenty years old, your maximum heart rate is roughly calculated as 200 beats a minute. Your target range during rhythmic exercise is 70 to 85 percent of 200, therefore, or 140 to 170 beats a minute. If you are fifty, your maximum heart rate is 170, and your target range works out to 119 to 145 a minute.
- For swimming, target ranges are always somewhat lower, 60 to 75 percent of the maximum rate. So if you are twenty, your target range is about 120 to 150 beats a minute. If you are fifty, it is about 102 to 128.

• To find out if you are in target range after you have been exercising vigorously for two or three minutes, stop and check your pulse immediately. To do so, place your index finger gently against the carotid artery at the side of your neck. Count the beats for 10 seconds, and then multiply by 6 to get the number of beats a minute. It is important to start counting beats without delay, otherwise the heart rate will have fallen too much to give you an accurate indication of your rate. To take your pulse, incidentally, you need a watch with a second hand.

• Here are some key points to bear in mind:

There is a great deal of individual variation, so target ranges are merely a rough guide to comfortable and safe averages. Do not push yourself to meet any given target if it feels like a strain. It is more important to listen to your body than to aim for a statistical goal.

Exercising at lower intensity levels for longer periods of time can have benefits about equal to more vigorous activity for shorter periods of time.

If you are out of condition, your threshold for a conditioning effect is lower than it would be for someone who is exercising on a regular basis. Starting at the bottom of the fitness ladder means aiming for about 55 percent of maximum heart rate at the beginning of an exercise program and gradually increasing the rate to between 70 and 85 percent of maximum.

Your Basic Ageproofing Exercise Plan

One key part of your exercise life is a program you know you can count on to provide the basics. You want a program that can build up your aerobic endurance, strength, and flexibility. You want one you can easily use wherever and whenever you want to. And that means one which does not involve a great deal of gear or equipment. Your Basic Ageproofing Exercise Plan is just that. You can alternate and combine it with any or all of the other four plans as you like, using them in ways that are not only the most enjoyable but also the most beneficial from every point of view.

Your Basic Ageproofing Exercise Plan gives you a new kind of endurance, strength, and flexibility training that provides fast switches of exercises to benefit all the main areas of your body quickly, easily, and aerobically. It has been worked out for you by Michael O'Shea, the head of the Sports Training Institute in New York and a leading expert on physical fitness. All the plan takes is a jump rope, a stool, a pair of 5-pound wraparound cuff weights, an exercise mat, and motivation. The idea is to do each of the exercises as briskly as you can in order to get your heart rate into target range and keep it there.

There are sixteen simple routines in Your Basic Ageproofing Exercise Plan. Each one lasts either one minute or two minutes, for a total of twenty minutes. Done at a good speed, the series is a real workout for a person who is in top shape as well as someone who is in the process of getting there. If you are just starting and somewhat out of condition, go as slowly as you feel you need to at the beginning. You may find, for instance, that during the first few weeks you have to do some of the routines more slowly than others and you have to rest briefly between a couple here and there. But as you get in better shape, you will be able to go at a faster and more aerobic clip, moving directly from one exercise to the next. When you find that you can do each exercise comfortably for the length of time called for, gradually increase the number of repetitions you do within the allotted time for each exercise. In this way you continue to get greater and greater benefits from the plan.

YOUR BASIC AGEPROOFING EXERCISE PLAN

• *Run in Place.* 2 minutes. This is one of the simplest and most effective ways to warm up to an aerobic stint. Start slowly and gradually get your speed up. As you get used to running in place, try lifting your knees a trifle higher with each step. Always run on a surface that has some give to it—a wood floor or one that is carpeted. It is also a good idea to wear well-cushioned running shoes.

• *Step-Ups.* 2 minutes. Step up on a solid stool or small bench about 16 inches high, leading with your left leg and then bringing up your right one. Step down, again leading with your left leg. Repeat for 1 minute. Then do the second minute leading with your right leg. Instead of a stool you can use two standard steps of a staircase.

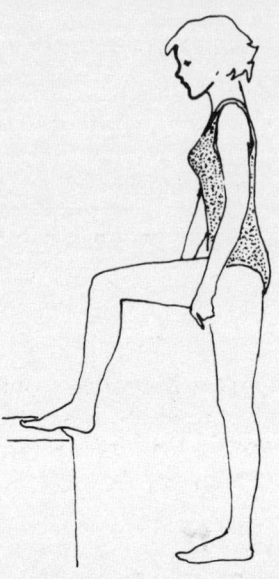

• *Sit-Ups*. 1 minute. Lie on your back with your knees bent. At first, do the exercise the easier way, with your arms crossed on your chest. After a few weeks try doing it the harder way, with your hands clasped behind your head. Rise to a sitting position. Slowly lower yourself back to the floor. Repeat. Do the exercise on an exercise mat or a carpet.

•   *Skipping*. 1 minute skipping is very strenuous, so do this exercise slowly at first until you are able to jump for a full minute without exceeding your target rate. When you can do that, gradually pick up speed.

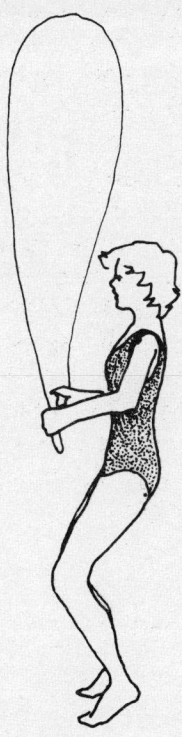

• *Hamstring Curls.* 1 minute. Wrap 5-pound cuff weights around each ankle. Lie on your stomach with your arms next to your sides. Lift your lower legs until they are perpendicular to the floor. Return. Repeat.

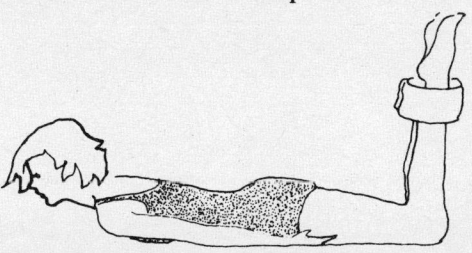

- *Push-Ups.* 1 minute. Lie on the floor, facedown, back straight, palms flat on the floor, elbows pointing out. Push yourself up until your arms are straight, keeping your body straight. Return. An easier version is to use your knees instead of your feet as the base point. For this version use a mat or a cushion to protect your knees.

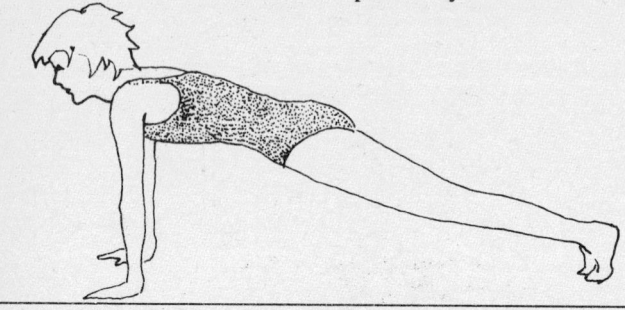

- *Jumping Jacks.* 1 minute. Stand with your feet together, arms at your side. Jump into an open position, arms and legs wide apart, so that they form an X. Jump back into closed position, with your hands meeting overhead and your feet together. Repeat. Do this exercise slowly at first until you can do it for a full minute without exceeding your target rate.

• *Leg Lifts*. 2 minutes. Lie on your right side, your legs extended in a straight line with your left shoulder and left hip. Lift your left leg as high as possible. Lower it. Repeat for 1 minute. After the first few sessions try doing this exercise with a 5-pound cuff weight wrapped around each ankle.

• *Chair Dips*. 1 minute. With your body straight and your back facing the floor, assume a slant position, as you hold onto the seat of a solid chair behind you with both hands. Let yourself down as far as you feel you can comfortably go. Return to your original position. Repeat.

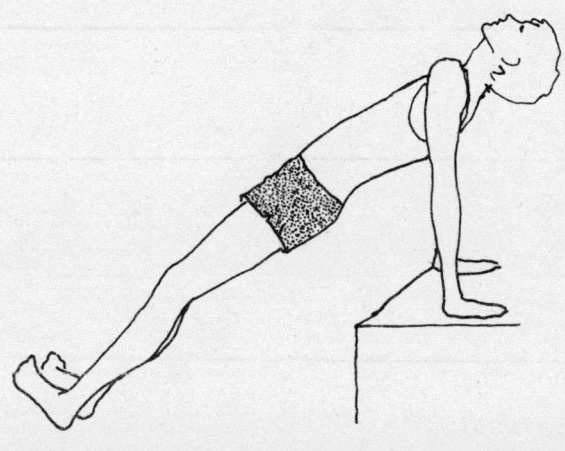

- *Skipping.* 1 minute.
- *Calf Steps.* 1 minute. Stand with just the balls of your feet on a very thick phone book or a solid block 3 or 4 inches high. Holding onto a chair or table and keeping your back straight, rise on your toes and then go back down. Repeat.

- *Shoulder Arcs.* 1 minute. Stand with your feet 12 inches apart, a 5-pound cuff weight wrapped around each wrist. Raise your arms sideways until they are at shoulder height and parallel to the ground. Return them to your sides. Repeat.

- *Jumping Jacks*. 1 minute.
- *Diagonal Touches*. 1 minute. Lie on your back with your knees up. Lift your head and shoulders off the floor and touch your right elbow to your left knee, or get as close as possible. Return to the floor. Repeat, touching your left elbow to your right knee. Repeat, first right elbow, then left.

- *Front Curls*. 1 minute. Stand up straight, with your arms at your sides and 5-pound cuff weights wrapped around your wrists. Keeping your upper arms close to your body, lift your lower arms to your chest. Return them to your sides. Repeat briskly.

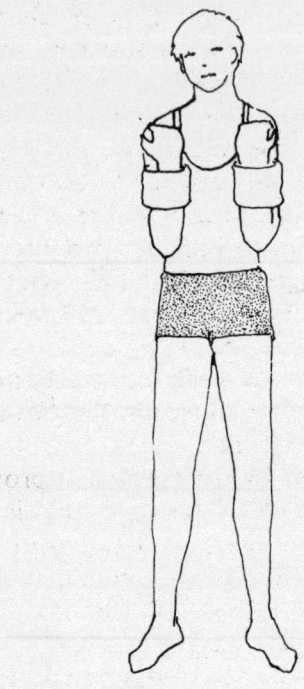

- *Run in Place*. 2 minutes.

Your Ageproofing Walk Plan

The easiest way to get started on an outdoor exercise program is simply to walk. Walking is the most natural form of exercise. You walk as a matter of course in going about your daily activities. You can walk just about anywhere, anytime, regardless of your fitness level or your age. You do not need special gear. You do not need to spend a penny. And walking is certainly a good way to get from one place to another these days, especially during rush hour, when buses and undergrounds are so crowded and traffic, such a jam. With all this going for it, it is no wonder that walking is now Britain's number one form of physical activity and that millions of men and women across the country make a point of walking regularly.

"Walking can provide you with an excellent basic program for a healthy heart and blood pressure and all-around fitness," says Dr. Ernst L. Wynder, president of the American Health Foundation and one of the world's leading authorities in preventive medicine. "If you walk at a fast enough clip, the benefits are similar to those you get from activities such as running. And walking is a lot easier on your joints." If you prefer to walk at a more moderate pace, however, you can still get a conditioning effect by walking longer and more often. Forty minutes of brisk walking five days a week, for example, may do just about as much for you as running three times a week for twenty minutes.

In starting out on Your Ageproofing Walk Plan, you should begin at a pace that feels comfortable and then gradually work up to a speed and distance that provide optimal benefits. As with any kind of exercise, this is particularly important if you have not been physically active for quite a while or are overweight. The program can fit into your working day very easily, going right through the week from Monday to Friday. If you have a job and do not live far away from your office, you can walk to and from work. If your home is quite a distance away, try taking the bus or subway to a certain stop and then walking the rest of the way. If you commute, you may find that a walk during your lunch hour is an enjoyable fitness break. More and more people are using their lunch hour to exercise and having something to eat at their desk when they return.

Walking is a very flexible form of exercise. It works for you in any number of different ways. If you decide that it is better to break your daily walk into two separate stints, covering one half your quota going to work and one half going home, you can still get plenty of benefit. At first, perhaps, five times a week is more of a mental and physical commitment than you feel up to every weekday in a row. No problem. Begin with just three days a week, walking on Monday, Wednesday, and Friday. Gradually shift from three to four and then five days of walking. But if you love to walk, all you have to do is find the level on the plan at which you want to start and progress accordingly.

On days when the weather is bad, you have Your Basic Ageproofing Exercise Plan to switch to. This will give you the indoor workout you need in order to maintain all the fitness mileage you have chalked up by walking. You can alternate your Basic Plan with any of the other indoor plans —swimming, dancing, or racquetball—or combine all of them. Each of the plans, it is important to emphasize, mixes well with any or all of the others.

On the days when you walk, you may want to do four simple exercises that the President's Council on Physical Fitness and Sports recommends. If you do them first thing on getting up in the morning, you will be all set to walk out the door.

WALKING STRETCHES

• *Knee Pulls*. Lie flat on your back and pull both knees up to your chest. Hold 15 seconds. Repeat for 1 minute.

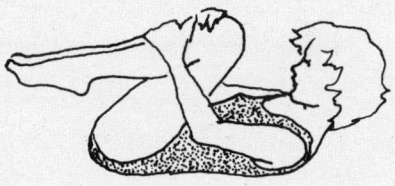

• *Sit-Ups*. 1 minute. Lie on your back with your knees bent. At first, do the exercise the easier way, with your arms crossed on your chest. After a few weeks try doing it the harder way, with your hands clasped behind your head. Rise to a sitting position. Slowly lower yourself back to the floor. Repeat. Do the exercise on an exercise mat or a carpet.

• *Stretch Out.* Stand barefoot at arm's length from a wall, with your feet together. Place your forearms vertically against the wall and lean on them. Drop your buttocks so that there is a straight line from the back of your neck to your ankles. Hold the position for a full minute. Return to your original position. Rest for a few seconds. Repeat. Do at least 3 repetitions a day. Step back a little further away from the wall each week so that you stretch your calves more and more all the time. When you reach a 3- to 4-foot distance from the wall (depending on your height and arm length) you will have reached your maintenance distance.

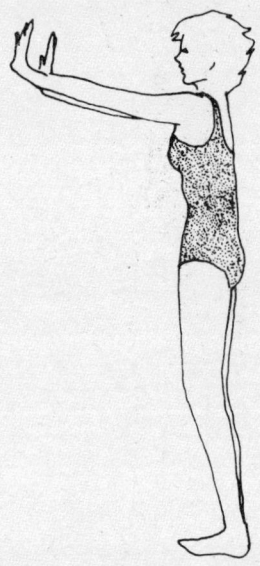

• *Reach and Bend.* Stand with your feet slightly apart. Reach above your head as high as you can, keeping your heels on the floor. Then flex your knees a little and bend from the waist, touching the floor with your fingers if you can. Hold 10 seconds. Slowly come back to a standing position, bringing your head up last. Repeat for 1 minute. Do not bounce or try to force your hands to the floor.

YOUR FOR-STARTERS PROGRAM

Stage	Distance	Miles per Hour	Time
Week One:	½ mile	2½ mph	12 minutes
Week Two:	1 mile	2½ mph	24 minutes

YOUR FOR-STARTERS PROGRAM (*cont.*)

Stage	Distance	Miles per Hour	Time
Week Three:	1½ miles	3 mph	30 minutes
Week Four:	2 miles	3 mph	40 minutes
Week Five:	2½ miles	3½ mph	42 minutes
Week Six:	3 miles	4 mph	48 minutes
Week Seven:	3½ miles	4 mph	52 minutes
Week Eight:	4 miles	4 mph	60 minutes

YOUR FOR-KEEPS PROGRAM

Walk regularly, maintaining 4 miles at 4 mph as your basic goal. If you feel you can comfortably walk further and faster, by all means do so. The only limit to intensity, duration, and frequency is your own level of endurance. Here are some useful walking pointers.

• Hold your head up, not down, as you walk.

• Let your arms swing free.

• Walk heel to toe. Your foot should meet the ground heel first. Then you roll forward onto the ball of your foot, pushing off from the ball and the toes.

• Wear comfortable shoes with good cushioning and a low heel. Running shoes are best.

• Check how long it takes to walk a mile. In a city like New York, it is easy to figure out distances; twenty regular blocks north–south equal a mile. If you go twenty New York blocks in 20 minutes, you are walking at 3 mph. The simplest way to gauge the distance if you live in the country or suburbs is to measure off a mile with your car.

• Walking can do a lot to help you lose unwanted pounds. Here is a chart showing you the number of calories you are likely to burn off as you walk:

2 mph	150 calories per hour
3 mph	300 calories per hour
4 mph	420 calories per hour

Your Ageproofing Dance Plan

Dancing is an extremely enjoyable form of physical activity and it happens to be a wonderful way to get exercise as well. It can meet all of the requirements for intensity, duration, and frequency that lasting fitness calls for. It is also unrivalled for developing flexibility. And the varied movements in quick succession provide the wide range of stress that is so important for bone health. As dancing is something that even very overweight people can do very well, it is a particularly beneficial type of exercise for those who have to count calories. There could not be a more positive way of dealing with excess poundage.

A special advantage of dancing that everyone with a job should take note of is that you can go out dancing after work, stay on the floor until all hours, and go right to sleep when you get home. This is a key point, because the same cannot be said of most other strenuous activities. Vigorous exercise, such as jogging or working out with weights, usually interferes with sleep if done at night. The reason that dancing is such an ideal type of exercise to do at night is that it is so rhythmical. Only swimming comes close to being as soothing as dancing.

"The fact that you can go on dancing for hours at a time, be it in the evening, afternoon, or morning, makes a difference," says Artie Phillips, a well-known New York ballroom dancing instructor and coach. "You could not possibly jump rope or run up and down stairs for such long stretches of time," he adds. "And one of the problems that overweight people have when they are trying to take off pounds is that they can only do spurty types of exercise—little bits of running or whatever—and the effects are not lasting. It does not amount to anything long-term. But if you have been dancing for an hour, you have been moving constantly for an hour—moving *and* burning calories."

The most energetic kinds of ballroom dances, Mr. Phillips says, are mambo, Charleston, fast swing, and hustle. Freestyle, he explains, is whatever you want to make it, so it too can be very energetic or it can simply be a way of marking time. Jazz steps and tap steps, many of which you can mix in with freestyle dancing, also call for a lot of calorie-burning and are easy to pick up, fun to do. Ballet, on the other hand, requires many hours of training at the barre before a level is reached where you can fully enjoy the beauty of the movements or expend as much energy as in the other forms of dance that are more readily mastered. Aerobic dancing is often a mish-mash of calisthenics, jazz, ballroom, ballet, disco, and jogging. Each class, each teacher, has a different blend of these basic ingredients—which, as Mr. Phillips points out, is equivalent to saying that any batch of steps you throw together in your own individual program can, if sufficiently vigorous, be called aerobic dancing too.

In order to make up Your Ageproofing Dance Plan to suit your own tastes and abilities, Mr. Phillips gives six key pointers.

- Dance by yourself for half an hour every day at home, so that you can have a regular dance schedule that you stick to. Do a series of genuine dance steps in a fixed order. Add to the series as you get better.
- Try a mixture of different dance steps rather than just limiting yourself to one or two. You will get a greater benefit, because more types of movement will be involved.
- Tape a half hour's worth of good dance music. Choose pieces that have a sure beat. Listen to various radio stations to get music that has the kinds of dance rhythms you want.
- Practice in whatever sort of shoes you feel most comfortable wearing, or just dance barefoot.
- You do not need a smooth wood floor to dance on. A rug actually has certain advantages in that it prevents you from sliding around. What's more, if you cannot move well on a rug, you are not moving the way you should and simply need more practice.
- If you would like to brush up any steps, take a few classes. There are plenty around. Check with your local leisure center.

Here is a basic set of five dance routines to get you started in Your Ageproofing Dance Plan. You can add to the steps in each routine, interchange them with other steps as you find ones you like to do, or simply use them as a guide in planning a mixture of your own. The music for each of the dance routines below has four counts to the bar or measure. A step that lasts two counts is called a slow step. A step that lasts one count is called a quick step. The terms "slow" and "quick" are only relative. A slow step is twice as long as a quick step for any given piece of music, but it may actually seem quite fast when you dance it. There may also be other step lengths, such as double-quick, which lasts half a count.

Each dance has a basic step sequence in which there is usually a mix of different-length steps. Often the basic sequence covers two bars of music, or a total of eight counts, with the steps in the second bar a reverse of those in the first. Sometimes the basic sequence may add up to six counts, so it takes two sequences—twelve counts in all— and three musical bars—of four counts each—in order to come out even.

YOUR AGEPROOFING DANCE PLAN

Swing

Swing has a basic step sequence of six counts. The first and third counts each have a pair of double-quick steps. The other four counts are quick steps. You can count it out this way: one and two, three and four, five, six.

Here is the footwork for the basic swing figure:

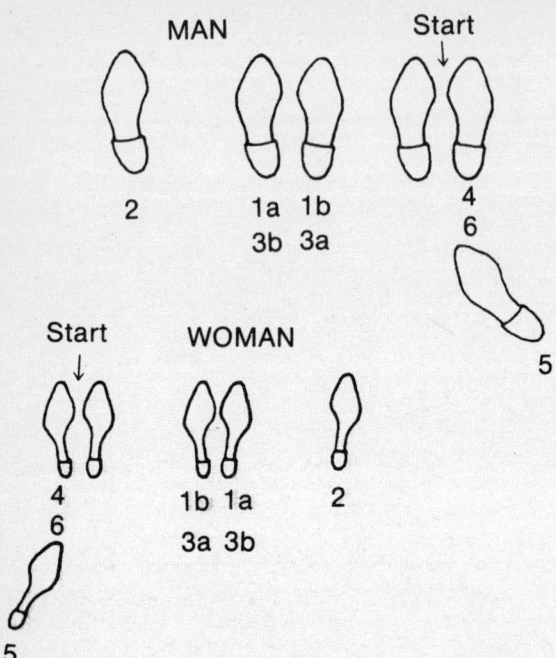

Count	Man	Woman
1 and 2	Step to left with left foot (double-quick). Bring right foot left to meet it (double-quick). Step to left with left foot (quick).	Step to right with right foot (double-quick). Bring left foot right to meet it (double-quick). Step to right with right foot (quick).
3 and 4	Step to right with right foot (double-quick). Bring left foot right to meet it (double-quick). Step to right with right foot (quick).	Step to left with left foot (double-quick). Bring right foot left to meet it (double-quick). Step to left with left foot (quick).

| 5 | Step diagonally back to right on left foot (quick). | Step diagonally back to left on right foot (quick). |
| 6 | Rock forward on right foot (quick). | Rock forward on left foot (quick). |

Samba

Samba is a fast Latin dance, with each four-beat bar taking about one second—for a total of sixty bars a minute. You dance samba with relaxed knees, a slight bounce, and a sort of oscillating movement. Your feet go forward while your body goes backward, and they go back while your body goes forward. Samba music has an unmistakable syncopated beat.

Here is the footwork for the basic samba figure:

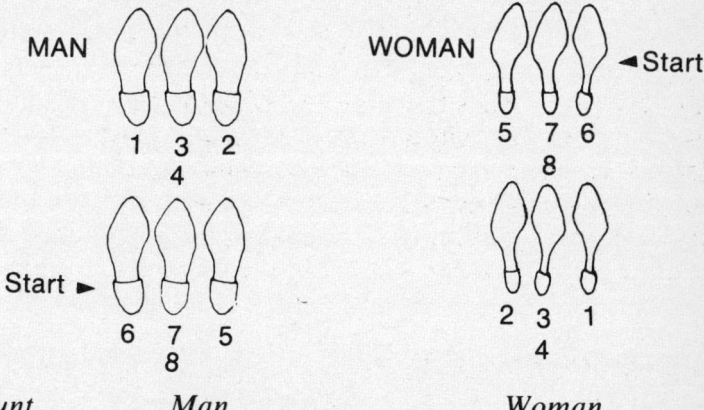

Count	Man	Woman
1 and 2	Step forward on left foot (long quick). Bring right foot close to left foot, and put partial weight on it briefly (double-quick).	Step back on right foot (long quick). Bring left foot close to right foot, and put partial weight on it briefly (double-quick).
3 and 4	Bring left foot over to right foot, and put full weight on it (slow).	Bring right foot over to left foot, and put full weight on it (slow).

5	Step back on right foot	Step forward on left foot
and	(long quick). Bring left	(long quick). Bring right
6	foot close to right foot,	foot close to left foot, and
	and put partial weight on it	put partial weight on it
	briefly (double-quick).	briefly (double-quick).

7	Bring right foot over to left	Bring left foot over to right
and	foot, and put full weight	foot, and put full weight
8	on it (slow).	on it (slow).

Charleston

The basic step technique of the Charleston is six quicks. The second and fourth quicks are hops instead of steps.

Here is the footwork for the Charleston hop:

MAN   WOMAN

1   3   3   1
2   4   4   2
5   6   6   5

Count	Man	Woman
1	Step on left foot	Step on right foot
2	Hop on left foot, raising right foot in back.	Hop on right foot, raising left foot in back.
3	Step on right foot.	Step on left foot.
4	Hop on right foot, raising left foot in back.	Hop on left foot, raising right foot in back.

5	Step on left foot.	Step on right foot.
6	Step on right foot.	Step on left foot.

Mambo

Mambo, with its built-in Latin hip movement, could not be faster or more fun to do. The basic step sequence goes: quick, quick, slow, quick, quick, slow. Mambo's special characteristic is that the sequence starts on the second, heavily accented, beat of the four-count bar—*not* on the first beat.

Here is the footwork for the basic figure:

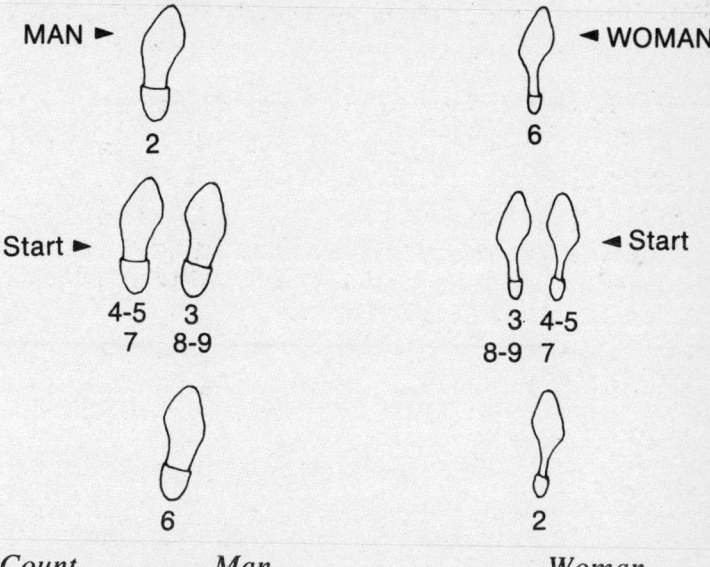

Count	Man	Woman
2	Step forward on left foot (quick).	Step back on right foot (quick).
3	Rock back on right foot (quick).	Rock forward on left foot (quick).
4-5	Short step back on left foot and hold (slow).	Short step forward on right foot and hold (slow).

6	Step back on right foot (quick).	Step forward on left foot (quick).
7	Rock forward on left foot (quick).	Rock back on right foot (quick).
8-9	Short step forward on right foot and hold (slow).	Short step back on left foot and hold (slow).

Polka

Polkas have very fast four-beat music with a strong accent on the first beat and an unmistakable bounce. The basic dance sequence is eight quick counts covering two bars of music.

Here is how the footwork for this basic figure goes:

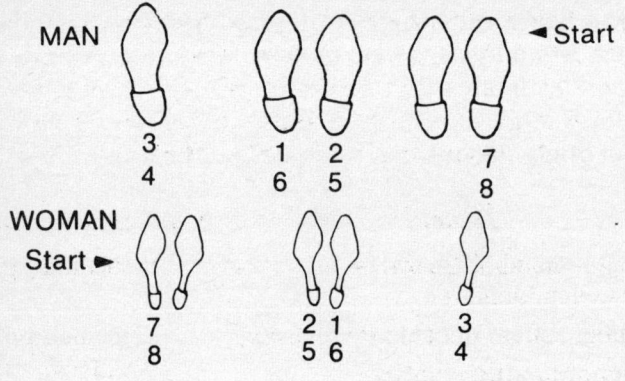

Count	Man	Woman
1	Step to left.	Step to right.
2	Bring right foot together with left foot.	Bring left foot together with right foot.
3	Step to left.	Step to right.
4	Hop on left foot.	Hop on right foot.
5	Step to right.	Step to left.
6	Bring left foot together with right foot.	Bring right foot together with left foot.

7	Step to right.	Step to left.
8	Hop on right foot.	Hop on left foot.

You can use this same pattern of step-step-step-hop to do turns or to go forward and back. The hop on the last beat of each measure and a relaxed bouncing action are typical of the polka.

When you go out dancing in the evening with friends, check the places with really fast dancing. Good swing spots are opening up all over the map. Places with rhythm bands are marvelous. They usually have a mix of fast and not-quite-so-fast Latin music.

A great gimmick to use if you are trying to shed pounds by dancing, is a calorie counter. It can tick off the number of calories you burn doing various types of dancing. Then you can figure out which footwork combinations give you the highest counts together with the most enjoyment. Here are some estimates that sports physiologists have come up with for energy expenditure and total calories counted per hour in doing dances that have different speeds.

Dance	Calories per Hour
Hustle, mambo, Charleston, fast swing, polka	600 and up
Samba, square dancing, quick step	550 and up
Viennese waltz, cha-cha	450–550
Rhumba, merengue, tango, fast fox-trot	300
Slow waltz, slow fox-trot	200–250

Your Ageproofing Swim Plan

Swimming can do wonders for your looks, your health, and your overall fitness from head to toe. "In many ways, it is the ideal exercise," says Dr. Willibald Nagler, chairman of the department of rehabilitative medicine at The New York Hospital-Cornell Medical Center and a noted orthopedist in the world of sports. "It can yield lasting benefits throughout your whole life." It appears that quite a few people agree, around the world. Even in Great Britain, where the weather is less conducive, it is one of the most popular forms of exercise.

You can look to swimming to provide an excellent aerobic effect. Like other activities that use the big muscles in a steady, rhythmical way, it tones and strengthens your lungs, heart, and blood vessels so that they do a better job of taking in and distributing oxygen throughout your body. A special benefit of swimming is that more than any other sport it improves the size and functional capacity of your lungs. The resistance of the water forces you to breathe more efficiently. The diaphragm muscle becomes stronger, the chest wall gets more flexible, and the air passages of the lungs open up. Swimming, in effect, helps you learn to breathe properly.

As your lungs absorb more oxygen, your body produces more blood to transport it, and the fitness of your entire vascular system is enhanced. All of this has a decidedly stimulating effect on your immune system; the increase in the number of red blood cells and in the volume of plasma bolster its ability to ward off infection. If you can become acclimated to swimming in cold water, this can have an even more positive effect. "People who swim regularly in cold water," Dr. Nagler says, "look younger and keep in better shape than others the same age—and they are usually very fit and healthy throughout their later decades."

Swimming in cool or cold water can also, as you saw in Ageproofing Your Breasts and Ageproofing Your Thighs, have a beneficial influence on fat distribution. This is why it can be so helpful in getting rid of stubborn fat in sex-specific areas, such as women's hips and men's midriffs. There is also one further, long-term advantage to the type of fat-shift swimming induces. It counters the loss of subcutaneous fat which otherwise occurs almost invariably in later years. This can make a conspicuous difference in how the skin looks—plumped-up and smooth instead of wrinkled and prunish.

The visible effects swimming has on your muscles are even more noticeable. Few forms of exercise other than dancing engage every muscle in the body as swimming does. Arms, shoulders, chest, waist, hips, buttocks, and legs all get a good workout. What's more, your body moves symmetrically with both sides being kept in balance—a key point. And although the resistance of the water works your muscles in much the same manner that weights do, there is virtually no risk of injury, because the movements are so slow and rhythmical.

Swimming is also the easiest of all sports on your joints because your body is always buoyantly supported by the water. This safety factor is especially important for people who are overweight or have joint problems. They do not risk stress on any of their joints, in contrast to other sports like running. Swimming is therefore one of the few sports that people can engage in strenuously, no matter how heavy they are, without fear of chronic damage. As you can see, by looking at the chart below, it is an excellent means of weight loss as well.

CALORIES PER MINUTE

	7½ Stone	9¼ Stone	10½ Stone	12 Stone
Backstroke	8.5	10	11.5	13
Breast Stroke	8.1	9.6	11	12.5
Freestyle	7.8	9.2	10.6	12

Your Ageproofing Swim Plan has been worked out for you along the lines of the YMCA's program. It provides you with a choice of strokes—freestyle or crawl; backstroke; breast stroke; or any combination of these three that you feel comfortable with. Used together, these strokes can give you an even more comprehensive workout than you can get with any one stroke by itself.

Interspersed with each lap set in which you do regular strokes is one in which you work only the legs and, after the initial series, one in which you work only the arms. These are an important part of Your Ageproofing Swim Plan, because they zero in on various muscles you should make a special point of keeping strong and firm.

To work only your legs, use a kickboard. This is a rectangular slab of compressed plastic that is usually curved at one end. It supports the upper part of your body, allowing you to cover distance as you practice your kicks instead of just hanging on to the rail at the side of the pool. A kickboard is a very good means of achieving faster, more expert leg action in the water, and it gives your legs a trimmer appearance in the bargain. To get the best results, be sure to hold the board stretched out in front of you and kick under the water, so that your feet scarcely churn the surface.

For concentrated work on your arms, use a Pull-Buoy. This effective little contraption is made of two lightweight plastic foam cylinders about eight inches long that are linked together. Place the cylinders so that one is above and one below your thighs as your body extends flat-out in the water. The Pull-Buoy forces your legs to remain close together and high in the water. Because it prevents you from making the slightest kick motion with your legs, you have to use your arms to propel yourself through the water, an unbeatable way to tone and strengthen them as you improve your strokes.

Each full set of laps—strokes and leg and arm workouts —is followed by a Breather Break for either 30 or 60 seconds. Use these short intervals to check your pulse rate if you think you may be exceeding your target rate—which, for swimming, is only 60 to 75 percent of your maximum heart rate. If you are over the 75 percent cutoff point, slow down for the remaining laps or even do a few less. After all, each person has a different level of fitness, so it is important to take the individual factor in exercise requirements into account. When you feel you can do so comfortably, start to increase the number and speed of your laps, as outlined for you on the program.

YOUR FOR-STARTERS PROGRAM

Begin with this progressively vigorous sequence and continue as indicated, doing the number of laps designated below for each successive week in a standard-size pool.

Week One	*Week Two*	*Week Three*	*Week Four*
20 min	20 min	30 min	30 min
Swim: 4 *Kickboard:* 2 *Break:* 30 sec	*Swim:* 4 *Kickboard:* 2 *Break:* 30 sec	*Swim:* 4 *Kickboard:* 2 *Pull-Buoy:* 2 *Break:* 60 sec	*Swim:* 5 *Kickboard:* 2 *Pull-Buoy:* 2 *Break:* 60 sec
Swim: 4 *Kickboard:* 2 *Break:* 30 sec	*Swim:* 4 *Kickboard:* 2 *Break:* 30 sec	*Swim:* 4 *Kickboard:* 2 *Pull-Buoy:* 2 *Break:* 60 sec	*Swim:* 5 *Kickboard:* 2 *Pull-Buoy:* 2 *Break:* 60 sec
Swim: 4 *Kickboard:* 2	*Swim:* 4 *Kickboard:* 4	*Swim:* 4 *Kickboard:* 2 *Pull-Buoy:* 2	*Swim:* 5 *Kickboard:* 2 *Pull-Buoy:* 2
Total: 18	*Total:* 21	*Total:* 24	*Total:* 27

Week Five	*Week Six*	*Week Seven*	*Week Eight*
30 min	30 min	30 min	30 min
Swim: 5 *Kickboard:* 3 *Pull-Buoy:* 2 *Break:* 60 sec	*Swim:* 5 *Kickboard:* 3 *Pull-Buoy:* 3 *Break:* 60 sec	*Swim:* 6 *Kickboard:* 3 *Pull-Buoy:* 3 *Break:* 60 sec	*Swim:* 6 *Kickboard:* 4 *Pull-Buoy:* 3 *Break:* 60 sec
Swim: 5 *Kickboard:* 2 *Pull-Buoy:* 3 *Break:* 60 sec	*Swim:* 5 *Kickboard:* 3 *Pull-Buoy:* 3 *Break:* 60 sec	*Swim:* 6 *Kickboard:* 3 *Pull-Buoy:* 3 *Break:* 60 sec	*Swim:* 6 *Kickboard:* 3 *Pull-Buoy:* 4 *Break:* 60 sec
Swim: 5 *Kickboard:* 3 *Pull-Buoy:* 2	*Swim:* 5 *Kickboard:* 3 *Pull-Buoy:* 3	*Swim:* 6 *Kickboard:* 3 *Pull-Buoy:* 3	*Swim:* 6 *Kickboard:* 4 *Pull-Buoy:* 4
Total: 30	*Total:* 33	*Total:* 36	*Total:* 40

CHAPTER 7

Your Ageproofing Sleep Plan

Getting enough sleep on a regular basis can have a profound and lasting effect on every organ, tissue, and cell in your body and go far to ageproof your looks and health and maintain a high level of fitness throughout your life. As some of the most recent scientific findings indicate, sufficient sleep may add years to your life.

Two Kinds of Sleep

In order to understand what your sleep needs actually are and what you can do to make sure you meet them, it helps to have some idea of what sleep itself involves. Sleep is not just a single process. There are two quite different kinds of sleep, and you experience both in the course of the night. They alternate repeatedly from the moment you go to sleep until the moment you wake up. One kind is called REM sleep; REM is short for Rapid Eye Movement. The other is called non-REM.

REM Sleep

Rapid eye movement sleep is actually dreaming sleep. During periods of this kind of sleep, your brain is very active, in some ways even more active than during your waking hours. Although your lids are shut, your eyes are constantly darting about as if they were trying to see what is happening in all directions at once. Your heart beats faster, your blood pressure rises, and your breathing becomes more rapid. Men experience noticeable sexual arousal, and there is evidence that women experience similar intervals of arousal. In contrast to this stepped-up activity in vital organs and functions, however, there is a blocking of all voluntary muscle activity for the full length of each REM sleep period. The muscles are relaxed almost to the point of total paralysis. You could not move if you wanted to.

Non-REM Sleep

During the other kind of sleep, non-REM, which is in so many ways the reverse of REM sleep, your brain is relatively inactive, and even though there may be some dreaming, there is not the wealth of mental imagery there is in REM sleep. Your pulse rate and blood pressure are at normal levels, your breathing regular, and your eyes still. Tone returns to your voluntary muscles, and you can move about easily. Non-REM sleep has four distinct levels, or stages, each one taking your into a deeper state of sleep. You descend from stage one through stage two, down into stage three until you finally reach stage four. Then you ascend again to stage one and switch for a certain length of time into REM. At this point, the cycle starts anew.

A fascinating point is that the regular repeated switches between non-REM and REM throughout the entire time that you are asleep seems to be a nightly version of an ongoing rest-activity cycle that is also present during waking hours and is about 90 to 100 minutes long. You start off your night's sleep with a period of non-REM, and this is followed by a period of REM, so completing one basic cycle. A total of four or five cycles occur in the course of the night as a rule. The two kinds of sleep are believed to fulfill separate but complementary functions. Non-REM sleep serves to restore your body's tissues physically, through protein synthesis after all the wear and tear of the preceding day. REM sleep helps keep your mental processes in the peak of condition by sorting out and organizing all the input from the day before and readying your brain and central nervous system as a whole to deal with whatever occurs during the day ahead. Although at the start of life, when the brain is undergoing very rapid development, sleep periods contain fairly equal amounts of non-REM and REM, the proportion gradually shifts during early childhood to a preponderance of non-REM. From about eight years old on, the ratio is 75 to 80 percent non-REM to 20 to 25 percent REM, and it remains so pretty much throughout life.

Sleep Needs

How much sleep do you actually need? Requirements vary a great deal from one individual to the next. Einstein needed a good thirteeen hours at a stretch, whereas Thomas Edison thrived on two-hour snatches now and then around the clock, and Napoleon cantered off to his victories on no more than four or five a night. But even though people can be categorized to some extent as either short sleepers or long sleepers with distinguishable personality traits—short sleepers tend to be more rational, pragmatic, and extroverted and long sleepers to be more intuitive, creative, and introverted—there are certain basic guidelines that apply to just about everyone.

You need enough sleep each night to look well the next day. You do not have to be told that too little sleep shows in your face. That much is obvious. And although plenty of people pride themselves on being able to make do on very few hours a night, they obviously have not looked in the mirror. A good night's sleep gives the muscles of your face and neck as well as your whole body a seven- or eight-hour respite from fighting the pull of gravity. The restorative processes of sleep temporarily dispel the frown lines, brow puckers, lip pursing, and other typical signs of daily tension, anxiety, and worry. A key point that too few sleep-skimpers realize is that a good night's sleep helps keep the skin smoother and firmer not only on a daily basis but over the years as well. If you get the sleep you need every night, there is less likelihood that facial lines and sagging skin will become a chronic problem. Lines and sagging are to a large extent the result of expressions and gestures that are exacerbated by fatigue and the stress and tension it triggers—as well as by gravity's unremitting tug for a greater number of hours at a stretch. The less sleep a person gets, the more indelibly lines may become etched and the greater the amount of sagging that may occur.

Sleep, of course, affects more than your looks. Recent studies have produced fascinating evidence that what is considered an adequate amount of sleep for most people is not enough for efficient functioning during the day. Prompted by findings that children age ten to twelve who averaged about nine hours and forty-five minutes of sound sleep a night exhibited boundless energy and alertness during the day, researchers went on to test young adults who were getting about eight hours sleep a night. The volunteers were simply asked to stay in bed one hour longer each morning. This resulted in forty-five minutes extra sleep a night and a marked improvement in daytime alertness as measured by rigorous tests. The study made it quite clear that insufficient sleep impairs mental functioning and indicated something further as well: most people are chronically sleepy during the day.

The message is obvious. The way to get more out of your day is to get more sleep at night. This flies in the face of much of the current advice on ways to get more mileage out of your day by sleeping less. To many, cutting back half an hour every night for an annual saving of 182 daytime hours may at first glance seem like the most time-wise tip yet. But in the light of these new findings it turns out to be penny wise and pound foolish. The most practical and profitable thing you can do is to try to get an additional half-hour of sleep each night, at the very least. Chances are you will feel full of energy and much more alert the next day and get greater mental and physical benefits out of every hour.

Obviously not everyone has the ability to sleep the maximum amount each night. The very fact that so many men and women complain of insomnia means there are plenty of people who are unable to get as much sleep as they need and would like. Even among those who do not have insomnia, demands imposed by work schedules and social life cut into sleep time. On weekdays, people usually have to get themselves up and out of the house far earlier than they are ready to do, and they drag themselves to their office half asleep. And when people work all day, the evenings are the only time they have to be with family and friends, so the hour at which they go to bed tends to be quite late. If you have to get up early every weekday morning, try to get to bed at least a half hour—and if possible an hour—earlier at night in order to avoid shortchanging yourself of needed or wanted sleep. See if you can do this on a regular basis, not just one or two nights a week but every night.

The Regularity Rule

Regularity is probably the single most important sleep habit to aim for. A bedtime hour that works for you and that you can adhere to comfortably is a key factor in helping you get as much good sound sleep every night as you need and want. There are several reasons for this. Habits are built-in cues. They act as powerful triggers for the body's vital biological rhythms. Many people who have to leave for work every weekday morning at eight o'clock, and therefore have to wake up at, say, seven o'clock, do so automatically day after day without need of an alarm clock. Why? Because their body's internal clock system, which controls the rhythmical timing of events in every organ, tissue, cell, and function of the body, provides its own wake-up call. That internal clock has been set to go off at seven sharp.

The cycle of sleep and wakefulness is closely linked to a host of other daily and nightly rhythms in the body which it influences and by which it is influenced. The sleep-wake cycle cannot be separated from the rest of this intricate clockwork without risk of discomfort, fatigue, and stress, all of which occurs because the very fine and complex tuning of the events taking place in the body's myriad organs, tissues, cells, and functions is disrupted.

The intermeshing system of bodily rhythms—the sleep-wake cycle among the many others—has an inborn period of about twenty-five hours. This is normally compressed into the more compact framework of the twenty-four-hour day—the time it takes for the earth to make one full rotation on its axis. Social cues, such as mealtimes, office hours, the arrival of the mail, or walking the dog, together with the sequence of daylight and darkness and other recurring daily patterns, keep the body's clock system synchronized to this twenty-four-hour day, a little as though the body's clock were constantly being adjusted in order to keep the same time as the sun clock. Irregular sleep habits compromise the synchronizing process, so the more you can go to bed at a set hour and get up at a set hour, the better.

The importance of regularity does not therefore stop with sleep habits. It holds for all your main daily habits. A well-balanced daily pattern is much more vital than most people realize. In order for your body's infinitely complex system of rhythms to function as it really should and run like clockwork, it should be geared to a reasonably predictable schedule of events. Your body needs to know well ahead of time what you expect to do regularly each day at given times so as to see that the cascading rhythms of, say, various hormones and enzymes and peptides all mesh and flow in a well-ordered and well-timed sequence. Whatever you do in the morning is bound to affect the state of your body in the afternoon, evening, and night. So your sleep patterns are bound to hinge on the rhythm patterns before and after.

Shift Stress

You can see why, from the point of view of your body's rhythmical functioning in general and your sleep-wake rhythm in particular, it is advisable to minimize occasions that demand sudden shifts in your time of sleep. These can disrupt the body's intermeshing rhythms. The most common and vivid example of this is jet lag. Some rhythms return to their normal pattern very quickly, but others remain disrupted for days or even weeks. It may be quite a while before you are able to enjoy the fully restorative benefits of sleep that you would under normal conditions, when your day is going along at a predictably normal pace and follows a predictably regular schedule of events.

The disruptive effect that repeatedly stressful occurrences, such as frequent flights across more than three time zones, have on your rhythms can have far-reaching consequences for your looks, health, and overall level of fitness. Observations by leading experts in the newly emerging field of biological rhythms have disclosed that pilots who regularly make east-west flights across the Atlantic, and keep crossing numerous time zones, appear much older at the end of a three- or four-year period than pilots assigned to fly north-south runs, who are never obliged to cross time zones. The stress to the body's rhythmically run system caused by constant changes in sleep-wake schedules can actually be read in people's faces, and what is read there reflects the chronic deteriorative changes taking place throughout the body. There is, moreover, growing evidence that such stressful shifts can markedly shorten the lifespan.

If you maintain a basic daily pattern, free of undue stresses to your body's vital rhythmical functioning, your sleep-wake rhythm is not likely to undergo any conspicuous amount of change as you get older, certainly not until very late in life. What this means is that the sleep problems increasingly experienced by people with the years do not for the most part seem inevitable consequences of aging processes but rather problems that any and all can get the better of.

Exercise Prescription

Among the several aspects of sleep believed to be affected as people grow older is the total amount of sleep they are able to get. But findings from noted authorities in sleep research indicate that the total amount of sleep people get does not really change all that much over the years. There does appear to be a great deal more variability in sleep time during the later decades, with a fragmented sleep pattern that breaks up into fewer hours of sleep at night and more naps in the daytime. This fragmentation seems, however, to be largely the result of the lower levels of physical activity among older people. The way to help prevent it is to step up daytime activity in whatever ways and to whatever extent a person can and wants to.

Waking at frequent intervals during the night, which is only part of the problem of fragmented sleep, has been singled out as one definitely age-related change in the basic sleep pattern. It is a common occurrence and is seen quite frequently in men from age twenty on—as a matter of fact, the number of nightly awakenings start to increase among young boys after they have reached puberty. Women, in contrast, show a more gradual increase in nightly awakenings—only from about age forty on, but with a considerably greater frequency in extreme old age. Here again, however, age does not seem to be the sole, or even the key, factor. The cause is almost invariably linked to certain chronic deteriorative changes taking place over the years, such as sleep-associated breathing difficulties, which are seen in at least 50 percent of all men and women over sixty-five. The problem can undoubtedly be prevented in many instances, or if under way even partially reversed, by adhering to a sufficiently vigorous, regular program of cardiorespiratory exercise. None can do more good than swimming.

Deteriorative change and chronic disease seem to be the main underlying causes of whatever losses in REM sleep occur during later decades, even though people usually lay the blame on aging changes. The fact is that biological aging does not seem to have anything to do with any slight reductions in REM sleep that may take place up until extreme old age. Where there is a discernible decrease in the REM component of each basic sleep cycle during the night, this is more likely to indicate such critical changes as loss of cerebral blood flow, lack of sufficient oxygen, and reduced brain function—in other words, a pathological condition. If there is simply less total REM sleep in the course of the night but the REM component of each cycle remains intact, this is usually due to older people's habit of waking up much earlier and therefore missing one or two basic sleep cycles, particularly those richest in REM, which happen to be the ones closest to morning. But the same holds true for every person who gets up early, regardless of age. If you sleep only five or six hours at night, you are bound to experience fewer basic sleep cycles and therefore less REM.

In looking at non-REM sleep for evidence of change over the years, you really have to consider the various stages of non-REM sleep separately. The amount of time people spend in stage one sleep actually increases throughout life, with men experiencing a higher percentage of this very light type of sleep than women from puberty on. Time spent in stage two sleep rises from the early adult years to the middle years and later drops again. Stage three sleep exhibits still another lifetime pattern: in women it may rise slightly and in men it may fall off slightly. It is in stage four sleep that the most conspicuous and consistent difference between younger and older people is seen. But even here, although by age fifty a quarter of the men and women in this country no longer have any stage four sleep at all, there is still a wide range of individual variation, and a substantial number of elderly women appear to retain stage four sleep perfectly well. The reason for the decline or disappearance of stage four sleep is not clear. It may be that it is no longer needed. On the other hand, exercise and physical fitness have been shown to increase stage four sleep, and it may be that less activity and a lower level of fitness in older people brings about a corresponding drop in their deepest level of sleep. If such is the case, maintaining physical activities at an age-proofing level might prevent or even restore losses of stage four sleep.

A program of regular, vigorous exercise is without a doubt one of the surest ways there is to get a good sound sleep, provided, of course, that you do not exercise too late at night, as that is apt to rev you up too much. The cutoff point for most kinds of strenuous exercise should be the hour before dinner, no later. If, however, you find that the late evening hours are the only ones left in your day, there are certain activities that you can go in for without sleep trade-offs. Dancing is the best choice of all. You can dance until all hours and then fall right to sleep the moment you hit the bed. This is because for most people dancing is such a rhythmic activity. The only two sports that even begin to approach it in this respect are swimming and, for whatever use this information may be to you, cross-country skiing. A long walk after dinner, which can also be quite tonic and soothing, is probably what most people will find the simplest solution to the matter of after-dinner exercise.

Diet Prescription

The caffeine present in coffee—and also in tea, cola drinks, and even chocolate—can, as everyone knows, be so enduringly stimulating that it interferes with a person's ability to get to sleep. If you find that you have trouble falling asleep at night when you have had coffee at some point in the afternoon or evening, simply limit your coffee intake to breakfast and midmorning or lunch at the very latest.

In contrast to caffeine, however, there is one food substance that actually induces sleep: tryptophan. Tryptophan is an amino acid essential to the diet and important in the synthesis of protein. While it is present in a wide number of protein foods, the most effective source is milk. If you have trouble getting to sleep and staying asleep, dietary tryptophan can be helpful. There are two simple things you should do in order to get the best results. Eat plenty of carbohydrate-rich foods for dinner at night—vegetables, fruits, and grains—and go easy on protein, eating no more than Your Ageproofing Diet Plan suggests. Protein foods contain other essential amino acids besides tryptophan, and these compete with tryptophan for passage across the blood-brain barrier that so carefully monitors the kind and amount of substances that can enter the cerebral blood flow and gain access to the brain cells affected by sleep-inducing trypto-phan. The idea is to keep protein—and therefore competi-tion—low in the evening, except for milk and milk products at dinner and bedtime. The tryptophan in milk, yogurt, and cheese reaches the brain very quickly, and through a series of interactions with brain hormones and enzymes acts not only to induce sleepiness but also to improve the quality of your sleep all night long. There is no safer or more effective sleeping pill on the market today than this natural compo-nent of one of the most nutritively complete and beneficial foods there are in the diet. I love to sleep and I also love yogurt at bedtime. I am sure it is no mere coincidence that I sleep so well and love yogurt as much.

YOUR AGEPROOFING SLEEP GUIDELINES

- Keep regular hours. This applies not only to bedtime and rising but also to the whole structure of your day. Sleep is part of a daily cycle involving many other body processes.
- Do not economize on sleep. Instead, see if adding thirty or forty minutes to your usual sleep quota does not im-prove your daytime alertness and vitality.
- Remember that regular, vigorous exercise is excellent for improving your sleep, provided it is not done too late in the day.
- Alcohol is not a good nightcap. It fragments sleep patterns and, through a rebound effect, tends to wake you up three or four hours after you have gone to sleep.
- Sleeping pills are also destructive of sleep patterns. Use them only for a brief emergency period and as prescribed by your doctor.
- Caffeine's sleep-disturbing effects may last longer than you realize. Some people should avoid even afternoon coffee breaks. There is, however, a great deal of individ-ual variation.
- Hunger can keep you awake, so a light bedtime snack is often a good idea. A cup of yogurt or a glass of milk is especially helpful.
- If you cannot sleep, do not worry. Get up and do some-thing enjoyable or useful. If you begin to feel sleepy at some point, go back to bed.

CHAPTER 8

Your Special Ageproofing Guidelines

Your Ageproofing Alcohol Guidelines

Alcohol is the active ingredient in all the fermented and distilled beverages that people all over the world have been drinking for thousands of years—long enough for them to be more aware of the risks than they are.

Immediate Effects

Of the many swift and predictable ways in which alcohol acts, its most important effect is on the central nervous system. Alcohol lowers brain mechanisms that control and integrate. A small amount of it has the effect of releasing inhibitions and producing a sense of well-being and relaxation, but larger amounts interfere with balance, coordination, and various mental functions, and do so more and more as the amount is increased. An inevitable series of changes take place, including slurred speech, staggering gait, blurred vision, impaired concentration, judgment and memory, and very often aggressiveness and depression as well.

Long-Term Effects

The manifestations of alcohol's complex and contradictory effects give the lie to the poet's claim that alcohol is the elixir of perpetual youth. Moderate drinking does not appear to be hazardous to people's health and looks, and an occasional spree need have no lasting effects. But heavy drinking over the years can be extremely harmful. The toll includes cardiovascular damage; high blood pressure; cancers of the mouth, throat, and esophagus—especially among smokers —and the liver; cirrhosis; inflammation of the pancreas; anemia; accelerated osteoporosis; and impairment of the brain and other parts of the nervous system. The deteriorative changes to which alcohol contributes so conspicuously are bound to make the body look, as well as feel and act, old. The ravages of outright alcoholism are of course appalling.

Three Basic Factors

How much alcohol affects a person is determined by its level in the blood at any one time. This depends on several factors. One is weight. The heavier a person is, the more blood there is, and so, other things being equal, it takes proportionately more alcohol to achieve a given level in the blood. If you happen to be on the light side, this is all the more reason to make sure you drink very moderately, if at all.

A second significant factor is the speed of drinking. The body can get rid of alcohol only so fast and no faster. A 150-pound man will take about an hour to metabolize the alcohol in a single shot of whiskey. If his drinking does not exceed one shot of whiskey per hour, the alcohol in his blood does not have a chance to build up to an excessive level. It follows, of course, that the slower people drink, the better off they are.

A third factor that has to be considered is the type of beverage a person is drinking—and, specifically, the percentage of alcohol it contains. Beers have the lowest concentrations of alcohol, most of them being 5 percent by volume. Regular wines are about twice as strong as beer, with an alcoholic content of 10 to 13 percent. Contrary to what people often think, this has nothing to do with a wine being light or full-bodied; a light wine can easily contain a higher percentage of alcohol than a heavy one. Fortified wines, like sherry, Madeira, and port, are close to 20 percent alcohol. Distilled spirits, such as gin, vodka, whiskey, and brandy, are between 40 and 50 percent alcohol. This is expressed as "proof" on the label, proof being equivalent to twice the percentage. An 80-proof vodka, for instance, is 40 percent alcohol. Pure alcohol is 200 proof.

What this means in practical terms is that wine has about twice the alcoholic content of beer, fortified wine has twice that of regular wine, and spirits twice that of fortified wine. These proportions are important to bear in mind because it is the amount of alcohol you consume that counts, not the kind of drink the alcohol happens to be in. Interestingly, traditional glasses take all these percentages into account. A 12-ounce glass of beer equals a 6-ounce glass of wine equals a 3-ounce glass of sherry equals a 1½-ounce shot of whiskey.

Civilized Drinking

Very good pointers on how to drink sensibly can be gleaned from those peoples of the world who have used alcohol down through the centuries but not abused it. Italians, Greeks, Spaniards, Jews, and Chinese are a few of the groups among whom the social tradition of moderation is very strong. The beverage is usually wine or beer. It is thought of as something that accompanies food, rather than something consumed by itself. Abstinence is accepted socially, but drunkenness is not. Here are some pointers that such drinking customs provide.

- Eat while you drink: food slows alcohol consumption.
- Drink slowly and for pleasure, not for a quick fix.
- Have a drink only if you feel you really want it. Do not feel you have to have it just because you are offered one.
- Do not drink to relax or, as so many mistakenly do, to help you relieve stress or cope with problems. It does none of these things.
- Do not drink on your own.
- Set moderate limits for yourself.

What are moderate limits? A couple of drinks a day is a useful rule to go by. And not every day: try to have a dry day between every two or three drinking days each week. It is also a good idea to give up drinking for a week or so every now and again, to make sure there is no real dependence on alcohol. One time not to drink is just before bedtime. A nightcap may help get people to sleep, but as noted in the preceding chapter, alcohol has a profoundly disturbing effect on sleep rhythms and therefore on the quality of the sleep.

Your Ageproofing Anti-Smoking Guidelines

According to The Royal College of Physicians smoking is the single most important cause of avoidable illness and premature death in the United Kingdom. It causes nine out of ten deaths from lung cancer; the majority of deaths from bronchitis and emphysema; and it is also a major factor in coronary heart disease, the commonest form of death in Britain today. It is now as important a cause of death as were the great epidemic diseases such as typhoid, cholera and tuberculosis that affected previous generations. In England and Wales alone about 95,000 people are killed by smoking each year. It has been estimated that out of every thousand young men who smoke in this country, one will be murdered, 6 will die in road accidents and 250 will die prematurely as a result of their smoking. On the average, women live seven-and-a-half years longer than men, who until recently were much heavier smokers. Now that women are smoking so much more, however, male and female expectancies may converge. In 1981 about a third of the total deaths from lung cancer were in people aged under 65. These are a few of the indisputable facts about cigarette smoking.

Legal Street Drug

Most of us certainly know that smoking is dangerous. And most of the smokers in this country would like to stop, as many perhaps as nine out of ten. Millions try every year, but only about 20 percent succeed in quitting for as much as a year. Why do cigarettes have such a grip on smokers? There has been an extraordinary amount of misunderstanding about what cigarette smoking actually is. Until a short time ago, it was seen as just a very complex and tenacious psychological habit. But experts now view it differently. They have concluded that for most smokers it is a genuine drug addiction. Authorities taking this stand include The Royal College of Physicians, The World Health Organization, The American Psychiatric Association, and the U.S. Department of Health and Human Services. As a matter of fact the U.S. Department of Health and Human Services describes cigarette smoking as "the most widespread example of drug dependence in our country" and one causing more illness and deaths than all other drugs combined. Cigarettes are what you might call a legal street drug. They may, moreover, be the most addictive drug around, and the one that causes the most relapses.

In trying to give up a drug—any drug—one of the most important things is understanding just what it does to people. What is it in tobacco that causes addiction? The main, if not the only, factor is without a doubt nicotine, a chemical substance related to cocaine and morphine but found only in the tobacco plant. Acting through specialized receptors on cells in the brain and muscles, nicotine triggers a series of reactions, including changes in brain waves and release of hormones affecting the central nervous system, a rise in pulse rate, and a slowing of peripheral blood circulation. Nicotine can relax or stimulate, produce moments of euphoria or act as a depressant. It has quite a paradoxical mix of consequences.

Although the immediate effects of nicotine are not worrisome, the long-term effects are. Together with carbon monoxide, the most lethal of the gases in tobacco smoke, it is known to be a factor in heart disease. It may also increase the cancer-causing effects of the huge variety of tiny particles in the tar of cigarette smoke. But by far the worst thing about nicotine is that it hooks the smoker to tobacco, a product with numerous lethal ingredients. Cigarettes are a particularly addictive source of nicotine because the lungs are by far the most efficient way of absorbing it. This leads to a higher concentration of nicotine in the blood than achieved with other forms of tobacco and one that smokers strive to maintain by reaching for a cigarette—or fix—every thirty or forty minutes. Superimposed on this fairly stable level of blood nicotine are the individual highs that occur with each puff, which send a fresh rush of nicotine from the lungs to the brain in 7.5 seconds, twice as fast as it takes a drug like heroin injected into the arm to reach the brain. In other words, cigarette smokers "mainline" through the lungs. The average smoker of a pack and a half a day is getting over 100,000 kicks a year.

No Safe Cigarette

All this helps explain why switching to low-nicotine, low-tar cigarettes is no solution. The widely advertised low numbers do not refer to the actual nicotine or tar content of the cigarettes but to the yield when the cigarettes are smoked by a standard machine. People do not, however, smoke like machines. Recent studies show that smokers of low-yield cigarettes have much the same amount of nicotine in their blood as smokers of higher-yield cigarettes because they compensate by taking more puffs, inhaling more deeply, smoking more cigarettes, or even blocking the ventilating holes in the filters. The tar intake goes up in tandem. A cigarette in the 1 to 5 milligram (mg) tar range can readily deliver 15 to 20 milligrams of the stuff to an assiduous smoker. People who smoke have got to stop kidding themselves. They must simply face the fact that there is no safe cigarette. Although it is true that lung-cancer death rates are somewhat lower among smokers using filtered or low-tar cigarettes, they are still much higher than among non-smokers. And no reduction of heart risk is seen with the low-yield cigarettes. In fact, there are good indications that heart risk may have risen.

Getting Unhooked

Quitting is the one and only answer for anybody who smokes. Some smokers can manage to do this without too much trouble—they may be light or casual smokers. The addicted smoker, on the other hand, will have to contend with withdrawal symptoms such as craving a cigarette, irritability, anxiety, depression, trouble concentrating, sleep disturbances, drowsiness, and constipation. Some people gain weight as a result of metabolic changes, increased appetite, or both. The U.S. Department of Health and Human Services makes four basic points that can be extremely helpful for people trying to quit:

- Acknowledge that drug dependence may be involved. If you have trouble quitting, it is not because you do not have enough willpower.
- Quitting is a long-term process. Craving often recurs at intervals months after the last cigarette. Relapse is common—and the only thing to do is quit all over again.
- Ninety-five percent of those who stop do so on their own. But some people are helped by a stop-smoking clinic or cessation group. These can be found all over the country and to find the most convenient in your area, contact your Local Health Education Office. Also you can contact ASH (Action on Smoking and Health), 5-11 Mortimer Street, London W.1.
- The support and encouragement of family and friends is crucial.

A nicotine chewing gum called Nicorette has been used for a number of years in Canada, England, Switzerland, Sweden, and elsewhere and is now available in the United States as well. The gum eases withdrawal and reduces the chance of relapse by providing an alternative and safer source of nicotine at a lower level of intake for a transitional period, according to researchers. In one test the quitting success rate doubled among users of the gum.

Your Ageproofing Health-Check Guidelines

Periodical medical checkups are of vital importance for your health and well-being, especially to help protect you against the degenerative diseases that develop insidiously over the years and decades. The earlier that today's major killers and cripplers are detected, the better the chances of successful action against them. And spotting risk factors and warning symptoms in good time often makes it possible to avoid the disease altogether. Periodic visits to the doctor also give him a chance to get to know you, both medically and personally. Starting with a "baseline" appraisal of your physical condition, the doctor can more easily evaluate any changes that may occur later on.

There are no hard and fast rules about how often someone who is well should have a medical examination or what checks should be included in it. There is a great deal of variability from one individual to the next, and recommendations from different medical organizations differ. The best thing is to agree on a schedule with your doctor that works well for you. Here are some guidelines to help you in making your checkup plan.

The most comprehensive recent review of the whole medical-checkup question comes from the American Medical Association. For young men and women between twenty-one and forty the AMA recommends a medical examination every five years. After age forty the AMA suggests checkups at one- to three-year intervals, depending on a person's occupation, health, medical history, and other individual characteristics. For people not much beyond forty-five the interval between checkups might be closer to three years. For those over sixty-five a one-year interval might be preferable. Some people, obviously, will require more careful surveillance than others.

As to what goes into a checkup, the one constant is the actual examination, when the doctor asks an assortment of questions and then looks at, feels, listens to, and taps various parts of your anatomy that are readily accessible. What else remains to be done, and how often, depends on your age and the doctor's judgment. An overall checklist compiled from the AMA review includes:

- Height and weight
- Blood pressure
- Vision
- Hearing
- Skin
- Breast examination for women
- Mammography for women
- Pelvic examination for women
- Cervical smear for women
- Rectal examination
- Stool test for occult blood
- Sigmoidoscopy (visual examination of
    lower intestine with flexible instrument)
- Blood cholesterol
- Electrocardiogram
- Blood glucose
- Urine analysis for sugar and protein
- Red blood cell count
- Tuberculosis
- Venereal disease
- Rubella check for women

Routine chest X rays are not on the list, as they are no longer recommended by most authorities.

There are several things to bear in mind about tests. The simplest ones should not be overlooked, because they can be of great value. A decrease in height, for example, is the clearest sign of osteoporosis. Modern laboratory techniques and computerization make it possible to gauge a whole range of blood variables at a very modest cost. This is a real bargain. The streamlined testing done by health maintenance organizations can also hold down expenses, but it does not take the place of the judgment of your own doctor—to whom, of course, the results can be referred.

Checkup recommendations from groups dealing with major killers and cripplers are naturally of special importance, and the most specific ones come from the American Cancer Society. They can be summed up thus:

CANCER CHECKS

Men and Women 20 to 40

• Have a cancer-related checkup every three years. It should include examinations for cancer of the mouth, thyroid, skin, lymph nodes, breast and ovaries or testes and prostate.

Men and Women Over 40

• Have the above checkup every year.
• Add to it a digital rectum examination for colon and rectal cancer.
• After age fifty add a stool occult blood test every year as well as a sigmoidoscope examination every three to five years after two negative tests one year apart.

Special Recommendations for Women 20 to 40

• Breast Cancer Checks: Besides the doctor's check mentioned above, do a self-examination every month and have one baseline breast X ray between the ages of thirty-five and forty.
• Uterine Cancer Checks: Have a pelvic examination every three years and a cervical smear test at least every three years after two negative tests one year apart. This also applies to young women under twenty who are sexually active. (The Royal College of Obstetricians recommends an annual cervical smear test.)

Special Recommendations for Women Over 40

• Breast Cancer Checks: Besides the yearly examination by a doctor and the monthly self-examinations, have a breast X ray every year or two from forty to forty-nine and every year from age fifty on.
• Uterine Cancer Checks: Have a pelvic examination every year, a cervical smear test every three years, and an endometrial tissue sample check at menopause if at risk.

Advice on key checks for heart and blood vessel health comes from the American Heart Association:

CARDIOVASCULAR CHECKS

- One major recommendation is to have your blood pressure checked at least once a year. This is particularly important because high blood pressure has no symptoms to speak of in its early stages.
- A person whose total blood cholesterol is below 200 should have it checked at less than five-year intervals to make sure it has not gone up.
- If a person's total blood cholesterol reading is over 200, a test should be done for the two key cholesterol fractions, low density lipoprotein (LDL) and high density lipoprotein (HDL). LDL is the fraction that causes trouble, and HDL is the fraction that is protective.
- If LDL is below 100, heart risk is low, regardless of HDL. If LDL is above 200, heart risk is high, even if HDL is high.
- In nine out of ten people, LDL levels range from 100 to 200. For them, the ratio between LDL and HDL is important. The higher the ratio, the greater the risk. If LDL is only twice as high as HDL, heart risk is very low. If LDL is five times HDL, heart risk is very high.
- More frequent checks are obviously called for as risk goes up. If high-risk cholesterol levels do not respond to simple lifestyle changes, a doctor usually prescribes medication.

The National Society for the Prevention of Blindness in the United States recommends an eye examination every two years. This is especially crucial for spotting glaucoma, which has no symptoms until a lot of damage has been done but which can be readily treated if caught in time.

Finally, how often should you see your dentist? Most dentists recommend a visit every six months, but it is a good idea to check with your dentist about your particular requirements. Some people need checkups at more frequent intervals.

CONCLUSION

Your Ageproofing Potential

Throughout my book I have stressed the fact that you have it in your power to ageproof your looks, your health, and your whole body from head to toe. You can see for yourself that there are no set limits to what is possible. There is no known cutoff point to how much you can do. This is really the most extraordinary thing about ageproofing. It means that you can go far toward your goal of peak fitness and function throughout life, probably a good deal farther than you or anybody else yet realizes. It means that you need never take no for an answer—I certainly do not.

Your ageproofing potential is there for you to discover, and it can be largely what you choose to make it. The challenge is indeed exciting, but realizing your ageproofing potential does take motivation.

Motivation is what revs you up, drives you forward, and keeps you going strong against all odds. It is a mix of willpower and enthusiasm. The two work together to fuel and spark your every move and help you reach your goal in each new endeavor. Lack of motivation is what slows people down year after year and decade after decade. It compounds the disuse and abuse of physical and mental abilities, the widespread degenerative changes in looks, health, and fitness, and the devastating chronic diseases that so many people blame on aging processes.

How do you go about developing motivation? The very fact that you are reading these words shows that you want to do something, and that in itself is a start. What you want to do now is begin concentrating on your willpower. Will-power gives you the drive and determination to hang in there and keep trying when everyone else is giving up and dropping by the wayside. Being able to count on this willpower edge when you need it can make a big difference in everything you do in life.

Willpower is something that you really can never have too much of. And the way you get more is to use more. Willpower creates willpower, so use it every chance you get. Little by little you can build up your reserves to the point where you always have plenty you can count on. Each time you deal with a situation that is more difficult than usual, this makes it easier to handle an even harder one the next time around. Each time you exercise your willpower this way it gets stronger. At work here is the same kind of overload principle that underlies physical conditioning. The strength that your willpower, like your body, can develop by means of gradual overloading stands you in good stead as you come to grips with the various problems facing you from day to day. But it must be done gradually. This is important. Otherwise you soon reach what is called a super-saturation point; when substances are added to a fluid all at once instead of by degrees, everything just falls out of solution.

Building up your willpower slowly and steadily to make it a source of inner strength can do a great deal more to protect your looks, health, and overall fitness throughout life than you may think. Over the past few decades, as you are undoubtedly aware, there has been a great deal of concern about the role that stress plays in modern life. Stress is being increasingly implicated as an important risk factor in today's major chronic diseases. You saw earlier how strong and direct a link it has been found to have with hypertension and indirectly with stroke and coronary heart disease. The key thing, however, is not the stress itself but how people cope with it. What may be stressful for one person may be stimulating for another. There is a tremendous amount of individual variation in the way different people react. So you have to give special thought to how well you cope with each stressful situation you find yourself in, not how stressful the situation itself is generally considered to be. The stronger your willpower, the better you can handle the stress.

It should come as no surprise that willpower can make a big difference in your looks by enabling you to deal confidently and successfully with problems, so that they are not a source of undue stress. Your looks invariably reflect your thoughts and feelings, and your thoughts and feelings invariably reflect your ability to cope with stress. Those that are unduly stressful work against your looks. Those that are stress-free work for them.

The effect that willpower can have on your health at various periods of your life, while not as obvious as what it does to your looks, is certainly far-reaching. If people feel that they are in control of situations and are able to deal effectively with them, stress does not seem to have any negative effects on their health. It may, as a matter of fact, provide beneficial stimulation. But if they do not feel in control and able to cope, that is another story altogether. A whole cascade of stress hormones is released into the circulation. Although this revs you up physically to deal with a possible emergency, there is often too much of a reaction. It can have dire consequences, especially for immune defenses. The stress hormones suppress many of the powerful fighter cells, thus lowering the body's ability to defend itself against foreign invaders and toxic substances and ward off disease. Instead, the body is left exposed to many of the chronic, degenerative processes that underlie the development of today's big killers and cripplers.

The body's reaction to what is perceived as stress is regulated by the brain's key control center, the hypothalamus. The fact that the hypothalamus calls the shots, as it were, points to the very close relationship that exists between the nervous, endocrine, and immune systems. The interactions between the three systems are so complex that they almost defy deciphering. But enough is known about the ways they work together to reveal two basic things. One is that the nervous system, with the brain at its center, oversees and controls everything that goes on in every part of the body and at every level. The other is that the endocrine and immune systems work for and with the nervous system, providing information and carrying out instructions. The endocrine system signals what is going on metabolically in the body's organs, tissues, and cells. The immune system keeps the nervous system posted about the state of the body's defenses and any unfamiliar and unwelcome agents or substances that might pose a threat—as a rule, elements from outside the body, but occasionally ones from within. Besides furnishing information to the nervous system, the endocrine and immune systems act on neural orders based on this information, the endocrine system's job being to keep metabolic processes functioning properly and the immune system's being to maintain a strong watch against bacterial and viral invaders, toxic elements, and other threats to the body's well-being.

This interlinked functioning of the nervous, endocrine, and immune systems is turning out to be of very great significance, so much so that it now constitutes a special field of scientific inquiry known as psychoneuroimmunology. Because of the leading role played by the brain in this scheme, fresh light is being thrown on the relation between the mind and the body—suggesting that mental processes are extensively involved in physical ones and that the mind has a good deal more effect on the body's health than the conventional medical view holds. Old-fashioned precepts such as "It's mind over matter," "Where there's a will, there's a way," "You can do it if you just put your mind to it"— which were standard fare in the household I grew up in but which fell out of favor along with house calls and bedside medicine as well-couched psychoanalytic terms entered the language in their place—are now scientifically respectable. Conclusions being reached by the new research are still mostly tentative, but there is mounting evidence that physiological functions previously thought to be beyond voluntary control can actually be influenced or even directed by the mind—and the will. It gives you the feeling that you are on the threshold of a new mental and physical world, which scientists are only just beginning to explore and map out.

Many people have of course heard about the exceptional powers of yogis who are able to control such involuntary processes as heart rate and body temperature at will, bringing them down to levels so low that the yogis can remain buried underground for days at a time and emerge unharmed as though from the deep torpor of hibernation. Also familiar are the exploits of members of certain Eastern sects who walk as if in a trance on burning coals without any apparent pain or injury. It is fascinating to see how awareness of such little-tapped mental resources is developing in this country and with it a serious interest in how they may help prevent and treat major chronic disease.

One pioneering team of researchers uses what is called image therapy to help cancer victims in the fight against their malignancy by visualizing their immune system's white blood cells gobbling up their tumor cells. The results of this psychoneuroimmunological technique during the past decade have drawn the attention and acclaim of cancer and immunology experts the world over. Other researchers are finding increasing evidence that cancer patients who have a sense of control over their disease, are aggressive and even cantankerous in coping with it, and have a high expectation of success in the outcome, stand a far better chance of cure than those who feel helpless and hopeless and just give up and accept the disease without a fight.

This pattern is not unique to cancer. It is seen in other major disorders as well. It is one very good reason for learning to deal with difficult situations of various kinds—including but not limited to possible illnesses. Things like this show you why it is so important to develop strong willpower. Willpower may influence your body's functioning and lifetime fitness in many as yet unsuspected ways.

The workings of the other key component of motivation, enthusiasm, are just as fascinating as those of willpower. Here, too, the past offers clues of unexplained routes of control. Before the introduction of antibiotics forty-odd years ago, enthusiasm or some other strong emotion was one of the most effective medicines in the arsenal of bedside medicine. The wise family doctor prescribed it in large doses, carefully timed to bring the patient through the crisis of the disease. The rationale behind this was not spelled out in scientific detail. General practitioners were simply acting on experience gleaned from many years of house calls and hospital rounds, which suggested that if you could rouse patients from the sinking apathy of a serious illness like pneumonia by bringing them to a high emotional state, they could rally better against the illness and pull themselves through. Anger was as effective as joyous excitement; it was the intensity of the emotion that seemed to count. Such therapy is not too far removed from the traditional rituals of witch doctors, Shamans, and other healers of past times and more primitive ways of life. Nor is it unrelated to such sophisticated treatment as the laughter therapy that Norman Cousins used so brilliantly a few years ago to doctor himself and effect a cure from a severe illness for which the medical prognosis had been poor.

Just as the helpless-hopeless syndrome of patients who give in to illness and have low survival rates is symptomatic of clinical depression, so the enthusiastic peaks reached by those who stay on top of the situation and have high survival rates may not be all that far from mania. Depression is a frequent topic of discussion and an almost everyday concern, to judge by the amount of coverage it gets in the media. But how often do you see its counterpart, mania, featured by the press, TV or radio?

Life needs enthusiasm, fervor—a dash of mania. This is a key point when it comes to realizing your ageproofing potential. A good dash of mania may well be the only way of dealing with what is perhaps the most critical problem of aging: decreasing ability to deal with stress challenges. Ordinarily there is no noticeable difference in the way younger and older people go about their everyday routines, but they do respond differently to change. It may be something as traumatic as a death in the family, a bad accident, or a crippling illness. Or it may be something seemingly lower on the stress scale like switching to a better job or moving to a more convenient neighborhood. The younger person tends to respond more quickly and effectively than the older one. The difference is always present—there is not a survey that does not reveal it.

Most experts seem to assume that this decrease in ability to respond to stress challenges is part and parcel of inevitable aging processes. But is it? What is occurring here ties in very closely with findings about two other changes usually linked to aging: a decline in activity and loss of motivation. What all of this means, as far as your ageproofing potential goes, is that you want to do everything possible to counter the insidious tendencies that can lead to loss of motivation, less physical activity, and a lower response to stress challenges. You want to step up, not slow down, your daily pace —and start doing so as soon as possible. You want to increase your physical activity, not decrease it. You want to add to your share of positive stress challenges, not pull out and away. In other words, you want to get more involved in life, keep things on the upswing and not let them start on the downswing. And to every situation, add a dash of mania for a lively mix—it may well be the spice of your ageproofing potential!

ACKNOWLEDGMENTS

I wish to thank the National Institutes of Health for making research available and for reviewing my manuscript, and specifically the experts who took time and trouble at the National Cancer Institute; National Heart, Lung, and Blood Institute; National Institute on Aging; National Institute of Arthritis, Diabetes, and Digestive and Kidney Diseases; National Institute of Dental Research; National Institute of Neurological and Communicative Disorders and Stroke; and the National Institute of Mental Health. I am particularly grateful to Marc Stern, Chief, NIH News Branch, Office of the Director, for his generous assistance throughout the writing of my book.

Among the authorities whose work I have found particularly helpful are: Dr. Roy M. Acheson, Dr. Robert Ader, Dr. Jürgen Aschoff, Dr. Per-Olof Åstrand, Dr. Louis V. Avioli, Dr. Per Björntorp, Dr. Walter M. Bortz II, Dr. Barry M. Brenner, Dr. W. Virgil Brown, Dr. Robert N. Butler, Dr. William B. Castelli, Dr. Paul D. Coleman, Dr. William E. Connor, Dr. Ralph A. DeFronzo, Dr. Hector F. DeLuca, Dr. William C. Dement, Dr. Herbert A. deVries, Dr. Marion C. Diamond, Sir Richard Doll, Dr. Michael Easterbrook, Dr. John H. Epstein, Dr. Caleb E. Finch, Dr. Thomas B. Fitzpatrick, Dr. Samuel M. Fox III, Dr. William F. Ganong, Dr. Richard C. Gibbs, Dr. Mark Gold, Dr. Ralph Goldman, Dr. Robert A. Good, Dr. Robert N. Hamburger, Dr. Ernest L. Hartmann, Dr. Egil P. Harvold, Dr. Robert B. Heaney, Dr. D. Mark Hegsted, Dr. Howard F. Hunt, Dr. David J.

A. Jenkins, Dr. Norman M. Kaplan, Dr. Fred W. Kasch, Dr. Albert M. Kligman, Dr. Robert A. Klocke, Dr. Hans Kraus, Dr. Richard M. Krause, Dr. Daniel L. Kripke, Dr. Lawrence E. Lamb, Dr. Lance E. Lanyon, Dr. John L. Laragh, Dr. Allan J. Lazare, Dr. Arthur S. Leon, Dr. Sidney L. Lerman, Dr. Walter B. Mertz, Dr. Robert B. Millman, Dr. J. F. Moorhead, Dr. William P. Morgan, Dr. James B. Nicholas, Dr. Ralph S. Paffenbarger Jr., Dr. John L. Parrish, Dr. Charles M. Peterson, Dr. Salvatore V. Pizzo, Dr. Michael L. Pollack, Dr. Stanley I. Rapaport, Dr. Kaare Rodahl, Dr. Arthur Rook, Dr. Isadore Rossman, Dr. George S. Roth, Dr. Neil B. Ruderman, Dr. Michael A. H. Russell, Dr. Bijan Safai, Dr. Marvin M. Schuster, Dr. James H. Shaw, Dr. Roy J. Shephard, Dr. Gordon M. Shepherd, Dr. Maurice E. Shils, Dr. Israel Siegel, Dr. Pentti Siiteri, Dr. Everett L. Smith, Dr. Jeremiah R. Stamler, Dr. Bernard L. Strehler, Dr. Keith B. Taylor, Dr. Edgar A. Tonna, Dr. Peter V. Von Soest, Dr. Roy L. Walford, Dr. John F. Waller Jr., Dr. R. A. Weale, Dr. G. Donald Whedon, Dr. Jack H. Wilmore, Dr. Ernst L. Wynder, and Dr. Vernon R. Young.

I am also grateful to the following organizations for providing me with reports and research: American Medical Association, American Heart Association, American Cancer Society, American Lung Association, American Diabetes Association, National Society to Prevent Blindness, American Dental Association, President's Council on Physical Fitness and Sports, and the U. S. Department of Health and Human Services' Office on Smoking and Health.

Comprehensive reports that I have found especially useful include: Diet, Nutrition, and Cancer, commissioned by the National Cancer Institute and put out by the National Research Council in 1983; Rationale of the Diet-Heart Statement of the American Heart Association, Report of the Nutrition Committee, 1981; The 1984 Report of the Joint National Committee on Detection, Evaluation, and Treatment of High Blood Pressure; and the series of annual reports from the Surgeon General on the health consequences of smoking.

In connection with Your Ageproofing Program for Looks,

Health, and Fitness, I particularly want to acknowledge the help I received from Michael O'Shea, Arthur Phillips, Romana Krysanowska, Louis Licari, the YMCA of Greater New York, the YWCA, and the New York Health and Racquet Club.

And, of course, my warmest thanks and gratitude go to my editor, Carole Hall, and my agent, Don Cutler.

INDEX